Following
Sir Fred's Steps

Ashton's Legacy

Following
Sir Fred's Steps

Ashton's Legacy

Edited by
Stephanie Jordan
Andrée Grau

Proceedings of the Ashton Conference,
Roehampton Institute, London,
12–13 November 1994

DANCE BOOKS
CECIL COURT LONDON

First published in 1996 by
Dance Books Ltd
15 Cecil Court, London WC2N 4EZ

© 1996 Stephanie Jordan and Andrée Grau

ISBN 1 85273 047 1

Cover picture:
Frederick Ashton rehearsing David Blair
and Nadian Nerina in *La Fille mal gardée*.
Photograph by Zoë Dominic.

Book and cover design: Sanjoy Roy

A CIP catalogue record for this book
is available from the British Library

Printed in Great Britain by
BPC Wheatons Ltd, Exeter, Devon

Contents

Acknowledgements

'Following Sir Fred's Steps: a Conference Celebrating Ashton's Work', was held at Roehampton Institute, London, 12–13 November 1994, in collaboration with the Society for Dance Research, the Royal Ballet, and the Birmingham Royal Ballet. The conference committee consisted of: Stephanie Jordan (Head of Dance, Roehampton Institute; Chair), Andrée Grau (Senior Research Fellow, Roehampton Institute; Conference Administrator), Angela Kane (Senior Lecturer, Roehampton Institute), Ann Nugent (editor, *Dance Theatre Journal*), Jane Pritchard (Archivist, Rambert Dance Company and English National Ballet), and Bonnie Rowell (Lecturer, Roehampton Institute). The committee was supported by a group of advisors: Monica Mason (Assistant Director, Royal Ballet), Alastair Macaulay (critic, *Financial Times*), Pamela May (former ballerina, Royal Ballet), and Sir Peter Wright (Artistic Director, Birmingham Royal Ballet). A number of scribes documented the workshops, lecture-demonstrations and panel discussions: Henrietta Bannerman, Elizabeth Marshall, Frances Palmer, Helen Roberts, and Linda Willcox. The lecture-demonstrations and panels were video recorded by Robert Jude (Royal Ballet Video Archive). Lucy Carter, as technician, ensured that no technical problems occurred, Irene Glaister (Honorary Treasurer, Society for Dance Research) helped with the original planning of the budget, and Jenny Johnstone, as secretary to the conference, was pivotal to the organisational success. Thanks finally to David Leonard (Dance Books), our publisher, and to Sanjoy Roy (Dance Books), who gave invaluable editorial assistance in putting this book together, and also produced the typographical design.

I would like to thank everyone for their commitment, including all of those who have not been named individually, students and staff helpers, and other supporting personnel. Without all their hard work, the conference and this book would not have been possible. Last, but not least, I would like to thank the Arts Council of England, the Linbury Trust, Miss V. L. Clore's 1967 Charitable Trust, and the Roehampton Institute for giving us financial support and believing in what we were trying to achieve.

Andrée Grau
Conference Administrator

Preface

This volume represents something more than straight 'proceedings', although the aim was to maintain the feeling of the conference. After the event, authors were encouraged to re-submit their papers: comments, debates, or discussions arising from the weekend could be incorporated, and ideas could be developed further without the constrictions of a twenty-minute presentation. Many of them took up this opportunity. Except for minor details, the papers were not 'edited' as such, as we felt it was more important to keep the individual style of each author rather than go for an overall unifying style.

In addition, prior to final editing, participants were asked to verify the accuracy of their biographical details, when they had not provided them themselves. Similarly, transcripts of all the workshops and lecture-demonstrations were sent to the presenters for comments and checking. We are immensely grateful to everyone involved for taking time out of their very busy schedules not only to check that no misinterpretations had crept in, but also occasionally to reword or develop slightly what they had said in order to give a fuller picture. We hope they will find our editing faithful to their words.

I trust that readers will enjoy what, I think, is a rather splendid volume. For those who were unable to be present, it gives them a glimpse of a very stimulating weekend. For those who were fortunate enough to have been there, I hope it will remind them of how inspiring sharing knowledge about a great choreographer can be. For all, I am sure, the volume will be an invaluable working tool for years to come.

Andrée Grau
Conference Administrator

Introduction

What would Ashton have said if he'd known that there was to be a conference about his work? According to Anthony Russell-Roberts, Sir Fred's nephew, and administrative director of the Royal Ballet, he would probably have said, 'How deeply boring and I don't know why anyone should spend money on such a thing. But . . . I'm thrilled.' That was his way, perhaps, of giving us his blessing for Following Sir Fred's Steps!

The initial idea that there should be some kind of festival or gathering to celebrate Ashton's work came from Alastair Macaulay. It would, after all, have been Ashton's ninetieth birthday in September 1994, and there was a strong feeling in the air that it was time to make a new assessment of this choreographer's work, and to respond to the need to capture the memories of those who worked with him. The understanding of the Ashton style is easily lost, and likewise his works easily disappear from memory (although many have been recorded in Benesh Movement Notation since 1960 – see Appendix I). Indeed, many of us felt that we should address these problems as a matter of urgency. It emerged, happily, that his birthday was also being marked at this time by revivals of a number of his works, in Britain and abroad, and also in numerous publications and radio and television presentations. The role of our conference was to promote a special intensity of new thinking about Ashton, and at the same time to develop a range of new source material upon which future dancers and writers might draw. This was to be a unique collaboration between higher education, the two Royal Ballet companies, and the Society for Dance Research.

The conference opened with a pre-performance panel at the Theatre Museum, down the road from the Ashton programme at the Royal Opera House, Covent Garden, followed by a packed weekend at Roehampton Institute. It turned out to be a weekend full of love for Sir Fred, of generosity, fun and surprise. For me, it was particularly important to consider the radicalism and dangerous sensuality of the choreographer, as well as his wit, humanity and grace. David Vaughan, our opening speaker, was quite right to sound his warnings that we should look after Ashton's work a good deal better and show more of it; but, thanks to our contributors, so many challenging, fresh ideas emerged from the conference that an energy towards positive action developed naturally. Many of us discovered that there was much more to celebrate in Ashton's work than we would ever have believed. Clearly, there was no question of the relevance of Ashton today.

The conference also became an occasion for crossing many boundaries: the professional ballet world and academia, dancers and writers from several generations, Ashton enthusiasts from many different fields, including scholars, critics, notators, teachers, dancers and musicians. There were also many different kinds of presentation: lecture-demonstrations, papers, workshops, interviews, panel discussions and film screenings. Some contributors too demonstrated the particular value of moving across traditional territorial limits. Both the teacher Richard Glasstone and ballerina Katherine Healy gave academic papers, and Shelley Berg and Jill Beck, both academics with practical dance backgrounds, demonstrated a passionate involvement in reconstruction. Our audience was generous too in contributing information and asking provocative questions – quite often answering questions from the stage too! We welcomed people from many countries as well as from Britain (America, Australia, Canada, Austria, Denmark, Italy, Spain and Sweden). I shall not forget the special contribution of Alexander Grant, who was there throughout, and who not only had his own interview slot, but also spoke eloquently and regularly from the floor. Sadly, we missed the presence of Michael Somes, who was to have led the session on his revival of *Enigma Variations*. At the time of the conference he was already seriously ill. That marvellous final session, however, led by Sir Peter Wright, was flooded with memories of him.

But Following Sir Fred's Steps is only the start. I hope that there will be many further collaborations between the ballet and academic worlds. For the immediate future, there are already a number of reverberations stemming from the conference: the possible development of special training classes in the Ashton style, the reconstruction of lost works, the recovery of old film footage, and so on.

Certainly, I am delighted to offer this book as a document of the conference. It contains accounts of the practical sessions, transcriptions of the panels, as well as the papers, some of these slightly developed from their original form. There is, of course, no substitute for the dancing that featured so strongly during that weekend. It is hard for me to single out only a few examples: Antoinette Sibley and Anthony Dowell, exquisite movers themselves, while coaching the pas de deux from *The Dream*; the fascinating Solo Seal variations danced by students from the English National Ballet School and introduced by Pamela May; not to forget Monica Mason's teaching of a solo from *Birthday Offering* and Katherine Healy's illustrations of her own paper on *Romeo and Juliet*. Nevertheless, I am confident that the book will serve as a useful source for both Ashton practitioners and writers, and will be of interest to the many other Ashton lovers around the world. I hope that it will provoke more writing and more thinking about this wonderful choreographer's work.

Stephanie Jordan
Conference Chair
January 1995

Ashton Now

David Vaughan

The establishment of a national school of classical ballet de-
pends on the existence of three prerequisites: a great choreographer
whose works provide a repertory and define a style; a company (prefer-
ably with its own theatre) to present that repertory; and an academy to
codify and promote that style and to provide dancers trained in it. The
most obvious examples of this combination of circumstances have been
in Denmark, with August Bournonville; in Russia, with Marius Petipa;
in the United States, with George Balanchine; and here in Britain, with
Frederick Ashton.

The works of Bournonville, Petipa, and Balanchine have been maintained (with varying degrees of authenticity), but it is no secret that many
people believe that Ashton's work has been neglected by the company
and school whose first responsibility should be to preserve it. The
number of his ballets in the repertory of the Royal Ballet has undeniably
declined, and in the Royal Ballet School the Russian influence is in the
ascendant, while the Cecchetti system, the technical basis of the Ashton
style, is in eclipse.

Ashton, like Balanchine, his exact contemporary, was from the beginning a prolific choreographer able to provide on demand works that
could make up a well-balanced programme – the kind of programme one
used to see at Sadler's Wells or the New Theatre in the late thirties and
early forties: ballets like *Apparitions, Nocturne, Les Patineurs, A Wedding
Bouquet, Harlequin in the Street, Horoscope*, and later *Dante Sonata, The Wise
Virgins*, and *The Wanderer*. More than that, these ballets, by their technical
and interpretive demands, helped to turn young dancers into virtuosi,
even into artists, and they formed the basis of what has come to be
recognised as the English style of classical ballet, a style expressive of what
we like to think of as the English national character – lyrical, precise,
well-mannered, yet robust – but flavoured by Latin and Gallic elements in

1

Ashton's own temperament and background, a certain chic, a certain flamboyance, which counteracted any tendency toward gentility or dowdiness. More seriously, Ashton's own dance experience – his adoration of Pavlova and Karsavina, his work with Massine and especially with Nijinska, and his study of the Cecchetti system – all contributed to the technical foundation of this English style, giving it greater freedom of épaulement, faster changes of direction, and more amplitude of movement.

In the years following the Sadler's Wells Ballet's move to Covent Garden, and especially during Ashton's tenure as director of what had become the Royal Ballet, from 1963 to 1970, the process continued. *Symphonic Variations*, which Ashton called his choreographic credo, and the ballets that came after it, constituted a contemporary repertory equalled in its number of masterpieces only by that of New York City Ballet. Margot Fonteyn, Ashton's muse, later acknowledged as prima ballerina assoluta, was joined by younger artists like Nadia Nerina, Svetlana Beriosova, Antoinette Sibley, Lynn Seymour, David Blair, and Anthony Dowell, most of them the products of the Royal Ballet School, as were the dancers who made up a corps de ballet unrivalled in the Western world.

Ashton's creativity after his premature, even enforced retirement was diminished in volume, but not in mastery. Yet he often used to predict that before long his works would be considered passé and that most would fall into oblivion. It is true that only a handful of ballets even by the greatest choreographers tend to survive, and that on the whole they are the best ones. But it is also true that in Ashton's case a number have disappeared too soon, and their neglect may have been due to a feeling among those who took over the direction of the company that these ballets were dated and irrelevant.

In other words, we were taken back to the kind of criticism that Ashton often suffered in his earlier years – that he failed to deal with sufficiently serious subject matter – to which was now added the further condemnation that he was out of touch with contemporary life and its problems. Ashton may have been aware of this stricture when he wrote that 'ballets about current social happenings ... [are likely] to date as quickly as yesterday's newspaper' (1958, pp. 38–9).

I would be the first to agree that Ashton was often on shaky ground when he tried to be trendy, as in *Jazz Calendar*. But it is naïve at best to suppose that ballet is brought into the modern world when it concerns, say, the supposedly realistic depiction of sexual acts by people in jeans on a construction site. Apart from the fact that realism of that kind can be carried only so far in dance, the movement possibilities are limited. As someone once said: in ballet, people make love standing on their feet.

In his later years, Ashton's favourite subject was romantic love, a subject uniquely suited to dance expression. Who is to say that it is less representative of the human spirit than gang rape? I have often quoted Edwin Denby's observation that 'the more trivial the subject, the deeper and more beautiful is Ashton's poetic view of it' (1986, p. 426). The reverse is true of some choreographers, of whom one could say that the more profound the subject, the more trivial and prosaic is their treatment of it.

In any case, it is not seriousness of subject that makes serious choreography. In my view, the most important developments in the art form have come not from emotional expression but from formal innovation. What I am talking about here, clearly, is what has been called the Great Divide, or what Joan Acocella has termed the quarrel between the adherents of 'expressive' and 'pure' dance:

> One position is that dance is of value insofar as it is tells a story or at least expresses or portrays something in the way that literature or painting might. Opposing this is the view that dance has *autonomous* value, that it is capable of communicating something on the highest level of meaning through purely dance means, without resorting to imitation of the methods of painting or literature. According to this position, dance communicates as music does. (Acocella & Garafola, 1991, p. 1)

It is generally accepted that this Great Divide is also between Europe on the one hand and America on the other, but it is interesting to note that the two choreographers whom Acocella names as embodying the 'pure dance' view are Balanchine, who was American by adoption, and Ashton, sometimes called the most English of choreographers, who nevertheless felt more appreciated in America than at home.

In any case, expressive dance had once again reared its – dare I say? – ugly head in Britain as in Europe, and the damage to Ashton's reputation, and to the heritage of British ballet, was done. Certain works, of course, survived in the repertory, a handful of acknowledged classics: *La Fille mal gardée, The Dream, Cinderella, A Month in the Country*. True, *Monotones,*

3

Ashton's purest distillation of classicism, also survived, but he himself kept *Symphonic Variations* out for a number of years for lack of a suitable cast. And this fact pinpoints one of the basic problems: because Ashton's works were not being danced, nobody could dance them.

There were a few exceptions, of course – the dwindling number of dancers who had worked with him kept certain ballets alive when they were revived – *Scènes de ballet*, for instance. But too often revivals have looked like carbon copies at best. The last time *Enigma Variations* was performed by the parent company one saw dancers wearing the proper clothes and make-up and going through the motions they had learned, but the spirit of the ballet was gone. Roles like the mortal lovers in *The Dream* and the stepsisters in *Cinderella* have been performed in inexcusably broad and vulgar fashion. What is significant, though, is that in the hands of the few dancers I have mentioned, keepers of the flame like Lesley Collier and Nicola Roberts and Genesia Rosato, the ballerina roles remained pretty well inviolate. In other words, some part of the dance element survived. It is not the fault of younger dancers that even this dance element often eluded them: they were being asked for other qualities.

If Ashton's work is to live on as the patrimony of British ballet, it must be because the dance element will be kept alive through constant performance, careful teaching and coaching, and faithful staging. Young dancers must of course be allowed to interpret roles freshly, in their own way – one would not want them to dance them by rote, parrot-fashion, as it were – but at the minimum they will have to get the steps right.

Ashton was a master of structure, both in terms of what he called the 'scaffolding', the matching of the action to the music, but also in terms of the dictionary definition, 'the way in which parts are arranged or put together to form a whole', the bricks and mortar, if you like, of steps and transitions.

Alastair Macaulay (1994a) reported that people who saw the Birmingham Royal Ballet dance *La Fille mal gardée* in Turin 'exclaimed with amazement that never before had they seen ballet with the harmony, structure, and fluency of music – that watching it was like reading a score'. If you look carefully at *Scènes de ballet*, you will see that there isn't a single step in it that doesn't relate to the structure as a whole. This is equally true of unassuming ballets like *Les Rendezvous* and *Les Patineurs* – it is what has ensured their survival.

Ashton's genius is evident at every moment of *Daphnis and Chloe*, but I

4

will just mention here Chloe's dance to the flute solo in the third scene, which is built on half a dozen steps, and variations on them: arabesque piquée into failli to fourth position croisée; the 'folk' step of slapping the foot with the hand in front or in back, with rond de jambe; pas de bourrée with small développé à la seconde into soutenu; plié in fifth position soussus; little ballonnés on pointe – all varied with different ports de bras and gestures, such as the moment when she holds a pose in fourth position croisée with the arms in an 'archaic' Greek position.

This leads me to another important truth about Ashton: we all know that he was a consummate storyteller when he wanted to be, but he told his stories and created his characters through the steps: you know what his people are like and what they are feeling because of how they dance. As Alan M. Kriegsman (1991) has written, 'Ashton didn't subject the classical steps to the kinds of radical transfiguration that became Balanchine's signature'. Ashton's great innovation was the extension of the classical vocabulary as a poetic language. I would add too that his use of space, especially in his purest dance works, *Symphonic Variations* and *Scènes de ballet* and *Monotones*, was as unconventional in its way as anything in Merce Cunningham. Of *Scènes de ballet* he said, 'I . . . wanted to do a ballet that could be seen from any angle – anywhere could be front, so to speak' (Vaughan, 1977, p. 222).

Ashton's work, then, it seems to me, can speak to us as strongly today as it did thirty or forty or fifty years ago. It is classical, and it is modern. And indeed the situation now is more hopeful than it has been. This conference, and the gratifyingly large turn-out for it, are, I hope, both a symptom of and a stimulus to renewed interest in his work. The Ashton revivals at the Royal Ballet, plus *Enigma Variations* by the Birmingham Royal Ballet, move beyond the usual handful of ballets that have been danced in the past.

This is true with other companies, too: *Romeo and Juliet* is coming back into the repertory of the Royal Danish Ballet, thanks to Peter Schaufuss. *Two Pigeons*, which hasn't been in the Royal repertory lately, I believe, was revived in Turin. The Dutch National Ballet, American Ballet Theatre, and the National Ballet of Canada have acquired, or will acquire, *Symphonic Variations*. The Dutch National, where Wayne Eagling looks out for Ashton's interests, has also revived *Scènes de ballet*, a rarity among companies other than the Royal, and ABT also revived *Birthday Offering* a couple of years ago.

Since the death of Robert Joffrey, I'm sorry to say, the company he founded seems to have dropped most of its Ashton repertory, which was the most extensive outside the Royal Ballet – it even included *A Wedding Bouquet*. But I should like to see more Ashton ballets in American repertories – for instance, Pacific Northwest Ballet or Boston Ballet might have a stab at *Scènes de ballet* or *Rhapsody*. Alastair Macaulay (1994b) wrote recently that the Russian companies should also acquire Ashton and Balanchine ballets that use Russian ballet scores, so that they could learn 'how far their heritage has been absorbed in the West, and with what effect'. There may, inevitably, be some loss of what we might think of as the pure Ashton style, but the gain for those other companies – and for Ashton's reputation world-wide – would surely be considerable.

The other, related question is that of which ballets could or should be revived. I am resigned to the fact that I will never again see *Harlequin in the Street* or *Mephisto Valse*, two ballets I loved – unless it's in heaven. The reconstruction of *Les Masques* shown at this conference (see pp. 38–46), a ballet that gave me one of those moments of the shock of recognition of genius when I first saw it in the spring of 1939, gives hope that a revival might be possible. *Foyer de danse* could easily be revived from the film that exists, and might be an excellent choice for a smaller company like London City Ballet. *Les Rendezvous* has been out of the repertory for far too long, and I would hate to think that Ashton's fourth act of *Swan Lake*, that sublime elegiac poem, will not come back somehow, somewhere. Would it be worthwhile to try again with *Apparitions*, another ballet that meant a lot to me years ago? The ballroom scene, at least, is a masterpiece. Anthony Russell-Roberts has dropped a tantalising hint that the Royal Ballet may yet revive *Sylvia*. At all events, some important additions could be made to what one hopes would be the irreducible minimum of extant Ashton works – the Ashton canon. (Clement Crisp has written that he has made a list of thirty Ashton ballets that should be in repertory.)

Having introduced a personal note, I should like to end on it. Years ago, when I was serving in the army in World War II, I had the luck to be stationed in London for a while at the time when the Sadler's Wells Ballet was giving regular seasons at what was then the New Theatre. Needless to say, that was where I spent my free evenings. It couldn't last, of course, and before long I was shipped out to India. There I tried to assuage my feeling of deprivation by writing an essay, my first, on Ashton's work. There was another balletomane in the headquarters in Delhi, and I showed him what I had written. He said, 'You're in love with Ashton's ballets!' And I realised that he had perceived an important truth about me. It's why even today I take pleasure in the mere naming of the ballets I have mentioned in the course of this talk – 'title after title,' as Virginia Woolf said, 'to be laid upon the heart like an amulet against disaster.'

E. M. Forster wrote in his essay, 'The Raison d'Être of Criticism in the Arts':

> I love music. Just to love it, or just to love anything or anybody is not enough. Love has to be clarified and controlled to give full value, and here is where criticism may help. But one has to start with love; one has, in the case of music, to want to hear the notes. (1951, p. 117)

Or, to offer a paraphrase, one has to want to follow Sir Fred's steps.

References

Acocella, J. & Garafola, L. (eds) (1991), *André Levinson on Dance*, Hanover, NH: Wesleyan University Press.

Ashton, F. (1958), 'The Subject Matter of Ballet', in A. Haskell (ed.), *Ballet Annual 1959*, London, A & C Black.

Denby, E. (1986), *Dance Writings*, London, Dance Books.

Forster, E.M. (1951), *Two Cheers for Democracy*, London, Edward Arnold.

Kriegsman, A.M. (1991), 'Ashton's Royal Treatment', *Washington Post*, 16 March 1991.

Macaulay, A. (1994a), 'Turin falls for "Fille" ', *Financial Times*, 22/23 January 1994.

Macaulay, A. (1994b), 'Saison Russe', *Dancing Times*, September 1994.

Vaughan, D. (1977), *Frederick Ashton and His Ballets*, London, A & C Black.

The Influence of Cecchetti on Ashton's Work

Richard Glasstone

In the autumn of 1984, as a result of a discussion we had had when he came to watch a rehearsal of his ballet *Pas de légumes* at the Royal Ballet School, I received a most interesting personal letter from Sir Frederick Ashton. In this letter, Ashton spoke with great enthusiasm about the value of the method of training handed down by Enrico Cecchetti, and of the influence it had had on him, via his studies with Léonide Massine, Marie Rambert and Margaret Craske. He wrote as follows:

> Having received my first tuition in ballet from Massine, a pupil and great advocate of Cecchetti and his system, and then on to Rambert in 'my rather rickety beginnings', I have always had the greatest respect and gratitude for the Cecchetti method and what it gave to me – with further tuition from Craske. If I had my way, I would always insist that all dancers should daily do the wonderful ports de bras, especially beginners. It inculcates a wonderful feeling for line and correct positioning and the use of head movement and épaulement which, if correctly absorbed, will be of incalculable use throughout a dancer's career.

Much has been written about the influence of Bronislava Nijinska's work on Ashton's choreography, in particular her innovative use of the torso. But Nijinska's twists and bends of the upper body – admired and absorbed by the young Ashton – were grafted onto a base of academic classical technique, as was also to be the case with Ashton's own choreography. Nijinska had started studying with Maestro Cecchetti even before joining the Imperial Ballet School. In her autobiography (1981) she speaks warmly of her studies with him, both at the Imperial Ballet School and later, when she and her brother Vaslav shared Pavlova's private lessons with the Maestro. Then, in her Monte Carlo diary of 1911 (Cecchetti having just arrived from St Petersburg to give the Diaghilev company classes), Nijinska wrote that 'Maestro Cecchetti has faithfully preserved the positions of the whole body according to the geometrical proportions and exact equilibrium developed by Blasis'. Commenting on the strict routine of Cecchetti's method of teaching, Nijinska went on to say that this 'develops in the student's body an absolute "habit" to assume the correct position automatically and to preserve this correct position not only on the floor but also in the air' (1981, p. 334).

Clearly, then, the precision and control of the *danse d'école* constituted the foundation upon which Nijinska built her edifice of choreographic invention. Ashton was inspired by Nijinska's marvellously original use of the upper body, but, like her, he recognised the importance of the classical basis which underpinned her choreography.

Invited by the Camargo Society to arrange a ballet for its first performance in 1930, Ashton was quoted in the *Dancing Times* as follows:

> The idea so often expressed that classical technique is hampering to artistic expression is erroneous and misleading. A sound training, such as one receives through the method of Maestro Cecchetti, embodying as it does a complete and pure theory of movement, awakens within the dancer a response to any style he may be called upon to interpret – and this is surely the ultimate aim of every true artist. (Ashton, 1930, pp. 124–5)

Ashton did not study with Cecchetti himself – the Maestro had left London for his native Italy not long after Ashton began his first classes with Massine. He says that it was from Massine that he learned 'about style and about the beauty of port de bras' (Vaughan, 1977, p. 7). Massine himself attributed his own understanding of the use of the upper body to classes he had with Cecchetti with the Diaghilev company; he talked of Cecchetti's influence on port de bras 'co-ordinating the movements of the arms and the head in order to develop épaulement' (1968, p. 54). When Massine left London, he sent his young student to work with Marie Rambert. Rambert had also studied with Cecchetti, and in her autobiography she too stresses the beauty of Cecchetti's port de bras: 'when I was taught the Italian arms by Cecchetti I realised it was possible to have beautiful arm movements in classical ballet' (1972, p. 103). Rambert had disliked the stilted arm movements of the French Académie. Cecchetti's use of expressive gesture within the academic framework of classical port de bras was thus an important aspect of the teaching which both Rambert and Massine were to hand down to Ashton; it was to become one of the hallmarks of his style.

When Cecchetti left London, his studio was taken over by Margaret Craske, and it was here that Ashton learned many of Cecchetti's famous adagios and allegro enchaînements. These were arranged according to a set weekly pattern of study – different aspects of technique being emphasised on each day of the working week. To anyone who has danced these enchaînements and has also performed in Ashton's ballets, the link between the two is unmistakable. What Ashton did was to use this movement material as a springboard for his own choreographic invention. By altering an angle of the body, substituting a different arm or head movement, or varying the rhythmic emphasis of the steps involved, he would create a totally new dance out of Cecchetti's classroom exercises. One of the best documented examples of this is Peggy van Praagh's description of the creation of the pas de trois in *Valentine's Eve*, based on some of Cecchetti's Saturday steps (Vaughan, 1977, p. 115).

Many of the arm and leg movements in *Les Rendezvous* also echo that Saturday work, whilst the terre à terre batterie and nimble footwork of the pas de trois and the men's pas de six relate directly to Cecchetti's Friday batterie enchaînements. In this respect, it is interesting to note Ashton's own reputed 'ability to do small batterie' (Vaughan, 1977, p. 27). Part of one of those Friday beaten steps en diagonale was incorporated into the Fonteyn solo in *Birthday Offering*. The virtuoso element characteristic of much of Cecchetti's grand allegro found its way into Colas's solos in *La Fille mal gardée* (Vaughan, 1977, p. 308). Here the source was the men's classes being taught by Errol Addison at the time Ashton was choreographing *Fille*. Addison had been a favourite pupil of Cecchetti's, and in his day was himself something of a virtuoso. David Blair presented Ashton with Cecchetti-based material from Addison's classes which Ashton then reworked in his usual way, challenging Blair with feats of technical brilliance which trumped the original both by their technical daring and with those little extra elements of surprise that transform a classroom step into a choreographic gem.

One of the major difficulties of many of Cecchetti's allegro enchaînements lies in the rapid changes of weight and direction their correct execution demands. This aspect of his work is reflected in many of Ashton's dances, notably the Red Girls' duet in *Les Patineurs* and the pas de trois in *Les Rendezvous*. In both of these ballets – as indeed in much of Ashton's choreography – an important element of the movement texture is provided by the gliding motion of the Italian chassé – in which the whole foot slides along the floor, unlike the lighter, 'pointed foot' chassé of the Soviet Russian school. The gradual erosion of this characteristic step dilutes Ashton's style, as much as do the reduced amount of sideways bend and épaulement found in many young dancers today.

The ability to sense a centre of balance which deviates from the vertical was an important element in Cecchetti's teaching, and is frequently echoed in Ashton's choreography, not least in the added thrill of a renversé movement to punctuate a pirouette, as in *Symphonic Variations* and *Rhapsody*. Today's emphasis on high leg extensions often results in a concurrent neglect of the upper body movement (not to mention a reduction in complexity and speed of footwork). Classical ballet seems to have become an altogether more vertical and statuesque affair, eschewing those marvellous, dangerous-looking sideways bends and swoops of movement found in *La Valse*, as they were in many of Cecchetti's classroom steps.

There is a tendency nowadays for dancers – and choreographers – to indulge in a leg-dominated distortion of classical dance. By concentrating the focus of attention on the look of the raised leg in space, with scant regard for the relevant disposition of arms and legs, the harmonious balance between all the limbs is distorted in a way which is contradictory to the demands of Ashton's choreography – hence his plea for the corrective effect of exercises such as Cecchetti's port de bras, with their meticulous attention to maintaining a balance of movement not only between both arms, but also between the arms in relation to the legs.

One of the characteristic positions of the Italian school is the so-called 'Mercury' attitude. Blasis claimed to have adapted this from Bologna's famous statue, and it features widely in Cecchetti's classroom work, as it does in Ashton's choreography. One can trace its development from the original curved shape as used in *Leda and the Swan*, dating from 1930, to the more elongated, streamlined look found in *Monotones* thirty-five years later. This arm position is as much an Ashton hallmark as the famous 'Fred Step' (his signature enchaînement inspired by Pavlova's *Gavotte*). There is a wonderful photograph of Cecchetti coaching Pavlova as she assumes a variant of the Italian attitude arm position, as used in the Maestro's sixth exercise for port de bras and his grande préparation pour

Anna Pavlova with Enrico Cecchetti.

pirouette en dedans – a period pose prefiguring as modern a work as *Monotones* by some sixty years.

Ashton's style is in many ways synonymous with what is called the English school of classical ballet. Although Cecchetti died in 1928, during the 1930s – when English ballet was beginning to come into its own – Cecchetti's pedagogic legacy was still dominant in Britain. It dictated the type of dancer the young Ashton had at his disposal in his formative years as a choreographer. Many of the technical and expressive elements emphasised in their Cecchetti schooling were inevitably reflected in Ashton's dance invention.

Ninette de Valois has written that 'Maestro Cecchetti left a great imprint on the English school. The important aspects of his teaching will remain a part of the academic tradition of our English ballet' (1973, p. 46). She goes on to stress Cecchetti's insistence on the importance of head and body movements, explaining that 'we were expected to master the épaulement first', and she adds that 'although he had been a famous virtuoso dancer he demanded grace from women before anything else. Unity of movement was a fetish with him' (1973, p. 45). Are not these the qualities reflected *par excellence* in Ashton's work?

References

Ashton, F. (1930), 'A Word About Choreography', *Dancing Times*, May 1930.

Massine, L. (1968), *My Life in Ballet*, London, Macmillan.

Nijinska, B. (1981), *Early Memoirs*, London, Faber & Faber.

Rambert, M. (1972), *Quicksilver*. London, Macmillan.

de Valois, N. (1973), *Come Dance with Me*, London, Dance Books.

Vaughan, D. (1977), *Frederick Ashton and His Ballets*, London, A & C Black.

The Bourrée: a Myriad of Uses

Geraldine Morris

For Ashton, ballet was 'an expression of emotions and ideas through dancing' (1951, p. 33), and he invariably insisted that his aim was to make ballets with little mime or gesture, in which dancing was dominant. Ballet, he maintained, is not a good medium for storytelling, its purpose being to 'heighten beyond words certain situations and give a kind of poetic evocation' (Crisp, 1974, p. 172). In other words, he felt ballet to be an excellent vehicle for communicating matters which have more to do with feelings than with reason.

It may come as a surprise to hear that Ashton was not interested in storytelling, since the majority of his titles indicate otherwise; but if we examine his ballets it is clear that these are indeed expressive works whose *raison d'être* is the communication of fundamental human emotions. Indeed, his work has many layers, and although he frequently used narratives, they were superficial vehicles through which he could explore both the human condition and dance: the emotions and moods of the characters provided him with the structure, vocabulary and the imagery he needed for the dances.

Scholars have already noted Ashton's habit of re-using his own material. One example is the particular way he uses the bourrée couru and pas de bourrée to stress different qualities, such as mood, emotion, character or humour. Ashton was not opposed to using simple steps to convey his meanings, and the bourrée, in both its forms, is a step which is central to much of his choreography. Despite this, its place in his choreography has not been fully examined before. By looking at extracts from a selection of his works, I would like to analyse the ways he manipulates the bourrée to depict human emotion. We need to be conscious of the different ways he employs such steps because the sense or purpose of the work frequently derives from the particular movement and its treatment. Ashton had a very individual approach to academic dance. Simply by

14

altering the context of the action, its dynamic, or floor pattern, he was able to change the meaning of the movement.

The bourrée features in his choreography from *Façade* (1931) to *Rhapsody* (1980) and as David Vaughan has already noted 'one might suppose that all the possibilities of the pas de bourrée had long been exhausted' (1977, p. 401). But whether he used it as a long floating movement suggestive of other worlds for Lady Mary Lygon in *Enigma Variations* (1968) or as a stabbing aggressive action to communicate the efficient, bossy yet humorous character of Webster in *A Wedding Bouquet* (1937), it remains a simple travelling step on pointe.

The ballets selected to illustrate Ashton's use of the bourrée have been chosen for two reasons. First, they represent the different tasks he assigned to the bourrée; and second, coming from different periods of his career, they demonstrate that this was indeed an abiding theme of his work. I have not attempted to provide an extensive survey of Ashton's use of the bourrée, but rather a discussion of its manipulation to convey four human conditions or traits: mood, character, emotion and humour. Thus I have divided the paper into these four sections, each of which examines a different portrayal of the bourrée. Although chronologically 'character' should come first, I have chosen to start with 'mood' in order to avoid confusion with 'emotion'. Consequently, to provide balance, 'humour' has been left to the end.

I would also like to clarify my use of the word bourrée. In the text 'bourrée' stands for a pas de bourrée couru, the series of rapid travelling movements usually on pointe, and 'pas de bourrée' is used to describe the action involving three changes of weight.

Mood

Mood here describes atmosphere, and this section looks at the way Ashton uses the bourrée as a method for changing or creating the atmosphere in a scene, with reference to *Symphonic Variations* (1946). This was Ashton's first complete work for the Covent Garden stage. The bourrée occurs on more than one occasion. In the first ninety seconds it is mainly used pragmatically, to move the dancers from one position to another, but when it appears again ten minutes later its function is different: then it indicates a change of mood and becomes a metaphor for love.

It is important to notice the very remote way in which the three females dance the opening ninety seconds, because the mood changes shortly after the entrance of the central male dancer, giving way to a warmer, less frigid tone. The continuous action of the bourrée, in contrast with the initial hesitancy, contributes to the evaporation of the earlier aloofness, something which is reinforced by the introduction of curving arms. But the most significant change of mood occurs when, to use Ashton's own metaphor, 'the wound of love' (Buckle, 1947 p. 23) is inflicted at the end of the female solo: she is caught, in a series of rapid bourrées, mid-movement, by the male. Here, Ashton abruptly introduces a flow of continuous movement which gradually conveys an impression of perfect harmony. What starts as a joyous solo turns into something more profound, and it is the use of the bourrée in this duet which effects that change of mood.

Beginning with a gliding run, the movement of the duet sets the tone for this and the following section. After a pause there follows a series of smooth bourrées punctuated by two flowing jetés. The sequence is repeated four more times, creating an aura of ecstasy and peace. Ashton achieves this by using the bourrée to keep the female just on the ground on pointe, and as an unobtrusive preparation for the floor-skimming lifts. Because the dynamic is smooth and the floor pattern circular, we are almost unaware that any dance movement is taking place. Indeed it is the complete simplicity of the movement which establishes this serene atmosphere, an atmosphere which is echoed after the duet when all three couples move forward in unison. The smooth progression of the bourrée here provides a moment of sublime tranquillity. Ashton builds on this motif later by bringing in an extended version of the pas de bourrée which moves the dancers from one side of the stage to the other in a series of three pas de bourrées. What makes this so impressive is the way it propels the dancers effortlessly across a vast area of the stage generating a sensation of surging ecstasy. Both these sections, the duet and the sextet, begin with astonishingly simple bourrées and end with all six dancers motionless. The atmosphere has developed from intense joy to a mood of complete stillness and peace. And, in the final exuberant section which follows, the bourrée's absence heralds the end of the mystical mood, allowing the protagonists to return to the natural world.

Character

Ashton's ability to depict personal traits is the subject of this section, in which I examine Webster and Julia from *A Wedding Bouquet* (1937). This ballet was the result of a collaborative effort by Ashton, Constant Lambert and Lord Berners with decor, costumes and music by Lord Berners, and words taken from works by Gertrude Stein, principally *They Must. Be Wedded. To Their Wife* (*sic*). The scene is a conventional wedding. All the customs are observed: a bride in white, overdressed guests, bridesmaids, champagne and a cake. Undermining the occasion is the suggestion that the groom has already seduced many of the guests and is still somewhat attached to one, Julia. Although presented as a comic piece it has an underlying streak of bitterness.

Each of the female characters is introduced on stage by a bourrée. It is one of the central motifs, and is used to depict the personalities of the guests as they arrive for the wedding.

The frontcloth rises on Webster standing alone centre stage. From the way she performs the bourrée there is little doubt that this is a formidable, severe and bossy lady. Her opening movements, a series of runs from foot to foot on pointe with elbows and shoulders raised, are really a grossly exaggerated bourrée. Here the overstated movement conveys her rather frightening personality. Later in her dance she executes fast-moving bourrées peppered with relevés in a low attitude. These scuttling bourrées, fractured by the relevés, proclaim her fussy nature and the apparent urgency of her task. She normally moves in diagonals, the quickest way to get across the stage, and she always performs her bourrées with a stabbing quality to emphasise her aggression.

Other characters, Josephine, Violet and Thérèse, enter with bourrées each interrupted by an idiosyncratic gesture. Josephine, with parasol and huge hat, looks towards the wings in a deep bow. Violet does very fast bourrées interspersed with two sauts de basque; she is chasing Ernest and is obviously quite desperate to marry. Finally, there is Thérèse who comes on backwards at great speed and is only stopped from exiting by bumping into Violet. Clearly, she is in too much of a hurry to be of use to anyone. In many ways, though, it is Julia's entrance which provides a brief but compelling example of Ashton's ability to depict a range of human traits with great economy. She bourrées on from the left side of the stage moving swiftly but smoothly before abruptly collapsing from the waist into a deep bend, causing her long hair to flow over her head. The sequence is repeated and followed by rapid bourrées from side to side as she nervously twists a curl between her hands; one is reminded fleetingly of the Betrayed Girl in Ninette de Valois' *The Rake's Progress* (1936). Could it be that Ashton was making a similar connection too? Julia appears to be a distressed but somewhat demented female who, for no apparent reason, has been excluded from the wedding. The speed of her bourrée, the dejected gesture, the repetitive floor pattern and, like the Betrayed Girl, her en face épaulement, all combine to suggest this distressed, if somewhat imprudent damsel.

Human Emotions

In many ways this section overlaps with the previous. But only by separating the two can degrees of feeling be analysed. I shall look here at two duets from *A Month in the Country*, the first for Vera and Beliaev, the second for Natalia and Beliaev.

What is striking when comparing these duets is the similar way in which Ashton uses the bourrée, and yet manages to convey two very different kinds of emotion. The second duet displays a deep sensuality, while the first tends more to affection and warmth, although it is fair to say that Vera also communicates an overwhelming infatuation for Beliaev.

A slow lift opens the first duet, followed almost immediately with Vera moving away from Beliaev in a quick, short elated bourrée. Developing from the opening lift, the bourrée starts in the air and continues as she reaches the floor, generating the impression that she is still floating on the air. This sort of bourrée sets the tone for the duet: its staccato speed, its performance at arm's length, its air of playfulness and its elated quality is continued throughout. Later in the piece she bourrées rapidly around him again but he holds her as though she were a skipping rope or some other toy; the bourrée here conveys her fervour, but his more distant grip suggests merely amusement. Later the couple move together in a diagonal; she performs a swift bourrée while he walks alongside, a moment which is duplicated in Natalia's duet. But, as we shall see later, everything about it is different from Natalia's, the speed, the extension of her arm, the swaying motion Beliaev creates as they move along, and the finish of the sequence in a supported grand jeté. For Vera the moment is ecstatic, but for Beliaev it is just an affectionate frolic emphasised by the speed of the lift and the swaying bourrée. When the duet ends in a series of evenly executed rapidly turning bourrées it has elements of bliss, but the way Beliaev responds – frequently at a distance and only partially moving in unison with her – confirms that he is merely observing, standing outside the relationship. Clearly Ashton has used the rapid execution of bourrées as a way of portraying Vera's ardour, but by distancing Beliaev physically, he generates the impression of brotherly love.

Natalia's duet too is dominated by the bourrée, which becomes an important metaphor communicating the sensuality of the piece. Initially it occurs after a long low sustained arabesque – reversing the opening of the duet in *Symphonic Variations*, where the female is lifted into a low jeté; here Natalia bourrées back before sinking into a splits-like position. Whereas the airborne jetés of *Symphonic* evoke serenity and peace, the sinking reversal of this sequence conveys sensuality and passion; above all, it communicates the harmony that exists between the two.

Elsewhere the floor pattern of constantly changing pas de bourrée diagonals from her earlier solo is repeated, but now replaced by the bourrée and a more tranquil dynamic. Together they move diagonally downstage, Natalia bourrées, while Beliaev walks, just stopping for a moment to lift her off the ground. These bourrées have a tender quality that is absent from Vera's duet, their sensuality portrayed by the closeness of the couple, by the gentle lift and by the use of repetition. It could even be argued that the relaxed recurrence of the floor pattern from her first solo indicates a new-found depth and passion. Concluding the duet is a succession of bourrées which move from side to side: Natalia is held under the arms by Beliaev and moves in gradually diminishing lines. Interspersed with several slow back-to-back turns, they end almost on the spot, with arms dissolving into a shimmer. The pattern is similar to Julia's in *A Wedding Bouquet*, but the quality, effected by the extended arms and the position of the upper back, is altogether different. Strangely, apart from sensuality, it has also more of a broken, ruined feel to it than that of *Wedding Bouquet*. The bourrée's multiple possibilities evidently held much fascination for Ashton.

Humour

The portrayal of humour is one of the most difficult things to render successfully in any genre, but surprisingly the bourrée serves Ashton very effectively for this purpose. Both *Les Deux pigeons* (1961) and *The Tales of Beatrix Potter* (1970) show, as so many of his works do, that Ashton had a deep sense of fun.

Les Deux pigeons may not be one of Ashton's greatest works, but it is certainly one of his most enjoyable to dance, and this might be because of all the fun he put into it. The bourrée appears early on in the first act, but it is only when the Young Girl tries to save her lover from the arms of the Gypsy Girl that the bourrée becomes an agent for humour. As Macaulay observes, she works 'herself up into a tizzy of (hilarious) indignation'(1987, p. 2), and it is because of the way the bourrée has been choreographed that it is so funny.

Her solo, which is directed at the Gypsy Girl, begins with an arabesque step followed by a pirouette into a very quick pas de bourrée and rond de jambe. What makes it comical is the speed at which the movement is performed, causing the Young Girl to look ridiculous. Following this is a jerky sequence of travelling pas de bourrée in which the main thrust is downwards, each pas de bourrée ending in a low arabesque on a plié. Her arms flap in unison with the legs, and she appears to have lost control, both of her body and the situation, something that becomes more apparent as she continues these pas de bourrée round in a circle. The solo finishes in a succession of pas de bourrée, so quick they never come off pointe. Clearly she is out of her depth and this is evident both from the ever-increasing speed of the pas de bourrée and the effort it takes to perform them. To slow down this section of music would thus greatly impair the meaning. The Young Girl would simply look elegant, and her indignant frustration, so carefully written into the dance, would evaporate. The clumsiness of the Young Girl is accentuated by the pas de bourrée of the Gypsy Girl, who dances them with an earthy sensuality missing from her rival. Essentially then, the meaning, the characters and the humour are embedded in the choreography.

Comedy is intrinsic to *The Tales of Beatrix Potter*, but in the duet between Pigling Bland and Black Berkshire Pig, Ashton treats it differently. In many ways the idea of two pigs on pointe performing a pas de deux is so absurd that anything else is unnecessary; but Ashton uses it to parody his own work, and Petipa's. Pigling Bland enters backwards on pointe in a fast-moving bourrée, but it is only when he waddles to the stool at the end of the solo that his bourrées become comical. Instead of an academic bourrée, his feet move to an ungainly parallel second position, and for the rest of the episode his bourrées remain in this position. Ashton's teasing reference to the classics begins when Black Berkshire Pig enters with the développés from the Sugar Plum Fairy's variation. We recognise the moment, and it puts classical ballet, and thus comedy, at the heart of the scene. Elsewhere, the Pigs bourrée together using a similar arm movement to that used by the Ondines in Act I Scene 2 of *Ondine*. But it is towards the end of the duet that Ashton's wit is most evident.

Here the couple bourrée together backwards, the music swells as they turn round and round, Black Berkshire Pig is carried forward in a supported grand jeté only to drop onto the ground as Aurora does. By placing the bourrée in this distinguished company and by choreographing it with all the smooth flowing quality of the academic dance, Ashton, using his favourite step, displays his sense of the ridiculous.

The bourrée is only one example of the way Ashton 'changed steps' (Macaulay, 1984, p. 3) to suit his work. Clearly it is important in Ashton's canon, but what is central to the choreography is the specific way he uses it. He does not simply take academic dance and transfer it to his dances; instead, he uses it to create emotional content. So when Ashton claims that the subject matter of his ballets is dance, always dance, he is in a sense right. What he means is that dance is at the heart of his choreography and everything else – character, mood, humour, emotions – develops from it. Consequently, it is the way Ashton uses the movement, its speed, gesture, épaulement and context, that conveys the meaning of the work or character. Undoubtedly the responsibility for interpreting the work lies with the performer, but if the movement is understood in purely formal terms its capacity to convey human behaviour and feeling will disappear. Alternatively, should the performer interpret the work through the character alone, ignoring the carefully crafted choreography, the significance of the work may be lost. The steps will still be there, but, as T. S. Eliot aptly warns in *The Dry Salvages*, we will have 'had the experience but missed the meaning.'

References

Ashton, F. (1951), 'Notes on Choreography', in W. Sorell (ed.), *The Dance Has Many Faces*, 3rd edn 1992, Chicago, A Cappella, pp. 31–3.

Buckle, R. (1947), 'Abstract Ballet', *Ballet*, Vol. 5 No. 5, pp. 20–4.

Crisp, C. (1974), 'A Conversation', in S. J. Cohen (ed.), *Dance as a Theatre Art*, New York, Harper & Row, pp. 169–73.

Macaulay, A. (1984), 'Ashton at Eighty', *Dance Theatre Journal* Vol. 2 No. 3, pp. 2–7.

Macaulay, A. (1987), *Some Views and Reviews of Ashton's Choreography*, Guildford, National Resource Centre for Dance.

Vaughan, D. (1977), *Frederick Ashton and His Ballets*, London, A & C Black.

The Expanded Moment

Narrative and Abstract Impulses in Ashton's Ballets

James Neufeld

It is easy, particularly when speaking of ballet, to think of the narrative and abstract impulses as opposed. The first demands that the choreographer tell a story, providing the audience with character, incident, motive and continuity – above all, continuity, to link the individual events of the story into a coherent sequence. The other requires structural logic, the work's sense of wholeness deriving from the logical relationships of its constituent elements, not from narrative continuity. 'What happens next,' the central question narration seeks to answer, is meaningless in abstract ballet, except as an aid to the notator. Consequently, narration seems to move us through a sequential pattern, whereas abstraction allows for concentration on the pattern's constituent parts, taken in isolation, then considered together. Frederick Ashton, as one of this century's most eloquent tellers of stories in dance, thus seems to be at odds with abstraction, on the side of continuity and sequence, opposed to abstraction's lifeless reduction of human experience to pattern and form.

Our experience of Ashton's narrative ballets, however, is quite different. As a storyteller, he is often cavalier when it comes to continuity, glossing over reams of discourse with a few casual gestures that leave the audience scrambling to catch up. And our sense of the lasting power of his work comes over and over again from those still points, of which he is master, when narration halts and his choreography opens out a single situation into an expanded moment of rapture, pathos or sorrow, fraught with emotional significance. Those expanded moments assume a weight and power disproportionate to their duration or their storytelling function, and focus all of our attention on their contemplation, like the most powerful moments of abstract ballet. Ashton forces us to abandon our conception of the narrative and abstract impulses as antithetical to one another and asks us to see them instead as reciprocal. He has found a way to fuse the pure abstractions of classical ballet form with the living, human concerns of narration, to the mutual enrichment of both. His narration gains artistic force through his use of abstraction; his abstraction is humanised by his reliance on narration.

The opening of *The Dream* demonstrates, in miniature, Ashton's readiness to interrupt narration with an expanded moment of abstract contemplation. As the fairies enter in groups, each group freezes momentarily on the musical cue, its motion arrested in a backward glance of listening hesitation. (The same gesture is given to Titania alone, at the end of the pas de deux later in the ballet.) This freeze-frame effect, before the ballet's story has got properly under way, acknowledges the abstract nature of the choreography (here we have a group of trained dancers assuming a carefully planned position) while simultaneously making a narrative point (here we have characters who are listening, fearful of being followed). The abstract moment of arrested motion interrupts the narrative flow, but also expands upon the narrative point being made. Without the pause, which momentarily distracts from the sequence and continuity of the action, the audience might miss the point which the action is intended to make. The abstract emphasis on the dancers' frozen attitudes focuses attention on the narrative content being developed. Narration and abstraction have been fused.

The point, choreographically, is a tiny one, and must not be laboured. It accustoms us, however, to the method of operation that gives this ballet its haunting charm, for *The Dream* is interrupted by a much more extended 'backward glance': the pas de deux for Titania and Oberon that arrests the ballet's action, yet expands the moment into the abstract culmination of the entire work. In order to see this technique at work, it is necessary to consider briefly Ashton's treatment of his source material, Shakespeare's *A Midsummer Night's Dream*.

A literary purist could accuse Ashton of playing fast and loose with Shakespeare's text, of reducing a complex series of interrelated plots, each with its own thematic significance, to a simple romantic comedy. The Athenian context, with Theseus and Hippolyta its rulers, is gone completely. Gone too is the play-within-a-play intended to celebrate their wedding, and with it the complex commentaries on class distinction and the power of the imagination that conclude Shakespeare's play. The rustics are mere shadows of their Shakespearian selves, Bottom's famous soliloquy reduced to a few gestures. Inevitably, the play's most characteristic feature, its youthful verbal exuberance, defies translation into dance terms. The story is truncated, its verbal splendour gone, its thematic complexities simplified.

But Ashton's narrative daring is deliberate, not expedient. In choosing for his framing action the feud between Titania and Oberon, rather than the wedding between Theseus and Hippolyta, he shifts the focus necessarily to the mistaken infatuations of the Athenian lovers and to the arbitrary power of the flower, love-in-idleness, to misdirect their love. (It may have been the fact that the flower is the most easily visualised of the play's metaphors that led Ashton in this direction.) Recognising ballet's inability to deal with Shakespeare's verbal and thematic complexities, Ashton concentrates instead on the emotional territory – equally a part of Shakespeare's play – that ballet is uniquely equipped to portray. His one-act distillation of Shakespeare's drama becomes a comic scherzo on the arbitrary power, the foolishness and ecstasy of love.

The principle of selection at work in Ashton's scenario, then, is already one of reducing or eliminating narrative complexity in order to achieve concentration on emotional situations that can easily be portrayed in choreographic terms. Once his pared-down scenario is complete, the choreography itself follows the same principle, moving the action along tersely in order to dwell on the expanded moment of the pas de deux. The reversals of affection, the petty bickering of all the lovers, the silly, arbitrary power of fairy meddling in matters of love, all are subsumed in the pas de deux, which is at once specific to Oberon and Titania (in its narrative function) and universalised as a formal exercise in pas de deux (in its abstract guise). Specific narrative references remain, in the fluttering, fairy-like port de bras for Titania, and in Oberon's languorous rocking of her to sleep at the end of the duet; but the pas de deux itself does nothing to advance, clarify or embellish the narration. The point of reconciliation has already been made; the pas de deux is simply an expansion on it.

But 'simply' is the wrong word, for here the point is in the expansion, not in the forward motion of the narration. *The Dream* achieves its focus in this pas de deux, not in the truncated narration of Shakespeare's plot that precedes it. Ashton uses the pas de deux to give substance to the relationships that have been developed through the story, but those relationships quickly become secondary to the abstract quality of the pas de deux itself. The exquisite mirror-image arabesque for Titania and Oberon, their joined hands encircling the entire gesture, moves us both as an expression of their characters and as an abstract moment of dance. Narration and abstraction support each other at the heart of the ballet in a fashion both specific and general, both narratively eloquent and abstractly satisfying.

A Month in the Country poses an even greater challenge, which Ashton meets with even more radical means. Turgenev's play has almost no real action of the kind that can be conveyed in gesture or dance. It is, instead, made up of conversations – conversations interrupted, half-understood, evasive, or beside the point – out of which the emotional lives of its characters emerge by implication. Ashton prunes characters, situations and entire subplots (the marriages of Vera to Bolshintsov and Shpigelsky to Lizaveta) in order to focus exclusively on Turgenev's primary interest, the tortured relationship of Natalia Petrovna to those around her, and to the tutor, Beliaev, in particular. Ashton salvages just enough narrative incident (or, as in the search for the lost keys, fabricates it outright) to hold together the solos, duets and variations that make up the ballet. As in *The Dream*, these culminate in a pas de deux, this time for Natalia Petrovna and Beliaev. The pas de deux is an abstract form given emotional significance by its narrative content as the expression of the thwarted passion between the two lovers. The brief narrative preparation (again, an invention of Ashton's) of Natalia Petrovna's placing a rose in Beliaev's buttonhole summarises all the preceding context and allows the abstract, classical conventions of the pas de deux to generate their expressive emotional power. Once again, Ashton has managed to impute emotional, narrative significance to a basic dance vocabulary that is, in itself, abstract and without content. Furthermore, his narrative ballet has moved the story forward, not by literal dramatisation of events (there are so few to dramatise in any case), but by presenting a series of such expanded moments of emotional abstraction, linked by the briefest of narrative strokes to provide their context.

The ballet's famous conclusion, in which Beliaev enters unknown to Natalia Petrovna, lightly kisses the ribbons of her dress and, as a sign of his farewell, drops the rose she had earlier given him, illustrates powerfully the reciprocal relationship between the narrative and abstract impulses in Ashton's work. The narrative purpose of the gesture is clear. Another invention of Ashton's (to replace the passing of the note in which Beliaev bids farewell in Turgenev's play), it is necessary to confirm Beliaev's reluctance to depart and Natalia Petrovna's belated awareness of her loss. But the gesture of kissing the ribbons confirms also our memory of the pas de deux that went before. In so doing, it moves into the realm of abstraction, as the final element in the architecture of the entire work, and gives the moment an expanded significance far greater than its narrative function. Narratively, the gesture is simply a sentimental tearjerker; abstractly, it elevates sentiment and gives it substance.

Ashton has described his method of operation as operatic, and the comparison is apt. Just as, in opera, recitative moves the story along expediently, while the arias and ensembles expand upon the emotional situation in a vocabulary at once narratively effective and abstractly satisfying, so too in his ballets Ashton recognises the reciprocal nature of the narrative and abstract impulses. His narration concerns itself less with sequence and continuity than the literalist might like; his most powerful moments of abstract construction always operate within an emotional context that humanises them and gives them life.

Two brief contrasts with other choreographers may help to clarify the point. As the twentieth-century's pre-eminent exponent of abstract ballet, George Balanchine has isolated the formal vocabulary of ballet movement for our contemplation and pure enjoyment. In *The Four Temperaments*, for example, the dancers are bodies in motion, not characters expressing emotion, not even, despite the programmatic titles attached to each section of the ballet, concepts given human form. Balanchine's approach in this ballet allows for no confusion, no mixing of motives. The emphasis is on dance movement as abstract form, and the full appreciation of his style rests on our apprehension of the movement's mathematical, almost geometric purity in relation to the musical score.

In keeping with this emphasis, no extraneous distractions are allowed to interrupt the audience's concentration on the abstract purity of form. Any hint of acting, of facial expression to invest the movement with specific emotional significance, would distort the intention of the choreography. Yet in Ashton, the presence of such emotional 'distraction' is fundamental to his effect. To imagine the pas de deux of Oberon and Titania, or of Natalia Petrovna and Beliaev, without the expressive acting that anchors them in their narrative contexts would render them pointless.

At the other extreme stands the storytelling technique of John Cranko. His two Shakespearian ballets, *Romeo and Juliet* and *The Taming of the Shrew*, concern themselves first and foremost with getting the story across in all its detail. Cranko's ingenuity at finding gestural vocabulary to convey the events, sometimes even the language, of Shakespeare's dramas, knows no bounds. But the emphasis in his ballets is so relentlessly on sequence and continuity – on answering the question, 'what happens next?' – that they rarely pause to explore the emotional significance of what has just happened. When they do pause, they don't tap into the abstract power of ballet's formal movement vocabulary to explore their new-found emotional terrain. The balcony pas de deux in *Romeo and Juliet*, for example, is more a series of postures that give scope to the mimetic abilities of a dance actress than an opportunity for a ballerina to invest the classical dance vocabulary with the emotional significance of the drama engulfing her. Telling the story is central and sufficient to Cranko's purpose; Ashton, by contrast, uses story to gain entry to a corner of the country where Balanchine has planted his flag.

But Ashton, though he inhabits a part of Balanchine's country, does so on his own terms. *Enigma Variations* illustrates the fundamental dependence on narration that separates Ashton decisively from his great contemporary, and gives him his own inimitable character. Though *Enigma Variations*, essentially an abstract ballet, has no narrative source, Ashton finds it necessary to provide a minimal narrative framework in order to give his abstract choreographic ideas their full expression. In this ballet, the reciprocal nature of the narrative and abstract impulses provides the foundation for Ashton's choreographic structure. Far from being opposed to each other, the two are essential to his work.

Ashton's constructed storyline for *Enigma Variations* is vestigial at best. A number of friends are presented through variations characteristic of their temperaments; human relationships, particularly those binding Elgar, his wife, and his friend Jaeger, are suggested; a telegram arrives; a photograph is taken. The narration concerns itself more with the 'Englishness' of Victorian country life than with specific events in Elgar's own experience. We are disinclined to ask what happens next, content to contemplate on its own terms whatever movement Ashton chooses to put before us. In this sense the ballet, as evocatively costumed and decorated as it is, is an abstract suite of dances, not a sequential narrative construction.

Viewed in this way, the ballet's most telling moments are pure abstraction. In the Nimrod variation, Elgar, his wife and Jaeger stand upstage, their backs to the audience, then turn and move slowly forward. Their progress is mesmerising, barely dance, yet movement so carefully judged that it becomes in itself an object of fascination. In the same variation, at the end of a lift, the wife, supported by Elgar, reaches her hand out to

Jaeger and brings him back into the dance. Again, our concern for narrative sequence is obliterated in the grace and beauty of the movement itself. Moments like these have the power to arrest the forward motion of the ballet and, although the movement is not actually stopped, to freeze it momentarily in our consciousness, like the fairies' hesitant glance at the beginning of *The Dream*.

But once again, the experience of the ballet, particularly if one remembers the original cast, either in performance or in the 1969 film, belies any attempt to isolate its constituent parts in analysis. My own memory of performances seen in 1973 is dominated by the presence of Svetlana Beriosova, as Elgar's Wife, and particularly by the luminous serenity of her face. The moments in the Nimrod variation which I remember as particularly satisfying in an abstract vein are also the moments in which Ashton, inspired by his narrative framework of human relationships, gave to a particular ballerina a set of gestures particularly suited to her personality and temperament. Abstractly, the role of Elgar's Wife is central to the conception of the ballet, as mediator for all of its action. But narratively, the character of Elgar's Wife, especially as danced by Beriosova, gives this abstract role the narrative substance required to allow it to perform its central function in the ballet's construction.

So *Enigma Variations*, though essentially an abstract work, could never be taken for a Balanchine ballet. Its narrative line, however slight, is necessary to make its abstractions humane. Ashton is fully fluent in the abstract language of classical ballet, but he speaks it in order to engage the human spirit in response, and thus, inevitably, engages his narrative impulse. David Vaughan may have had these double gifts in mind when he spoke of the Ashton of *Enigma Variations* as a poet who uses the resources of classic ballet 'to achieve a nobility of discourse and carry a weight of metaphor that many would say are beyond its scope' (1977, p. 363). For Ashton, the discourse and the metaphor, narration and abstraction, are inextricably linked; that linkage is the source of his eloquence, the inspiration for his poetry.

References

Vaughan, D. (1977), *Frederick Ashton and His Ballets*, London, A & C Black.

Character and Classicism in Ashton's Dances

John Percival

Ashton is rightly honoured above all as British ballet's most 'classical' choreographer. Space forbids analysing the many possible definitions of that term, but it seems to me there are two reasons for this public perception. One is the nature of his work as a whole, springing from Ashton's life-long belief that all ballets which 'are not based on the classical ballet and do not create new dancing patterns and steps within its idiom are, as it were, only tributaries of the main stream' (Ashton, 1951, p. 92). In other words, anything outside the classical tradition was for him peripheral. The other reason for the general view of him as primarily a classicist is that his creations include, notably, a series of works in plotless pure-dance form. These amount to something like one third of his ballets; no other choreographer except his close contemporary Balanchine has matched them in quality or exceeded them in quantity.

Note, however (turning to another meaning of 'classical'), that very few of Ashton's ballets require only dancers of a pure classicism, the strictest perfection of technique, line and style. When the Royal Ballet in 1970, on Ashton's retirement, was reducing its numbers, he made a revealing remark to me: 'They're getting rid of all the character dancers; they won't be able to do my ballets'. I aim to show that in his plotless as well as his narrative works Ashton was always interested in the full potential of ballet, welcoming the grotesque as well as the lyrical, the comic as well as the romantic. He wanted expressiveness as much as display; character and classicism in his work are not opposites, but part of a wide spectrum.

I want to take one of his plotless dance works as my starting point: *Les Rendezvous*. Created in 1933, it can be seen as an important step in Ashton's process of evolving his pure-dance form. That task occupied him throughout his career, from *Capriol Suite* in 1930, his earliest sur-

29

viving ballet, right through to his last major work, *Rhapsody*, a full fifty years later.

Les Rendezvous is succinctly described in Koegler's *Concise Oxford Dictionary of Ballet* (1977) as a suite of light-hearted dances for young people in a park. Balanchine's *Complete Stories of the Great Ballets* says that 'young couples promenade and dance to give appropriate expression to youthful sentiments that take hold of their ebullient spirits. There is no plot' (1954, p. 309). Actually, the impression of couples is largely an illusion, apart from the two leading dancers, whose roles virtually follow the pattern of an extended pas de deux (entry, adagio, solos and coda) which is accompanied, distracted and interrupted by an ensemble. Although the ensemble dancers pair off at times, the women and men enter separately, and the men (but, surprisingly, not the women) have a pas de six to themselves. There are also a quick, perky dance for another solo woman and two men (Balanchine calls its music 'saucy and bouncing'), and a quartet for a pretty, Petipa-like group of 'little girls'. Although the score (ballet music from Auber's opera *L'Enfant prodigue*) consists of separate numbers, the ballet's sequence is carefully and formally structured.

This work is not necessarily perceived by the spectator as a plotless ballet in the same way as is Balanchine's *Serenade*, created the following year. It has humour, which prevents some from taking it seriously. The dancers – or some of them at any rate – are given titles in the cast list: the leading couple are called Lovers, the corps de ballet are Walkers Out. They have little touches of mime to perform: shaking or kissing hands, bumping into each other or sidestepping to avoid this. The leading man is blindfolded in a game. Pairs of men each lift up a woman and swing her amorously between them. But there is no story here, no development of character, and rather less emotion than in *Serenade*. The comedy, the incidents, are just a device to make the ballet more acceptable to an audience that was unused to ballets without a narrative basis. As Ashton wrote later, at this period he was eager 'to please my audience . . . entertain, amuse and charm them' (1951, p. 89).

His chief intention, declared at the time, was to provide 'a vehicle for the exquisite dancing of Idzikowsky and Markova' (Ashton, 1933) – and, he could have added, to show the young Vic-Wells Ballet as a whole at a higher technical level than had previously been expected of them. His remark seems to me to indicate that he knew very well what he was doing: helping to invent and establish a new kind of ballet where dance was supreme without needing literary or dramatic excuse. In fact he later described this as the first ballet in which he took his lead directly from the music, the method of working which he came to prefer.

Les Sylphides is usually taken as the first ballet of the plotless genre, evolved by Fokine almost accidentally from a more conventional earlier version, and it had to wait a long time for successors. Perhaps Diaghilev, by presenting *Cimarosiana* (and even the *Polovtsian Dances*) out of their original operatic contexts, helped establish the precedent for a ballet that was simply dancing without narrative. By the early 1930s, Massine, Balanchine and Ashton were all devising their own ways of tackling this.

In Ashton's case, having to start his choreographic career making small works for mostly inexperienced casts, he soon produced some pieces which, to judge from frustratingly vague accounts and snatches of film, we might well regard (if we could see them today) as sketches towards the non-narrative genre. It is difficult to believe, for instance, that anyone watched *Leda and the Swan* or *Mars and Venus* for their faint plots, and he also staged suites of dances to Purcell and Mozart. Certainly by the time of *Capriol Suite* he was trying out many of the choreographic ideas that made the basis of much later work: setting two men in rivalry for one partner, or enhancing the effect of the male dancing by making the men work as a group. And since music and costumes both derived from Arbeau's sixteenth century dance manual *Orchésographie*, and Ashton's dances evoked the same period, *Capriol Suite* has a unity that deserves classification as a ballet without story rather than a divertissement. (*Façade*, the following year, was in many respects a better ballet, but a less unified one, since each of its numbers presents a fresh set of characters who have nothing to do with each other.)

With two exceptional virtuosi to head his cast, Ashton in *Les Rendez-vous* displayed the classic technique in all its brilliance. But, as Ninette de Valois pointed out (1937, pp. 115–19), ballet dancers can be divided, according to their physique and disposition, into categories which have proved serviceable for two hundred years since Noverre's time. On one side was the danseur noble or ballerina, elegant in appearance, reserved in manner; on the other, the character dancers, rougher, more vigorous and robust, encompassing dramatic and comic roles. But those who fell between these types, she suggested, the 'demi-caractère' dancers, had the best of both worlds, often ranging into the territory on either side, and Ashton was always happy exploring their centre ground.

In this he was influenced by the two choreographers whom he took as his models, Bronislava Nijinska and Léonide Massine, both of them

31

primarily demi-caractère choreographers. The Nijinska influence on *Rendezvous* is well known, pervading the whole manner of the ballet with the amusing sophistication of *Les Biches* (certainly not the monumental power of *Les Noces*). But I want to suggest one specific resemblance that I do not remember reading or hearing mentioned before. Looking at the ballerina's main solo in *Rendezvous*, with its dizzy turns, its circlings and its deft reversals of direction, its insouciant carriage of the arms, its slight but gracious acknowledgement of homage from male admirers, its general shape seems to me to resemble an abstract and more classical – although still rather jazzy – distillation of the hostess's solo in *Biches* (the Rag Mazurka), although stripped of its predatory characterisation and heightened in the technical demands it made on Markova's virtuosity.

However, if Nijinska is the strong underlying influence, we should not forget that Ashton in *Rendezvous* actually makes a direct quotation from one of Massine's ballets, *La Boutique fantasque*. The way the six male Walkers Out, as a group, lift the ballerina to the height of their shoulders and carry her off at the end of the duet (Adage des Amoureux) comes straight from the end of the Dolls' night-time revolt in *Boutique*, when the Cossack soldiers lift and carry the female can-can dancer. Except that Ashton trumps his model: he makes the partner, instead of following quietly behind, sink adoringly to one knee – a more romantic touch.

It is easy to imagine Ashton himself performing that gesture – although not the rest of Idzikowsky's part. In fact, creating *Rendezvous* before he joined the Vic-Wells Ballet, he made no role for himself in it, although later he danced in the pas de trois. Ashton's roles in early years included the man in *Les Sylphides*, Siegfried in *Swan Lake* Act II, and the Prince in Andrée Howard's *Cinderella*. He knew how to give romantic leads the right atmosphere and style, and how to support his partner to show her at her best; he was enormously proud of having partnered Karsavina, Lopokova, Markova and Fonteyn. Some of the parts he created for himself in early ballets were romantic too, partly because he wanted to see himself that way, and partly for lack of anyone else to do them. But temperamentally and physically Ashton was better suited to character or demi-caractère parts (and that was no great disadvantage: a similar bent did not prevent Massine from being the most celebrated male dancer of the day). Ashton excelled in quick, small steps: as the Ballet Master in his own *Foyer de danse* he was repeatedly skimming round the stage in brilliant solos. His most characteristic roles, the ones in which he is vividly remembered, were droll, witty, often cynical, from the Dago in

Façade and A Personage in *Les Masques* through to the Stepsister in his own *Cinderella*. Incidentally, he played that role much more 'straight' than is usually seen nowadays, more like a slightly caricatured portrait of a real woman (with a make-up modelled on Edith Sitwell) than a pantomime dame. Remember, too, Ashton's film solos as Kleinzack in *The Tales of Hoffmann* and Mrs Tiggy-Winkle in *Tales of Beatrix Potter*. And the roles which de Valois created for him were comic ones, the Sergeant in her earthy anti-fascist comedy *Barabau*, and Valentin the waiter turned can-can dancer (a figure from Toulouse-Lautrec) in *Le Bar aux Folies-bergère*.

Given his experience and circumstances, it is no surprise that Ashton developed his treatment of pure-dance works on lines very different from Massine and Balanchine. Massine made his two first 'symphonic' ballets in the same year as *Rendezvous*, but the high heroic style of *Les Présages* and *Choreartium* is far removed from Ashton's light, elegant confection. Interestingly, when Ashton (in *Apparitions*) and Massine (in *Symphonie fantastique*) both treated the same subject in 1936, Ashton – working to music by Liszt selected by Constant Lambert – undertook a more literal narrative than the dream fantasy which Massine devised to Berlioz's symphony. A direct influence on Ashton from Massine's symphonic style can probably be seen only in *The Wanderer*, his 1941 creation to Schubert.

The closer parallel is between Ashton and Balanchine. By coincidence, the latter was making a ballet to Schubert's Wanderer Fantasy (under the title *Errante*) just about when Ashton made *Les Rendezvous*, and he was thenceforward to specialise more than any other choreographer in non-narrative ballets. Although he often took symphonic music as his base, he called the outcome 'classic ballet' – never 'symphonic ballet'. It is a useful reminder that the great achievement for which Balanchine is often credited, but in which Ashton shared, was finding a way to preserve and adapt the classical ballet tradition so that it would thrive for modern audiences without needing the props of story or drama. Balanchine went further down that route. Ashton, for instance, never followed him into the use of what is usually but erroneously called practice dress – that is, the uniform of tights and T-shirts for men, simple tunics for women, which Balanchine invented to make the choreography more easily legible (besides saving money on costumes). Even dances which Ashton made as *pièces d'occasion* had some element of design: *Monotones* is the starkest, and for that he himself added caps and belts to the dancers' all-over tights.

Also, Ashton never proceeded to the fully and exclusively musical starting point of some Balanchine ballets (*Concerto Barocco, Symphony in*

C, and so on). This was because of his continuing concern for expressiveness and character in dance. Consider how his pure-dance works developed over the years (the landmarks tended to come in groups with intervals between them). *Les Patineurs* in 1937 follows the *Rendezvous* precedent of a slight situational pretext on which to hang the dances – and I am tempted to claim *A Wedding Bouquet*, later that year, for the same category; if this ballet has a narrative, it is a very surrealist one (perhaps post-modern before its time!). Then in 1938, *Horoscope* had a theme rather than a story.

The early wartime ballets mark a stride towards complete self-sufficiency of music and dance without theme or pretext. I have already mentioned that *The Wanderer* had elements reminiscent of Massine in its structuring, but *Dante Sonata* perhaps assimilated more fully the principles of the 'symphonic ballet' while clothing them in a bold style partly invented for the occasion. Ashton followed the surges of Liszt's music in presenting the confrontation of the Children of Light (a pained, tortured lyricism) and Darkness (twisted and malevolent) to evoke powerful emotions.

The breathing-space of Ashton's war service, followed by the return of peace and the liberation of moving to a larger stage at Covent Garden, produced the celebrated series of pure-dance works leading from the glory of *Symphonic Variations* in 1946 to the more romantic *Valses nobles et sentimentales*, the nostalgic grandeur of *Scènes de ballet* and another symbolically or 'abstractly' treated theme, *Don Juan* during 1947–48. Also, the big waltzes for the corps de ballet of Stars in *Cinderella* draw upon the way he developed the ensemble choreography in *Scènes de ballet*, so that they become in effect miniature plotless ballets. (Ashton was so far ahead of any other British choreographer in his handling of the corps de ballet that this subject deserves a paper to itself.) One of the further group of plotless works he returned to in the middle of the 1950s, *La Valse*, is unusual in being almost entirely for the large corps de ballet, and *Homage to the Queen* too used a large cast for whom he invented a cascade of brilliant display dances. *Birthday Offering*, also from that period, fulfilled a similar function for the unprecedented group of no fewer than seven ballerinas he could by then draw upon. And those three works, like the group in the 1940s, reveal his choreographic range: *Valses nobles* and *La Valse* are in romantic mode; *Symphonic Variations*, *Scènes* and *Birthday Offering* more purely classical – but even the display solos of *Birthday Offering* were suffused with the individual style and personality of the women for whom they were created. Very different from these, and from each other, were *Don Juan* and *Homage to the Queen*: the former aiming to distil the essence of the Don Juan legend into dances almost as abstract as *Scènes*, the latter a bravura showpiece for the whole company. What they (and the short-lived *Variations on a Theme of Purcell* in 1955) had in common was encompassing classical, demi-caractère and character work.

This particular mixture is rare in non-narrative ballets (although Balanchine did also use it, for instance in *Four Temperaments*, *Western Symphony*, *Bugaku*). It should not be surprising that Ashton adopted it, however, since the mixture is customary in the big narrative ballets of Petipa which he took as a model for his own long ballets, including *La Fille mal gardée* which James Monahan justly praised as 'the best long ballet of this century... There is no other... to rival this one for neatness of overall construction... wealth of characterisation and super-abundance of felicitous dance... What is most remarkable is that it is very funny. For any ballet to be funny is rare; for a long one to be funny is quite extraordinary' (Monahan & Roboz, 1980, p. 44). To which I would add that here, as in *Cinderella* and *The Dream*, Ashton did not arbitrarily divide the serious and comic characters, but allowed the romantic leads to provide some of the fun too, and some of the comics to have their own moment touched by a sense of wonder.

And, since *Fille* and *Dream* are among the works which were in the repertory equally of the Royal Ballet's two companies when Ashton was directing them in the 1960s, let me quote what he said to me apropos of criticism that the touring company was treated less well than the London-based one. Insisting that for him they were equal but different ('like two sisters' was the comparison he used), he defined the difference as being a greater emphasis on classical and technical perfection at Covent Garden, while the touring company excelled at a demi-caractère quality and in theatrical impact. This shows that he was conscious of these linked aspects of ballet, and he told me that he was happy for his works to be performed with the emphasis either way.

As early as 1951, Ashton wrote that he had grown to work 'purely and selfishly for myself' (1951, p. 89), but few would find that easy to believe, looking at the works he made then and even much later. By the time he made the first section of *Monotones* in 1965, however, his new small-scale treatment of the pure-dance form explored a mode of choreography that was austere, calm, remote and personal, a response to Satie's music that deployed three exceptionally elegant dancers in an idiosyncratic plastique.

Luckily, his mastery was such that what pleased Ashton also delighted the public. And the works that followed over the next couple of years seemed designed entirely to please, yet each introduced some novelty into the plotless form. *Sinfonietta* combined swift, virtuosic dancing in demi-caractère style with a central adagio as experimental as *Monotones*, the ballerina being supported by a group of partners and never touching the ground. The dances of *Jazz Calendar* (which incidentally included a burlesque of *Monotones* in the Tuesday's Child section) were arguably as disparate as those of *Façade*, but made to hang more together partly by the consistency and boldness of Derek Jarman's design. This work perhaps, and certainly Ashton's next, *Enigma Variations*, represent an unusual form, a non-narrative ballet composed entirely in terms of character or demi-caractère dance. The pretence of a plot in *Enigma* can fool nobody; Ashton is presenting portraits to parallel those in the score – portraits which were originally given definition and contrast by an amazingly strong cast of experienced dancers, and which can lose their sharpness when comparable performers are not available.

There was another unusual short work, again in lyrical mood, the *Five Brahms Waltzes* for Lynn Seymour, before Ashton made his last substantial ballet, *Rhapsody*, in 1980, a work that bears many resemblances to *Les Rendezvous* in mood and manner, as also in its emphasis on virtuosity, again with the male role created for a foreign guest star, this time Barysh-nikov. With Lesley Collier as the ballerina, too, Ashton seemed to me to be trying to use her speed and sharpness to create solos worthy of his first inspiration, Anna Pavlova.

And he ended *Rhapsody* with just the same puckish, quizzical gesture for its leading man as he had given the 'little girls' at the end of *Rendez-vous*. Since he had made it a recurring motif in other works too (Puck in *The Dream*, for instance, the Blue Skater in *Les Patineurs*, and a melancholy variant in his own role as the Spectator in *Nocturne*), it seems perhaps as if Ashton chose quietly to draw attention to the continuity of his work over half a century. He himself defined that work in his 1951 essay:

Consciously all through my career I have been working to make the ballet independent of literary and pictorial motives, and to make it draw from the rich fount of classical ballet ... If the ballet is to survive, it must survive through its dancing qualities, just as drama must survive through the richness of the spoken word. In a Shakespearean play it is the richness of the language and the poetry that are paramount; the story is unimportant. And it is the same with all the greatest music, and dancing and ballets. In a ballet it is the dance that *must* be paramount. (Ashton, 1951, p. 92)

Indirectly, Ashton also reveals here what it was about his ballets that made him a great choreographer: the *richness* of the dancing, its variety, its purity and its earthiness, its lyrical and expressive qualities, its poetry and its comedy, its humanity and its humour – and the fact that they coexist in harmony. For Ashton, there was no clash between classicism and character; they were part of one great whole.

References

Ashton, F. (1933), 'Ballet and the Choreographer', *The Old Vic and Sadler's Wells Magazine*, December 1933.

Ashton, F. (1951), 'Notes on Choreography', in W. Sorell (ed.), *The Dance Has Many Faces*, 2nd edn, 1966, New York, Columbia University Press.

Balanchine, G., & Mason, F. (1954), *Balanchine's Complete Stories of the Great Ballets*, New York, Doubleday.

Koegler, H. (1977), *The Concise Oxford Dictionary of Ballet*, Oxford, Oxford University Press.

Monahan, J., & Roboz, Z. (1980), *British Ballet Today*, London, Davies-Poynter.

de Valois, N. (1937), *Invitation to the Ballet*, London, Bodley Head.

Approaches to the Revival of Les Masques
Research, Education and Performance

Shelley Berg and Jill Beck

When the possibility of reviving, *Les Masques* was first mentioned to us at the Dance Division of the Southern Methodist University, Texas, I thought how marvellous it would be to rediscover and restore a 'lost' ballet from the canon of Ashton masterpieces. The development and implementation of such a project, however, presented both myriad challenges and opportunities. Could we 'recall to life' a ballet that had not been performed in over forty years, and make the reconstruction process stimulating and meaningful for our students? How would we integrate the requirements of their education as young dancers and artists with the exigencies of research, rehearsal, and performance? Could we develop a coherent methodology for the process that could be enhanced and refined and used for future projects? The possibilities we divined in the experiment were greater than the perceived difficulties, and we embarked on the adventure.

Ultimately, our decision to proceed with the revival was based on consideration of four criteria: the quality and character of the ballet itself, its place in both the Ashton canon and as part of the larger frame of twentieth-century ballet, and the possibilities such a venture would entail as an educational programme. *Les Masques (ou Changement de dames)* was originally choreographed in 1933, a year that clearly marked a watershed in ballet history. Two ballets that exemplify the currents of change that define the era, George Balanchine's *Cotillon* and Léonide Massine's *Les Présages*, have recently been revived by the Joffrey Ballet, and it seemed important to us to complete this trilogy of 'lost' works by restoring an Ashton ballet of the same period. In terms of Ashton's own work, *Les Masques* seemed a significant antecedent of more widely known ballets such as *Apparitions* (1936), or ballets still performed such as *Les Rendez-vous* (1933). The ballet, designed in elegant black and white by Ashton's

38

close friend and collaborator Sophie Fedorovitch, is a scintillating comedy of manners; even its subtitle is wittily ironic, with dance as its subtext. A favourite Ashton theme, romantic love, with its vicissitudes and follies, was illustrated in the ballet's slight plot. Two masked couples meet at a ball or nightclub; they switch partners, and discover, deliciously, that the husband and wife have fallen in love all over again, and the lover has found his intended inamorata.

Les Masques is a chamber ballet for seven women and two men, set to Francis Poulenc's Trio for Oboe, Bassoon and Piano. It would therefore be possible to work with a small number of students as an experimental learning group without taxing the resources of the Dance Division. Peter Franklin White, a former member of Ballet Rambert and the Royal Ballet, was sufficiently familiar with the work to construct an initial staging of the ballet on the students. It was also feasible to perform the ballet with live music, which would be played by students in the University's Music Division. The ballet's emphasis on characterisation, stylisation and narrative would provide an unusually rich learning experience for students, who rarely have the possibility of developing roles that require interpretation. Finally, the project would form an integral part of the graduate dance programme's focus on dance direction and repertory. By placing the reconstruction of a work by a master choreographer at the centre of study, the students would have an active and compelling example of the working process necessary to carry a ballet from research through rehearsal to performance.

Research: the Sense of the Past

In the last ten years, a growing number of seemingly 'lost' ballets have been revived and reconstructed. These include Nijinsky's *Le Sacre du printemps* and Balanchine's *Cotillon*, both restaged by Millicent Hodson and Kenneth Archer for the Joffrey Ballet, and Nijinsky's *L'Après-midi d'un faune*, which was re-envisioned and scored from the choreographer's own notation by Ann Hutchinson Guest, and which had its American debut at the Juilliard School under the direction of Jill Beck. The realisation of each of these productions has underscored the importance of contextual research as an indispensable component of the reconstruction process. The dynamic relationship of an artwork to its time is essential in decoding its significance in the cultural canon; problematic and elusive elements such as performance style (which in the case of *Les Masques* included manners, deportment and etiquette) can be more readily identified and described when placed in a specific historical framework.

I began the research for *Les Masques* by collecting and assembling source materials from reviews, photographs, programmes, costume and set designs in the archives of the Theatre Museum and Rambert Dance Company in London, and the Dance Collection of the New York Public Library. Both Rambert and the Dance Collection had fragments of film, with rehearsal excerpts from 1934 and 1938 respectively; the former would prove immensely valuable as a model for performance style, stage and costume design, and as an *aide-mémoire* for White in the reconstruction process. The immediate restrictions of time and resources, however, delayed our receipt of the later film, which we hope to incorporate into our performance research. Jane Pritchard provided a thorough and exhaustive *catalogue raisonné* of artists who danced the ballet from 1933 to 1953, which will serve as our primary source for the gathering of oral histories and further performance details, and many dancers who performed *Les Masques* continue teaching and coaching, and can actively communicate the *élan vital* of the Ashton repertory.

Our first studio rehearsals with White were not scheduled until the fifth week of the school semester, which allowed the graduate dance students to prepare the ground with some initial contextual research. For these four students, the 1930s are as remote as the nineteenth century, but as *Les Masques* is a 'comedy of manners', they needed to develop 'a sense of the past' to begin to capture the mood and atmosphere of the ballet. Each student was assigned to prepare an annotated bibliography and short narrative summary on one of four topics: the music, theatre, film, and art and fashion of the early 1930s in England and America. They had read David Vaughan's *Frederick Ashton and His Ballets* (1977) and excerpts from Mary Clarke's *Dancers of Mercury* (1962), and various shorter works to give them initial historical background and information; but I wanted them to begin to dig deeper. What information could we glean on the fashion and art of the thirties that would help the dancers with their body posture and deportment? What were the popular themes in the plays and films of the period, and how were these reflected in the ballet? Had Ashton's work in the musical theatre, especially his collaborations with the black American dancer and choreographer Buddy Bradley, influenced his choreography for *Les Masques*, and if so, would we be able to see these cross-currents in the ballet? The information the students gathered was then shared with the group as a whole, so that a broad picture of the ballet's milieu began to emerge. This process also gave the students immediate and productive investment in the ballet's eventual re-creation.

Our joint investigations yielded interesting (if not entirely surprising) results. The students became acquainted with the stylistic conventions of art deco, with its emphasis on sleek, angular lines and sculptural form; this background gave them references for the beautiful period look of the ballet. The fashion mannequins and starlets of the thirties provided models for the sophisticated and glamorous look of the women who perform the roles of the Wife and His Lady Friend. They discovered the felicitous nature of creative synchronism. Ashton's gift for devastating parody is well documented, yet the scenario of *Les Masques*, with its ironic commentary on the morals and mores of café society, prefigured many parallels plots and devices in the early Astaire–Rogers movie musicals. The students found this both remarkable and strangely satisfying; it was almost as if they had reinvented history to valorise the achievements of the ballet stage over the popular cinema.

The act of research into the past brought both historical and contemporary social issues into high relief. The contribution of African-American culture to the development of twentieth-century music, dance and theatre has been an important theme in recent dance scholarship. In her article 'Balanchine and Black Dance', Sally Banes notes that Balanchine, like Ashton, worked with Buddy Bradley during the early thirties, and states that the former's collaboration with Bradley was 'a crucial one' (1994, p. 59). As a choreographer, Bradley brought together the dynamic body movements of African-American vernacular dance with the tap-dance steps and rhythms of jazz improvisation to create a bold and inventive style. Ashton also worked closely with Bradley, and the fruits of this association were evident in ballets such as *High Yellow* (1932) and *Les Masques*. While the blending of material from black dance with the ballet idiom was clearly manifest in *High Yellow*, with movements such as 'snakehips' being readily recognisable, Ashton's use of black vernacular forms in *Les Masques* seemed both more subtle and more theatrical. In the course of their investigation, the students discovered, for example, that there were indications that the role of Her Lover, originally played by Walter Gore, was meant to be a black man (Vaughan, 1977, p. 86). In an oral history session with the graduate students, White stated that he thought that, in Ashton's conception of the part, the emphasis should be placed more on the manner in which the character appropriated black vernacular movement as part of his effort to disguise his true identity. He believed that if there was anything 'shocking' for audiences about the original production of *Les Masques*, it came from the *frisson* of eroticism rather than miscegenation. Nevertheless, it became clear that in casting and teaching the ballet, we would need to be sensitive to the social climate of both the 1930s and the 1990s, and make clear Ashton's great admiration and respect for Buddy Bradley and the black vernacular dance tradition.

Education

Although the contextual research was a crucial element of this early part of the process, we were anxious to begin the next phase of the project: White's initial restaging of the choreography. Although many of the Division's students were already committed to a strenuous rehearsal schedule for the fall repertory season and were unable to audition for *Les Masques*, we assembled a cast of seven undergraduate and two graduate students to be the experimental group for White. All of the students involved in the project had access to the file of critical and historical material the graduate students had developed on *Les Masques*, and were encouraged to add appropriate new material as they discovered it. In addition, each student was asked to keep a personal journal or diary during the rehearsal process. They were asked to record not only details of steps and stage action, but their impressions of the ballet, a description of their character and their reflections on the reconstruction of the ballet as they experienced it. This was, in a sense, a trial run for the second phase of this project, which will take place in the spring semester. We hope to organise the cast of *Les Masques* into a co-operative learning group, using multimedia technology as part of the reconstruction process.

Although the performance and analysis of masterpieces of dance repertory are central to the tradition of dance history, we have not fully explored the educational potential of the process of reconstruction and revival. The reconstruction process should be accompanied by critical learning activities that can enhance the dancer's performance, enrich contextual information on the ballet and help both performers and directors develop critical insights that will make the performance experience more meaningful. We see this programme taking place in four phases. In Phase I, the dancers would engage in historical and textual research, aided by multimedia information on the ballet's history, choreographer, music, and design, as well as any supplementary material available for the reconstruction. Information can be shared and ideas discussed on a community 'bulletin board' for the learning group. In Phase II, during the rehearsal process, the dancers could share their feelings and impressions about learning their roles, the task of mastering and interpreting the ballet physically and musically, so that the bulletin board becomes 'a collective diary of responses'. By giving the dancers a formal arena in which to share and analyse their responses to the ballet and to their roles, they literally share in the ballet's re-creation. This type of process also allows the dancers time for thoughtful reflection and consideration, learning activities too often curtailed in the course of a busy academic schedule. While the performance section of the project, Phase III, is often a self-contained activity, the dancers and the ballet's director could use the technologies already developed to hone details of execution and interpretation. In Phase IV, audience reactions and comments could be added to the performers' own final commentaries and a concluding analysis of the ballet would be written by the director. (For discussion and further examples of this type of co-operative learning process, see Beck, 1991; Beck & Bowers, 1994.) Although the *Masques* project does not yet have all the components of an ideal interactive media project, the historical research and the dancers' journals of their thoughts and experiences have helped provide a contextual and analytical framework with which to learn and view the ballet. The reconstruction process to date has enabled us to plan a research and restaging model, fully integrated with interactive multimedia, for use in future restagings of *Les Masques*.

Rehearsal: What is Les Masques?

We began the rehearsal process by listening to the music for the ballet while White described the stage action. The idea that the ballet had a plot, a development and a dénouement (and wasn't *Swan Lake* or *Giselle*) came as a surprise to some of the dancers. The students taking part in this restaging found that they had to think about performing a ballet in a new way. They would be required to tell a story, to relate a narrative through movement and, most especially, gesture. Their dancing not only had to be accurate, it had to be evocative. Each dancer would need to develop a character with a distinctive personality, a personality that had to be convincingly conveyed to the audience. For most of the dancers, it was a challenging, and at times even frustrating experience. In today's dance culture, it is usually execution rather than interpretation that is paramount; the current pre-eminence of technique sometimes threatens to destroy the subtleties of style and meaning in ballets that rely heavily on the dancers' dramatic abilities. In learning *Les Masques* the dancers made a commitment to explore new and often unfamiliar ways of thinking about performance, and in doing so gained confidence in their abilities as both dancers and nascent artists.

Our rehearsal schedule was concentrated and intensive: we worked together three hours each evening and on Saturday mornings for two weeks. White often spent much of the day preparing material for rehearsal: listening to the music, making notes, and watching the snippets of tape from the original production to revive his own memories of a ballet last seen over forty years ago. As the dancers began to perform the steps and to try and recreate the ballet's action, he would often remember and describe a detail or a pose. Each tiny fragment illuminated more of the picture. The two young girls were all 'fuss and bother', with 'eyes that they knew how to use', and who giggled at every opportunity. The three ladies with fans were the epitome of youthful sophistication, too grand really to join in the action, but 'terribly with it and rather bored'. The four principal dancers had more emphatically drawn characterisations, which seemed clearly delineated by their movement styles and qualities. The roles created for Alicia Markova and Pearl Argyle, as Ashton himself noted, were 'complementary but opposing' (Vaughan, 1977, p. 86): while Markova was brilliant, vivacious and exotic, Argyle was quietly compelling and elegantly *soignée*. For Walter Gore's character of Her Lover, Ashton incorporated the sinuous gait and jaunty ebullience he extracted from his work with Buddy Bradley, while in his own role as the Personage, the choreographer emphasised sophistication and charm with just a hint of jaded boredom. We found that as the ballet took shape, the characters took on a life of their own, and we often knew instinctively if their gestures and actions lacked sufficient justification or motivation.

In each rehearsal, the unusual combination of performance problems in theory, dance 'archeology' in practice, and ballet history in action, presented a series of intriguing puzzles to be solved. The early entries in the dancers' journals demonstrate their commitment to the experiment, and, on occasion, their confusion and frustration with the process. One of the two young girls declared: 'It's all in feeling the characters work off each other. We're not supposed to think so much . . . I am trying to visualise feelings instead of thinking of one movement after another.' Tina Curran, who undertook to learn the part of His Lady Friend, noted that the 'gelling together' of the oral history material from White, the discussions of the ballet's historical context and the choreography gave the ballet 'more content and weight' for her: 'I completely see the value of developing a character study and revamping it as the reconstruction process continues,' she wrote. The dancers noted choreographic details that improved their execution of the steps. The three ladies observed that the lines of their movements were always extended by their fans, and this made them more aware of the shapes described by their arms and hands. Tina saw that the high, prance-like walks of His Lady Friend limited her movement through space, but gave her an important tool with which to define strongly her character's flirtatious gaiety. The two Young Girls realised that their bourrées had different meanings in different sections of the ballet, and they began to experiment with varied dynamics and attack in each sequence. Scott Warren, essaying Ashton's own role of the Personage, decided that the choreographer would never strike a pose without assuming an attitude to complement it, and he began to explore transitions between steps and phrases to give them greater continuity and coherence. In 'deconstructing' a work such as *Les Masques* these student dancers came to understand the value of artistry and virtuosity as holistic concepts, that the meaning of a ballet can be embedded in its choreography, if only they know how to look and to learn.

For the dance historian, *Les Masques* offers a compendium of Ashton's choreographic devices. There is, of course, the 'Fred Step', woven so poignantly into the trio for the Personage and the young girls. The stage action the choreographer devised as counterpoint in this section, for the Wife and the three ladies with fans, sets off the moment like a delicate, faceted jewel. The vivacious allegro dancing for the two young girls foreshadows the virtuoso roles Ashton would later create for similar pairs and quartets of 'little girls' in ballets such as *Les Rendezvous* and *Les Patineurs* (1934). His use of contrasting styles of movement for the mismatched couples in *Les Masques* is particularly ingenious: the Wife (Argyle) and the Personage (Ashton) share an elegant, stylised formality of movement, while His Lady Friend (Markova) and Her Lover (Gore) are more flamboyant, extroverted and devil-may-care. This device makes the final unmasking and pairing off of the couples all the more delightful and believable. The three ladies with fans work together as a chorus –

'like the Andrews Sisters', as White remarked – and comment on the foolish and sometimes scandalous behaviour of the principal dancers. Each dancer makes a vital contribution to the choreographic design and the coherence of the story; to watch this ballet being re-created once again is, to paraphrase Ashton on Petipa's *The Sleeping Beauty*, like having a private lesson in the craft of choreography.

The first stages of this challenging project have left us with as many questions as answers. We know that there are significant details of the choreography still to be identified and incorporated. There is, for example, an overhead lift shown in a photograph of Walter Gore and Sally Gilmour; where is that located in the ballet, or was it performed solely for a photo shoot? Were there changes to the choreography in later versions of the work, and, if so, how were they assimilated? How did later casts learn the ballet? Mary Munro, who danced the roles of one of the Young Girls and the Wife, notes that the dancers who performed *Les Masques* in the late 1940s were urged to read Stanislavsky's methodologies for creating a character; when was this rehearsal strategy added, was it helpful to the dancers, and how should we include it in our reconstruction techniques? Although we may use a panoply of resources available to us, from multimedia technology to oral history and anecdote, can we ever really recreate the 'aura' of the ballet's almost mysterious original quality? We believe that if we have the right ingredients to cast the magic spell, this sleeping Ashton ballet will have a beautiful awakening.

References

Banes, S. (1994), 'Balanchine and Black Dance', in *Writing Dance in the Age of Postmodernism*. Hanover, NH, University Press of New England.

Beck, J. (1991), 'Recalled to Life: Techniques and Perspectives on Reviving Nijinsky's Faune,' in J. Beck (ed.), 'A Revival of Nijinsky's Original L'Après-midi d'un faune', *Choreography and Dance: an International Journal*, Vol. 1, pp. 45-80.

Beck, R. & Bowers, D. (1994), 'Education in the Performing Arts: Repertory, Reconstruction Groups and Multimedia', Proposal for Meadows School of the Arts.

Clarke, M. (1962), *Dancers of Mercury*, London, A & C Black.

Vaughan, D. (1977), *Frederick Ashton and His Ballets*, London, A & C Black.

A Month in the Country
Multi-Layered Musicality and Meanings

Stephanie Jordan

In building the score for *A Month in the Country* (1976), and to the alarm of some purists, Frederick Ashton and John Lanchbery, who arranged the Chopin music, used their by now familiar 'welding' approach: arranging, reordering, editing and orchestrating existing music to suit the ballet's action (Vaughan, 1977, p. 394). Robert Irving, Lanchbery's predecessor at the Royal Ballet and later musical director of New York City Ballet, denigrated this cutting and pasting approach as 'mutilation'; the 'snip-snip' version of *The Dream* he considered like a 'film travelogue' (Irving, 1976). Yet, in *A Month in the Country*, what results is an integrated musical/choreographic work with an immensely rich and varied resonance between what is seen and what is heard, from both the detail of individual moments and the new large structure. Here is a multilayered interaction and a celebration of the duality between external appearance and internal feeling. Whether all these resonances were ever intended or indeed recognised, whether my readings are all shared by Ashton, Lanchbery and others, is unlikely. Ashton himself spoke very little about what he made and the process of making it. Yet, this dance text, now self-standing, presents a wealth of possibilities.

Perhaps too it was simply fortuitous that the Claudio Arrau recording of the three Chopin pieces that Ashton used determined the right order for the ballet – although it also happens to be the chronological order of composition. Possibly fortuitous too, is that one of the pieces is a set of variations on the 'La ci darem la mano' melody from Mozart's *Don Giovanni*; 'Give me your hand' – the Don's song of seduction to Zerlina. There is a certain irony here as we are asked to compare two men who share the capacity for devastating impact on the women whom they meet. But Ashton, we know, enjoyed connections between the different facets of a work – that Turgenev was friendly with Chopin and George

47

Sand, whom Beliaev mentions admiringly in the play; the dance set in 1850, when the play was written and only shortly after they were likely to have met; that the Russian upper classes looked West for cultural inspiration, commonly speaking French amongst themselves; and that Turgenev and Chopin both lived and probably met in Paris. Yet Ashton also liked to think that the household of *Month* could have been near the Polish border (Seymour, 1976) – nearer, in other words, to Chopin's homeland. Vera, Natalia's ward, plays Chopin offstage, according to a number of stage directions in Emlyn Williams' translation of the play that Ashton used (a copy is in the Ashton library at the Royal Ballet School – ironically not in the translation by Isaiah Berlin, who persuaded Ashton to use Chopin in the first place). Neither are these directions in the original Turgenev. The designer Julia Trevelyan Oman told me that it was her idea to have the piano on stage, for Vera to play at the beginning (personal communication, 14 July 1994).

Prompted by this kind of information, some of which has, after all, been fed to us in programme notes, I am teased by the connections with Mozart's *Don Giovanni*. Scenes from the opera decorate the walls of the set – another connection – as in the fashion of certain genre pictures and engravings of the mid-nineteenth century. That again was Oman's idea, but it encourages us to see connections between the Don and Beliaev. After all, the Don has been variously interpreted as quarry or victim as much as pursuer, liberator of women and idealist rather than straightforward vile seducer. Arlene Croce compares Beliaev interestingly to the Kierkegaard figure of an unconscious Don, object of love rather than lover (1976, p. 221). In his 1843 essay 'The Immediate, Stages of The Erotic or The Musical Erotic', Kierkegaard considers the abstraction of sensuality rather than the Don himself as the true seducer, epitomised, it happens, for him, in the musical Don Giovanni, not a speaking individual, but a voice, 'the voice of sensuousness, and we hear it through the longing of womanhood' (1959, p. 95). The erotic force of Beliaev is focal within *Month*, and it is interesting – though again I am not trying to argue unduly from the point of view of Ashton's intentions – that Ashton once toyed with the idea of calling his ballet *The Student*, after Turgenev's original title for *Month* (Kerensky, 1976). Ashton, who created a *Don Juan* ballet in 1948 (using Richard Strauss's score), was aware of at least one less conventional, more open, nineteenth-century, post-E. T. A. Hoffmann reading of this character. In an undated letter to the critic Edwin Evans, Ashton begged for more information about the epic poem by Lenau upon which the Strauss tone poem is based (Ashton, n.d.). The use of the 'La ci darem la mano' theme can therefore promote a fascinating range of imagery to enrich our view of the ballet.

Ashton tells us that the Mozart theme also suggested the operatic recitative/aria structure of the ballet to him, but the same contrasts are embedded within the Chopin score, quasi-recitative passages choreographed as silent acting. At any rate, Ashton and Lanchbery (and, in the early stages of the working process, Ashton's friend Martyn Thomas) used their opportunities, reshaping and repointing the score to enhance the action (see Jordan, 1978–79, and Jordan, forthcoming book).

The musical selection for *Month* is as follows:

Variations in B-flat major on a theme from Mozart's *Don Giovanni* ('La ci darem la mano') for piano and orchestra, op. 2 (1827).

Grand Fantasy in A major on Polish Airs for piano and orchestra, op. 13 (1828).

Grand Polonaise in E-flat major for piano and orchestra (1830–31) preceded by Andante Spianato in G major for piano solo (1834), which contains the longest section of uninterrupted piano solo music in the work (published together as op. 22).

The first two of the pieces are suitably sectional, conveniently marking off scenes in the action, and in the Fantasy, rapid, abrupt changes of mood serve the developing drama well. We hear that both Lanchbery and Ashton were constantly surprised and delighted at how well the music and dramatic structure fitted together. However, much of the 'fitting' was the result of considerable manipulation – even, at one point, to the extent of taking two bars out of one section and using them to link two other sections. But the joins are convincing and, perhaps most surprising, very little music had either to be composed or even transposed in key. Chopin's orchestration, which Lanchbery has described as 'at best slender and at times sketchy' (programme note, 1976), was considerably modified, often to point up the quality of recitative or conversation, or to reinforce the dance structure. For instance, in the Andante Spianato for piano only, which is the music for the major love duet between Natalia and Beliaev, Lanchbery transfers the Semplice section (a sort of interruption during the coda) to strings. Now this is even more of an interruption as a contrast with the intimate qualities of the piano, given too that the piano, to Chopin more than to any other Romantic composer, is a specific world closed off from the rest of music. The device works well dramatically, because Natalia, reminded of the social problems that their relationship will cause, stops dancing when the orchestra returns her to harsh reality. Then we return to the piano, to dancing, and to the abandonment to feeling.

The most significant alteration to the original Chopin structure occurs with the curtailment of the Polonaise and the ensuing return to material from the Variations and Fantasy; this material covers the official departure of Beliaev, Natalia's final solo and Beliaev's brief re-appearance to return the rose that Natalia has given him. Two separate sections of music from the introduction to the Variations are heard (the 'La ci darem' theme is clearly alluded to again, though we have not heard this actual section of the score before), and, finally, the part of the Fantasy entitled 'Thème de Charles Kurpinski' returns, the theme to which Beliaev dances and during which Natalia returns to see him before their duet. It is therefore already associated with Beliaev and Natalia. That theme is an obvious reminiscence motif, introduced for dramatic point, as is the other musical reference. It is as if early memories flood back, and we and the main protagonists are called upon to summarise a recent past that is rapidly disappearing before our eyes (and ears). There are also the matching sketch references back in time in the briefest of solos for Natalia – she bursts in, with references back to both her duets with Beliaev, the early Polacca and the later Andante Spianato – and then her husband interrupts her privacy. Thus Lanchbery and Ashton both devise a 'whole' structure out of three originally distinct pieces, and suit the dramatic development at the same time.

The ballet starts with the Variations, introducing the characters of the household amusing themselves together before any dangerous emotional entanglements have developed. Formality is emphasised: strict three-part form in individual Variations dictated by the Mozart theme. The ternary form comprises eight bars (theme A), which is repeated with minor variation, an alternative theme B for eight bars, and then the original theme A, eight bars returned for the last time: AA'BA'. Form is further simplified in that each eight-bar unit already contains repetition, in a classical eigtheenth-century antecedent-consequent structure, and there is tonal imperative for full closure at the end of the theme (a 'classical' self-contained system). The family atmosphere is informal, the music speaks of controlled emotion, learnt manners, socially acceptable behaviour, even if there is something of a pent-up excitement on stage. Mozart and the eighteenth century have a deeper meaning in relation to the narrative. It is interesting that the original Chopin starts with an extended turbulent introduction (which Lanchbery introduces at the end of *Month*) and then settles into these formal and conventionally-arranged variations. It is significant that Lanchbery and Ashton choose to start the action with formalism and tonal stability.

Also underlining stability – and this probably just happened rather than being intentional – Ashton and Lanchbery iron out the tempo shifts that Chopin stipulated between the early variations: ♩ = 76, ♩ = 92, ♩ = 63, ♩ = 92 becomes ♩ = 76 throughout. And the first two dance variations regularly mark aspects of this formal structure, the immediate repetitions after every four bars, confirming choreographically the musical formality.

Of course, everything rapidly opens up from Variation V – Beliaev's entry, appropriately – where the old three-part form starts to shatter (Lanchbery adds to the point by cutting the first written musical repeat), and the Variation ends 'open', in a different key from that in which it started. From then on, structures are rhapsodic, episodic, with plenty of tempo fluctuation.

The piano itself plays a number of different roles in the work. At the outset, it is the domestic instrument, the Mozart theme mimed by Vera on a piano onstage, before the dance variations begin. Soon, however, it becomes very much the personal voice – allusions to the actual role that it played in nineteenth-century music, as the voice of Romanticism. Liszt describes the piano as 'my eye, my speech, my life' (Newman, 1972, p. 87). And Romantic music is often described as having a speaking quality, with listeners in the nineteenth century known to respond concretely rather than abstractly; Roland Barthes, in our own times, observes that Schumann's music is always a *quasi parlando* (see Lippman, 1964; Barthes, 1985, p. 115). We are keyed into the nineteenth-century view of Chopin by the very thorough periodisation of the ballet: we hear music through those characters. And there is too the emphatic notion of the composer developing an individual style and expression, Chopin's, one of yearning, restlessness, and drawing-room intimacy. If the piano is like a voice, directly expressing feeling, Ashton goes further in making us feel that piano and dancer are one, and that dancer/piano sing as in an aria. As an instance of the piano indicating the highly personal, there is the duet for Natalia and Beliaev to the Andante Spianato. It is in this duet too that we see excellent examples of piano ornamentation, so easily read as musical gesture, become personal, become dance gesture. Indeed the ornamented Chopin style becomes the dance style of much of *Month*, which is correspondingly more florid, lacy, here than in many of Ashton's works; at the beginning of this duet, Natalia's style is immediately ornamented, even at a point when the music is still quite plain.

Earlier, the form of the Variations was discussed, and how music and dance forms together create meaning. Contrast the large form of the two most important duets, each of them so different from each other and so different from the earlier representations of formal symmetry. Vera's duet with Beliaev, she in love with him, demonstrates a continuity: Ashton masks repetition, varied repetition or recapitulation in the music. The ballet has now opened out emotionally. The form of the music too is open, moving from A major to an unresolved dominant of F-sharp minor; the narrative of the duet is consequently unresolved, emotionally unfinished.

On the other hand, Natalia's duet with Beliaev, however mutually passionate, stresses the timeless, the reverie; more than half the duet is musical coda (after a simple ABA form), a long, sensuous shimmer over the tonic chord, with a deviation in the Semplice section, only to emphasise the return of the shimmer. Interestingly, the music is taken at slower speed for the ballet than is indicated in the score. To the shimmer, Ashton choreographs gentle swaying lifts, side to side, and side to side again, and endless bourrées, seamlessly linking into lifts. The transient lurks, but the characters of this romance clearly want it to go on for ever. Of course, this static time sense makes the interruption of Vera and the ensuing dénouement seem startlingly abrupt and the consequences alarmingly rapid by contrast.

Looking at this duet in more detail from the television recording involves a certain degree of generalisation. Obviously there are differences between one performance and the next, and there is also the major contribution of Lynn Seymour and Anthony Dowell in the creation of this duet. Before this shimmering coda, the choreography demonstrates several points of independence from the music. The broader contours of the music are reflected, two lifts at the two climaxes in the middle section B and in the final section A, but it is interesting to note how florid, passionate the movement seems to be at the outset (when the musical theme is plain); how the movement quietens of its own accord; and how, when the opening musical theme returns, the movement to it starts much more peacefully than before, a simple, continuous turn in arabesque with changing standing leg and arms. For the recapitulation of section A, the movement is new, but the dynamic procedure – hasty and then quieter –is the same as before, again independent of any change in the music. Often, too, the choreography shoots its own accents across the music. Sometimes musical ornament has a counterpart in the dance, sometimes the dance uses the musical idea, reflects it and carries it further – as in the flourish of linked hands with arching of the back. It is as if the dance has its own shape of turbulence and quiet that is more extreme than the music; it pulls against the music to create energy, added passion, from conflict until resolution in the coda with the music – the image of 'for ever' – in the coda. Likewise, in Natalia's variation there are independent dance rhythms and accents creating lively conversation with the music. This independence of dynamic and rhythm between music and dance is a feature of Ashton's musical/choreographic style, the dance at times matching, at times counterpointing the music. However, *A Month in the Country* is one of Ashton's most sophisticated and complex examples of this kind of dialogue. As explained earlier, the work is one in a series that forges narrative to specially arranged, existing music, and purists have worried about this technique. Yet these Chopin pieces are not among his best known, and I have tried to show how the musical score, as it has been masterfully arranged, acts both in dialogue with and in enhancement of the choreography. In terms of both form and meaning, it is one of the richest integrations of music and narrative choreography in the repertoire.

References

Ashton, F. (n.d.), Letter to Edwin Evans, New York Public Library Dance Collection.

Barthes, R. (1985), 'Day by Day with Roland Barthes,' in M. Blonsky (ed.) *On Signs*, Oxford, Blackwell.

Croce, A. (1976), 'The Royal Line', in *After Images*, New York, Vintage.

Irving, R. (n.d.), unpblished autobiographical material.

Irving, R. (1976), interview with Tobi Tobias, Oral History Project, New York Public Library Dance Collection, July–December 1976

Jordan, S. (1978–79), 'A Month in the Country: the Organisation of a Score', *Dance Research Journal*, Vol. 11 Nos. 1 & 2, pp. 20–4.

Jordan, S. (forthcoming) *Music in Twentieth-Century Ballet* [working title], London, Dance Books.

Kerensky, O. (1976), 'Frederick Ashton Meets Ivan Turgenev', *New York Times*, 25 April 1976.

Kierkegaard, S. (1959), *Either/Or* (1943), Princeton, Princeton University Press.

Lippman, E. A. (1964), 'Theory and Practice in Schumann's Aesthetics,' *Journal of the American Musicological Society* 17, pp. 310–45.

Newman, W. S. (1972), *The Sonata since Beethoven*, New York, W. W. Norton.

Seymour, L. (1976), interview with John Gruen, 'The Sound of Dance', WNCN-FM, New York City, 26 April.

Vaughan, D. (1977), *Frederick Ashton and His Ballets*, London, A & C Black.

My Dearest Friend, My Greatest Collaborator
Ashton, Fedorovitch and Symphonic Variations

Beth Genné

> It is impossible for me to write about Sophie Fedorovitch without the deepest emotion, for in her death I lost not only my dearest friend but my greatest artistic collaborator and adviser. (Ashton, in Fleet, 1955, p. 22)[1]

With these words Ashton paid tribute to artist Sophie Fedorovitch after her accidental death in 1953.

Sophie Fedorovitch and Frederick Ashton came from different worlds. In personality and temperament, too, they may have seemed mismatched. Fedorovitch was born and raised in Minsk, and studied painting in Cracow, Moscow, and war-torn St Petersburg. Born in 1893, she was eleven years older than Ashton. With her blunt, almost gruff manner and her solitary, Spartan style of life, she had no interest in appearances or social life. Ashton, an Englishman, born in Ecuador, raised in Peru and schooled in England, was well spoken, sociable, and attracted (when they met at least) to the frivolous social world of the twenties and thirties. Yet, personally and professionally, they were profoundly connected. In this paper I'd like to examine the nature of their friendship and collaboration by discussing their work on *Symphonic Variations*, the ballet that Ashton considered to be their 'most successful' and 'most flawless' work (Fleet, 1955, p. 22).

Ashton and Fedorovitch met in 1925, introduced by Marie Rambert. Rambert had met Fedorovitch in 1921 in Enrico Cecchetti's studio, where she had come to study and draw the dancers of the Ballets Russes while they rehearsed for Diaghilev's historic production of *The Sleeping Princess* (Rambert, 1972, p. 119). Fedorovitch also came occasionally to watch Rambert's dancers, and one day Rambert invited her and Ashton to lunch after class. Ashton was immediately attracted to the young Polish artist: 'I was fascinated,' he told David Vaughan 'by her appearance

55

– she was the first woman I had seen who wore her hair cut very short, and she dressed in a very singular way – she was a *garçonne* type, with a marvellously beautiful choirboy's face' (Vaughan, 1977, p. 12). After lunch the two continued their conversation at the Express Dairy in Notting Hill Gate, and from that day became the closest of friends. Looking back at that afternoon, twenty-eight years later, Ashton described it as a profoundly important event in his life: 'the greatest luck I ever had,' he has written, 'was when she walked into Rambert's studio . . . and I loved her from that day' (Fleet, 1955, p. 23).

At Rambert's urging, Fedorovitch and Ashton collaborated one year later on their first ballet, *A Tragedy of Fashion*. The ballet only ran for a few performances, but their experience with *A Tragedy of Fashion* would change both their lives. Ashton, who had perceived himself first and foremost as a dancer, began gradually to think of himself as a choreographer. And Fedorovitch, who had established herself as a painter, would come to devote her career to set and costume design. Between 1926 and Fedorovitch's death in 1953, Ashton and Fedorovitch would collaborate on eleven works.

Fedorovitch was far more than just a designer for the Ashton ballets. Ashton discussed every aspect of the ballet with her – not just its decor and costumes, for importantly, Fedorovitch was as interested in the dance as its decor. 'She loved the ballet for itself,' wrote Richard Buckle, 'not only because it gave scope for her work' (Fleet, 1955, p. 32). Fedorovitch was a regular viewer at Sadler's Wells and Ballet Rambert performances not just those which contained her own decor. She saw the visiting companies. She made friends with the dancers, and tracked the development of their careers with interest.

She was also Ashton's best friend. 'Sophie understood Fred better than anyone in the world,' insisted Margot Fonteyn (1975, p. 99). Fedorovitch believed in Ashton and in his talent wholeheartedly. Indeed, she was as concerned about his career as her own. She made it possible for him to continue dancing at a crucial early stage in his career. *A Tragedy of Fashion* had failed to result in any steady employment for Ashton, who was in dire financial straits. He needed to support his mother as well as himself. (The two were sharing a tiny two-room flat in London.) Fedorovitch persuaded a friend to give Mrs Ashton money, and convinced her to let her son go on with his dance classes (Dominic & Gilbert, 1971, p. 30). She then made sure that he attended class! Maude Lloyd remembers 'Sophie acting as Fred's alarm clock', calling him up every morning to make sure he got to class on time, a practice that she would continue until her death (personal communication, 1992). She lent him money to audition for Nijinska, and she found him work as an English tutor to one of her Polish friends when he desperately needed it (Dominic & Gilbert, 1971, p. 31). And when she died, she left him the bulk of her estate (Vaughan, 1977, p. 269).

Yet despite this maternal stance, Fedorovitch did not indulge Ashton or give him unconditional praise. She was not afraid to be critical, nor did she hesitate to push him when she felt he needed it. 'She did not spare one's feelings when she felt that the hard word had to be said,' wrote Ashton. 'One accepted it because it was always right, shared with sense, and given without ulterior motive, purely for one's private or professional well being . . . Amongst so much that I miss, I miss the gentle bullying' (Fleet, 1955, p. 23).

Ashton, then, was unshakably sure of Fedorovitch's love and support, and trusted as well her keen critical judgment. She served as a sounding board as he tried out his ideas. More importantly, she brought, in Ashton's words 'a real individuality and vision of her own . . . which enriched one's choreographic conception . . . Our endless conversations before, during and after a ballet was finished are among my fondest memories . . . My work with her gave me my happiest times in the theatre' (Fleet, 1955, p. 22).

The trust was mutual. Those who knew her describe Sophie Fedorovitch as an extremely shy person, who often muttered things so softly that she could be almost incomprehensible. There seems to have been no such problem with Ashton. Just as she called him every morning, he would call her every night, 'no matter how late', to continue their endless conversations (Vaughan, 1977, p. 269). Fedorovitch must have felt confident enough of Ashton's understanding and friendship to open up to him, and he probably saw a side of her that few did. Ashton felt that their work together gave Fedorovitch some of her happiest moments: 'Her happiness knew no bounds', he has written, 'when she believed we had reached true artistic unity' (Fleet, 1955, p. 22).

This ideal of 'artistic unity' is an important one, stemming directly from the ethos of the Diaghilev Ballets Russes, on whose productions both Ashton and Fedorovitch had been nurtured. Diaghilev, as we all know, had revolutionised the art of dance by making the designer an equal partner to the choreographer and composer. Ashton and Fedorovitch had thrilled to the Diaghilev productions. And Fedorovitch, in the tradition of Diaghilev's artists, was a major contributor to Ashton's ballets. But unlike those later Ballets Russes productions in which, as André Levinson has described, dance sometimes seemed to take second place to decor (Acocella & Garafola, 1991, p. 68), Ashton and Fedorovitch took dance as their top priority. As Ashton wrote, Fedorovitch 'believed firmly that nothing must hide the dancing or impede the dancers, and that the background should not distract' (Fleet, 1955, p. 22).

The hallmark of Fedorovitch's style, then, was her simplicity and economy of means. With a few well-placed touches of colour and line, she was able to give a sense of time and place and create a mood without cluttering the dancers' space or distracting the viewer's eye from their movement. The limited spaces and budgets of the Sadler's Wells and Mercury theatres, where she and Ashton mounted their earliest works, may have initially forced her into this position; but it was a position that was natural to her, and one that she maintained when creating for the much larger opera house stage.

Ashton's and Fedorovitch's central commitment to dancers is revealed clearly in their method of working. In contrast to choreographers like de Valois, who came into the studio with a preconceived plan which she then set on the dancers, Ashton worked out his choreography in the studio, on the dancers themselves, using their own special qualities and ways of moving to develop his ideas.

Similarly, for Fedorovitch, the design was not a finished product, but, in Ashton's words, 'only a point from which to depart' (Fleet, 1955, p. 22). Her decisions about cut and line were made only when she had seen not only how the material looked when draped on a particular dancer, but more importantly, when the dancer 'moved' in the material. Matilda Etches, the couturière who carried out Fedorovitch's design ideas, describes this process: 'Sophie would bring her sketches ... I would fold or drape a length of stuff until the mood and feeling of the sketch was captured. At the fittings ... the method would always be the same. No sooner would the costume be on the dancer than Sophie would say in her gruff voice, "move" – the dancer would move with pins falling and lengths of diaphanous stuffs trailing to the floor' (Fleet, 1955, p. 37).

Even then, the costumes were not 'set in stone'. Ashton remembers Fedorovitch's willingness to modify her designs as his ideas developed from day to day: 'She always attended as many rehearsals as possible, and as she saw the choreography develop, was capable of completely altering her conception to enhance the choreography and the dancers still more' (Fleet, 1955, p. 22).

This process of evolution and change, with the dancer and the dance at the heart of it all, was the key to the success of the Ashton–Fedorovitch collaboration. The working methods of both were based on the constant refining of an initial idea or constellation of ideas. As Ashton has said: 'It's not what you put into a ballet, it's what you take out' (Vaughan, 1977, p. xix). Fedorovitch agreed. 'Her method of designing', Ashton has written, 'seemed to be a process of elimination, clearing the stage of all unnecessary and irrelevant details (Fleet, 1955, p. 22).

Symphonic Variations

Nothing better illustrates this than the making of *Symphonic Variations*. By tracing the evolution of Ashton's initial ideas for this ballet and Fedorovitch's designs for them, we can almost watch them at work on that paring-down process that was the hallmark of their collaboration.

In 1946, the Sadler's Wells Ballet, housed before the war at the Sadler's Wells theatre, was given a permanent home at the Royal Opera House in Covent Garden. The move was significant: as David Vaughan has pointed out, it was one way of acknowledging the company's place as 'Britain's national ballet in everything but name' (1977, p. 202). It gave them too, for the first time, a full-size opera house stage on which to perform, and with it the capacity for much larger audiences. The inaugural performance at the Opera House, attended by the royal family, was the company's signature work, *The Sleeping Beauty,* in an expansive – and expensive – new production with sumptuous costumes and decor by Oliver Messel.

Ashton marked the move with a new ballet to César Franck's *Symphonic Variations* for piano and orchestra. As this was their first work for the new stage, both he and Fedorovitch were aware of the significance of the occasion. And as the Sadler's Wells resident choreographer, Ashton must have felt a special responsibility to prove to others (and to himself) that he could fill the vast new space and hold its huge audience. He was nervous, and so were his dancers. As Margot Fonteyn remembers, 'The Covent Garden stage, so much bigger than those we had worked on all our lives, still made us all uneasy. Fred had never encountered the problem of filling a large area' (Fonteyn, 1975, p. 99).

Ashton and Fedorovitch, as usual, worked together 'ardently' (Ashton's word) on *Symphonic Variations,* planning every aspect of the work, holding their 'endless conversations' on the phone, over meals, on walks and bicycle rides. In addition to her role as set and costume designer, Fedorovitch was 'as much involved in the choreography as the dancers' (Fonteyn, 1975, p. 99). She also soothed Ashton as he struggled with his anxiety about the 'weight' of the occasion and problems of stage size. Fedorovitch 'was beside him at rehearsals, and sat up with him at night, giving comfort and wisdom in her strange mumbling way and making him laugh when need be' (Fonteyn, 1975, p. 99).

As usual, Fedorovitch was ready to modify her decor and costumes as Ashton's ideas developed. This was especially needed with *Symphonic Variations,* for it changed many times in the choreographer's mind before the opening date. Initially, Ashton had planned a fairly elaborate narrative, in part inspired by his studies of mystics like St Teresa of Avila and St John of the Cross. He had planned too for a sizable corps de ballet to fill the opera house stage, but as work on the ballet proceeded, his elaborate scenario fell by the wayside and he trimmed the corps de ballet down to just six soloists – three men and three women – telling Fedorovitch not to bother working on the corps costumes (Vaughan, 1977, p. 206).

Further changes were made when the premiere of the ballet was postponed at the last minute because of an injury to Michael Somes, and Ashton, for the first time, had more time to do revisions before the opening night. These revisions and the making of *Symphonic Variations* were, as David Vaughan has pointed out, done in closed rehearsal for the first time, perhaps an indication of the intense level of concentration that Ashton demanded. (Before that company members had been free to watch him at work; Vaughan, 1977, p. 206.) Fonteyn remembers the particular intensity and care with which revisions were made, and Fedorovitch's constant involvement: 'When we started to rehearse it all again, Fred took out a lot of things and simplified and purified the choreography... I remember a lot of discussions and all sorts of different ideas and versions and several different endings, and Sophie Fedorovitch at the rehearsals and coming in each day to say what she thought' (Dominic & Gilbert, 1971, p. 83). Pamela May remembers Fedorovitch's contribution to the final moment of *Symphonic Variations.* At one point Ashton proposed that everyone leave the stage at the ballet's end, but Fedorovitch argued that it should conclude with the dancers on stage in the opening pose, and Ashton took her advice (see p. 162). May remembers too that Fedorovitch even persuaded her to dye her hair blond to dramatise the contrast with Fonteyn's dark and Shearer's red hair (personal communication, 1992). In this way, everything, even 'tiny details were discussed and reworked as though it was an architectural plan for a building that would last for ever' (Fonteyn, 1975, p. 99).

Abstracting the English Landscape

In the end, *Symphonic Variations* was daringly simple and abstract. The white backcloth, punctuated by green washes of colour at centre and sides, was inscribed with a curvilinear pattern of black lines continued in a small overhead drape. The costumes, all white for the women, white with touches of black for the men, allowed them complete freedom of movement to execute Ashton's endlessly interesting choreographic patterns. As A. V. Coton wrote: 'Nothing whatever is stated of place, person, condition or circumstance' (Vaughan, 1977, p. 208).

Yet, however hidden, Ashton's original scenario still underlay the dance and decor. In its initial form, the 'dominant' theme of *Symphonic Variations* was the seasons. 'At the beginning I meant it to be winter with the three women moving alone coldly, unfertilised,' Ashton told Richard Buckle. 'When the man begins to dance he introduces the spring: and the last part of the ballet represents to a certain extent the fullness of summer and the plenty of harvest' (Buckle, 1947, p. 23).

This seasonal imagery is reflected in *Symphonic Variations'* set, which was directly inspired by the English countryside in spring. Fedorovitch had a country cottage, a transformed barn at Brancaster in Norfolk, where she often took refuge from the stress of London life (Fleet, 1955, p. 18). Ashton and Fedorovitch were bicycling there in the spring when, as Ashton tells it, 'One day we came up a hill and suddenly there was the most marvellous glade, filled with sunshine, and this had the most terrific effect on us; I said, "This is the colour it's got to be, a sort of greenish yellow" '(Vaughan, 1977, p. 209).

This sun-filled country glade clearly appears in Fedorovitch's preliminary sketches, only to be gradually refined and abstracted until only a suggestion of it remains. In what appears to be the earliest of Fedorovitch's sketches, trees lean gently in from either side of the stage.[2] Curving clusters of lines suggest a canopy of leaves. Slanting rays of sun stream down on a clearing in the middle, and a ground line which rises gently on either side may suggest the slope of the hill up which Ashton

Figure 1. Sophie Fedorovitch: preliminary sketch for *Symphonic Variations* decor; pencil. Collection of James L. Gordon, London.

Figure 2. Preliminary sketch for *Symphonic Variations*. Collection of James L. Gordon, London.

Figure 3. Preliminary sketch for *Symphonic Variations*. Collection of James L. Gordon, London. It is this sketch (I believe it to be the penultimate of the series) that Ashton had framed and hung in his house in Suffolk. When the frame was dismantled for reframing after the sale of Ashton's property, four other preliminary sketches were discovered in the backing of the frame. This is convincing proof to me that Ashton and Fedorovitch saw them as a related suite of sketches.

Figure 4. Sophie Fedorovitch: final set for *Symphonic Variations*. Photograph by McDougall, Group Three Photography.

and Fedorovitch bicycled to discover this sylvan spot (Figure 1). As the design evolved these natural images disappeared, replaced by curving shapes which follow, abstract, and extend the original line of trees and shafts of sunlight. As if responding to music, these shapes take on a rhythmic quality. They dynamise the space, and the separate elements which make up the original pencil sketch move towards fusion into one unified design.

But trees are not the only source for imagery here, for this is a particularly modern countryside. Marie Rambert recalls that Fedorovitch told her that the black lines that undulate across the backdrop also reflected her fascination with 'telephone wires patterned against the immense green fields' of Norfolk (1972, p. 204). And Pamela May remembers Sophie 'muttering something about electricity and the illustrations of patterns made by electrical currents she'd seen in a book' (personal communication, 1992). In the later colour sketches for the *Symphonic Variations* set, the lines of wires, trees, and sunlight are conflated and increasingly simplified as Fedorovitch experiments with various configurations (Figures 2 & 3). In the final set, the linear patterns are ruthlessly pared down (Figure 4). Trees, sunlight and wires are unrecognisable, but a sense of the enclosing shape of the glade remains: the lines bend in protectively. A canopy of branches is suggested by the overhead drape. And the colour, a luminous green, retains the seasonal reference. Christian Bérard sensed it when he called the decor 'lily of the valley' (Vaughan, 1977, p. 209). So did Diana Gould Menuhin, when she described the set as 'vegetal' (personal communication, 1988).

The three men who pose quietly at the back of the stage for the first part of the ballet seem part of this 'vegetal' world. The black lines of the backcloth are picked up in their costumes at ankle, arm and torso.[3] These lines connect them definitively to the backdrop, and when they finally move to the front of the stage to dance with the white clad women, they seem to be emerging from the greenery at the back of the stage, symbols – as in Ashton's original scenario – of spring and fertility.

The Norfolk countryside was not the only factor in determining the 'look' of *Symphonic Variations*: the new space of the Opera House played a crucial role. As mentioned earlier, it worried Ashton and Fedorovitch. The easy way out would have been to fill the stage with a large group of dancers and extensive decor, as Robert Helpmann did in his first ballet for the new stage, *Adam Zero*. But Ashton and Fedorovitch treat the empty space as an asset, revelling not only in the ability of the dancers to move and stretch in the distances that separate them, but in the distances themselves. As Mary Clarke said to me, 'Space is part of *Symphonic Variations*. It is a ballet, in part, about space and the distance between figures.' In these spaces, too, there may be a hint of those 'immense green fields' of Norfolk that Fedorovitch loved.

Images of Classical Art

Many critics have seen *Symphonic Variations* as Ashton's affirmation of classical dance, a renewing of his allegiance to the *danse d'école* and at the same time his own reworking and revitalisation of it. The *danse d'école* in part celebrates the idealised Western human body, as first articulated in visual form by ancient Greek sculptors (Macaulay, 1987, p. 6). This visual ideal was reinvestigated and renewed by Renaissance sculptors and painters at the Italian courts where dancing masters, influenced by the same ideals, developed the techniques from which ballet's present-day vocabulary has evolved.

Resonances with ancient Greek imagery – Greek sculpture in particular – are very clear in *Symphonic Variations,* not only in the extended moments of stillness in which the dancers, like statues, rest on either side of the stage, but in the all-white colour scheme for the women's costumes and in their pleating and draping.[4] Both men's and women's costumes fully reveal the dancers' shapes, and Ashton has them stand with the contemplative serenity of Greek statues, not on two alert and ready-to-move legs, but in contrapposto – on one weight-bearing and one relaxed leg – the standard contrapposto pose modified slightly by crossing the relaxed leg in front. This casual pose, so at odds with traditional ballet positioning, seems at first a strikingly modern gesture, but its roots are deep in Greek artistic soil (Figures 5 & 6).[5] Cynthia Harvey remembers Ashton telling her to do the contrapposto poses 'as if you were a Greek statue' (personal communication, 1994). The dancer originally at the centre of *Symphonic Variations*, it must be remembered, was Margot Fonteyn, whom Ashton once described as having 'the proportions of Venus and the mind of Minerva' (Gilbert, 1979). Ashton calls attention to those proportions with her extended contrapposto poses, and silently he draws an analogy to her sculptured predecessor, the goddess of love and fertility (Figures 7 & 8).

My guess is that this is where Fedorovitch may have had a real impact on the choreography, for she knew the vocabulary of Greek and Roman

Figure 5. Men standing near the Gods, section of the east frieze of the Parthenon, c. 440 BC, British Museum (Lord Elgin collection). Note the crossed foot figure second from the right.

art well; her academic art training would have ensured that. And of course, within walking distance of Covent Garden were the collections at the British Museum, where rows of silent men and women stand in calm contrapposto along the Parthenon frieze.

But while reminiscent of Greek prototypes, Fedorovitch's costumes, like Ashton's choreography, are also a modern reworking of the style, and they reflect as well her own particular interests as a designer. Pleating was a favourite Fedorovitch device – almost a trademark. And the short skirts, pleated hip bands and bandeau tops of her female dancers also hint at forties fashions.

Fedorovitch's costumes also enhance and enrich Ashton's choreographic arrangement. Subtle differences in the draping and line of the costumes provide visual variety within an overall unified scheme, and at the same time subtly differentiate dancers' roles – especially during the ballet's opening, when the figures stand for so long in repose. The central male and female figures differ slightly but distinctly from the side, or pillar, figures. In the original cast, Fonteyn, who stands centre stage in the opening moments, anchors the group of three women with the V-shaped line of her skirt. The pleated band which swathes her hips is firmly gathered at the centre. In contrast, the hems of her companions on

Figure 6. Brian Shaw in the first cast of *Symphonic Variations*. For this pose, Ashton seems to have drawn elements from the poses of the Parthenon frieze figures at furthest left and second from the right (see Figure 5). In addition, the opening pose taken by the two side men in *Symphonic Variations*, with one arm placed diagonally across the chest and the foot in the crossed over position, is related to the figure second from the right (see Figure 5). Photograph by Baron.

either side are cut on a diagonal, and the bands which enclose their hips lack a centre accent. The men's costumes echo this visual arrangement: the V-shaped line of Somes' blouse, and his two full sleeves, accentuates his central position, while the diagonal cut of his companion's tops, echoed in the black lines that loop diagonally over their hips and circle the single bare arm of each, parenthesise his figure. (This feature has since disappeared: in recent productions all men wear the same single-sleeve top.)

Figure 7. Margot Fonteyn in *Symphonic Variations*. Photograph by Zoë Dominic.

But *Symphonic Variations* is not only a ballet about repose; it is about movement. Fedorovitch's costumes were made to dance in – not only allowing maximum freedom of movement to the dancers, but enhancing that movement. No better example of this exists than in the ballet's final section, which Ashton first marked 'the summer, the earth, the light, the dance of union, the festival'. Ashton responds to much of this final *allegro non troppo* section of Franck's dazzling variations with an equally dazzling series of choreographic variations on turning and circling: dancers spin on the ground and in the air, by themselves and in supported pirouettes; they circle each other and join hands in semicircular chains. In one of the most extraordinary series, the women revolve in sequence around the men while rotating themselves, like the earth around the sun.

Figure 8. Venus Genetrix (also called Aphrodite of Fréjus), Holkham Hall, thought to be a Roman copy of a Greek prototype. Whether or not they knew this as a Roman copy, Ashton and Fedorovitch would have thought of it as a Greek type. Holkham Hall is in Norfolk, where Fedorovitch had her summer home. Reproduced by kind permission of the Earl of Leicester and the trustees of the Holkham Estate.

Fedorovitch's costumes enrich this festival of circling and union. As the women turn and turn again, their skirts bell out like miniature whirl-winds, or – in line with the fertility motif – like flowers suddenly opening.

Fully part of this festival of music and dance, Fedorovitch's set, too, swirls. We have seen how, as her design evolved from literal glade to abstract design, the lines of trees and telephone wires took on new and 'musical' life, seeming to swing rhythmically across the Opera House

69

stage and over the heads of the dancers. To trees and telephone wires, then, perhaps we can now add the hint of a musical staff – or the strings of some gigantic lute playing for the festival of dancing below. Actually, we can add whatever we want, for whatever the original references, the descriptive function of these lines no longer matters. 'All these things', Ashton insisted when describing his original scenario to Richard Buckle, 'were only "put into" the ballet, if they were "put in", to be eventually refined and eliminated. I did not want to load the work with literary ideas; and I was quite willing for people to read whatever they liked into it' (Buckle, 1947, p. 23).

As with any abstract work, then, what counts in *Symphonic Variations* is not the story told, or message conveyed, but the feelings aroused. Ashton's dancers offer us the beauty of movement and the joy of dancing to music in the open, untroubled space shaped by the curvilinear patterns of Sophie Fedorovitch's set. Marie Rambert once observed that these lines 'seem to flow out of the music and into the dancing' (Fleet, 1955, p. 48). Thus the woman who first brought Sophie and Fred together bears witness to the artistic unity that these friends and collaborators achieved in *Symphonic Variations*.

Notes

1. In 1955, two years after Sophie's death from a gas leak in her flat, her friend Simon Fleet collected a number of written tributes from her friends and admirers. Called *Sophie Fedorovitch: Tributes and Attributes*, it was privately published and distributed to friends. It remains a major source on Fedorovitch's life and work. Ashton's remarks come from this work.

2. I am grateful to Jane Pritchard, who first alerted me to the existence of this sketch and the other preliminary sketches for *Symphonic Variations* which were kept with the final design and which came to light when Ashton's estate was sold. They now belong to James L. Gordon. In a letter to me, Jane Pritchard described the sketches and suggested that the more naturalistic came first. After seeing the sketches, I agree, and her suggestion seems all the more convincing in the light of Ashton's tale of the Norfolk glade.

3. The ankle bands have disappeared from subsequent productions. This may have been done with Ashton and Fedorovitch's approval.

4. Originally Greek sculpture was polychromatic Since the Renaissance, however, it has been white in the minds of artists, including Fedorovitch and Ashton.

5. It was, for example, a favourite Fred Astaire pose. It looks, too, like a

variation of a pose that Isadora Duncan, whom Ashton particularly admired for her moments of stillness, may have used; but a version of this pose was standard in Greek relief (see Figure 5). I would like to thank my colleagues in ancient art at the University of Michigan: Elaine K. Gazda, Margaret Cool Root and Molly Lindner, as well as Ivor Guest and Mary Clarke, for discussing parts of this article with me. Any mistakes are, of course, my own.

References

Acocella, J. & Garafola, L. (eds) (1991), *André Levinson on Dance: Writings from Paris in the Twenties*, Hanover, NH, Wesleyan University Press.

Buckle, R. (1947), ' "Abstract" Ballet: a dialogue between Richard Buckle and Frederick Ashton', *Ballet*, Vol. 4, No. 5.

Dominic, Z. & Gilbert, J. S. (1971), *Frederick Ashton: A Choreographer and His Ballets*, London, Harrap.

Fleet, S. (ed.) (1955), *Sophie Fedorovitch: Tributes and Attributes. Aspects of her art and personality by some of her fellow artists and friends*, London, privately printed.

Fonteyn, M. (1975), *Autobiography*, London, W H Allen.

Gilbert, J. S. (1979) (writer and producer), *Frederick Ashton: A Real Choreographer*, BBC Television, in association with RM Productions, Munich.

Macaulay, A. (1987), 'Notes on Dance Classicism', *Dance Theatre Journal* Vol. 5 No. 2, pp. 6–9, 36–9.

Rambert, M. (1972), *Quicksilver: An Autobiography*, London, Macmillan.

Vaughan, D. (1977), *Frederick Ashton and His Ballets*, London, A & C Black.

Mime in Ashton's Ballets

Tradition and Innovation

Giannandrea Poesio

Salvatore Viganò, the creator of nineteenth-century *coreo-dramma*, discussing his aversion to dance compositions derived from complex, allegorical literary subjects, wrote:

> I always try to structure my own works so that the spectator does not need any knowledge of either the past or of the future events to understand the content of the picture I draw. . . As the plot unfolds and as the human feelings are all clearly conveyed through dance, everyone can see and understand everything, without studying or referring to programmes or written explanations. (Viganò, in Ritorni, 1838, p. 199)

More than one century later, Frederick Ashton, discussing the same topic, affirmed:

> I personally do not like a ballet in which the audience has to spend three-quarters of the time with their noses in the program to try to find out what is happening on the stage . . . In my balletic ideology it is the dancing which must be the foremost factor, for ballet is an expression of emotions and ideas through dancing. (Ashton, 1951, p. 91)

It would be hazardous to claim that Ashton might have known Viganò's opinion: the latter's passage is a rare example of his writing, and was never translated into English before. Still, a parallel between the two choreographers is not simply fortuitous, for the two masters, apparently so different, present several points in common. On the one hand, Viganò created a distinctive and unique choreographic genre, that of *coreodramma*, from which Italian nineteenth-century theatre dance evolved; in addition, he formulated stylistic principles that were to characterise Italian ballet for more than one century. On the other hand, Frederick Ashton contributed considerably to both the creation and the development of British ballet, and, more particularly, to what is generally identified in the dance world as the 'English style'. The two masters, moreover, dealt with a particular use of the language of gesture, commonly and often erroneously called ballet mime. The 1981 conference on Viganò[1] demonstrated that despite what is generally written in dance history manuals, his *coreodrammi* were neither pantomimic displays, nor did they rely on the codified vocabulary of ballet mime. On the contrary, Viganò's choreographic canons prescribed a unique use of expressive gestures. These movements were fluidly interwoven with the dancing in order to render the latter more expressive and less artificial. Viganò refused to comply with both the formulae of French ballet – including those related to Noverre's *ballet d'action* – and the principles of conventional Italian mime language, namely a fixed vocabulary of expressive gestures stemming from the *Commedia dell'Arte* tradition. So did Frederick Ashton. In the same passage quoted above, Ashton affirmed that:

> I personally am not fond of the literary ballet, because it seems to me that there comes a hiatus in which one longs for the spoken word to clarify the subject. And these ballets seem to lead always more to miming than to dancing, thereby invading the functions of the drama or the cinema. (Ashton, 1951, p. 91)

This statement about the nature of mime and its relation to ballet requires a careful interpretation, for it could easily be misinterpreted. Ashton was not against expressive gestures as an integral part of dancing, as he demonstrated and affirmed on several occasions, for instance when planning some mime scenes (which were eventually omitted) for *Ondine* (1958), when discussing the structure of *La Fille mal gardée* (1960), or even when describing the way Pavlova used her hands on stage. Ashton's criticism was directed to the insertion of those overwhelming and often gratuitous gestural recitatives in contemporary ballets. Although he acknowledged the importance of expressive gestures and their contribution to the narrative of the work, he regarded long, conventional mime sequences as superfluous additions, if not as detrimental to the dance's purity. It was this particular attitude towards mime that led to both the creation and the development of an individual and distinctive language of gesture which is worth analysing.

In the first two decades of the nineteenth century, Viganò experimented with a range of expressive movements that could easily be integrated with the dancing. What he obtained was a unique vocabulary of gesture which did not interrupt or hinder the fluidity of the danced action, thus becoming an integral part of the dancing itself. Viganò derived this language from pre-existing formulae stemming from well-established Italian drama traditions as well as from the codified principles of the *ballet d'action*. He revised, adjusted and reworked those criteria to provide his dancers with a greater degree of freedom in expressing their feelings and those of their characters. An analysis of mime in Ashton's ballets reveals that the English choreographer too drew the fundamentals of his individual and unique language of gesture from pre-existing examples and formulae. Yet a conference paper cannot discuss thoroughly the various examples of mime in Ashton's ballets. This paper will therefore focus on the analysis of some significant historical and contextual factors which informed Ashton's language of gesture; its aim is to call forth further research on the topic.

It is generally acknowledged that the nineteenth-century Italian ballet mime tradition has been carefully preserved and perpetuated in twentieth-century England. It was in this country that great mime dancers from the famed Milanese Academy of Dancing established themselves as performers of great repute; among them were Malvina Cavallazzi and Francesca Zanfretta. The latter passed her art on to both Ninette de Valois, who invited her to teach at the Academy of Choreographic Art, and to Ursula Moreton. At Moreton's request, Zanfretta's classes were written by Sheila McCarthy and, as the eminent critic Kathrine Sorley Walker has affirmed, this set of notes 'was handed on in its complex and fascinating details to the Vic-Wells and its successor companies' (1987, p. 65). Zanfretta's recorded teachings became the reference source on ballet mime for many generations of English dancers. The influence of these teachings on Ashton can be detected in several ballets, where some canonic movements occur – for instance, the fairies' gesture for 'listening' in *The Dream* (1964). Still, Ashton never complied with the grammar of that language, and constantly filtered the rules of its syntax through a personal approach. Even when the most canonic gestures of the Italian tradition occur in his ballets – such as the popular gestures for 'to marry', 'to love', and 'to hear' codified by Zanfretta – they are never performed according to the precepts established by almost three centuries of practice. Ashton's choreographic rendering of these conventional signs is always smoother, less rigid than the original model. In his ballets, therefore, the use of space – an important component of Italian ballet mime – is reduced considerably, and gestures lack that flashy, flowery complexity that characterised the Italian style. The constant opposition between one gesture and another, one of the fundamentals of the Italian language of gesture – not to be confused with the balletic law of épaulement – is generally disregarded in Ashton's ballets, to provide the gesture with more spontaneity. The musical quality of the movements is different too: to the originally unrhythmical nature of the movements, Ashton juxtaposes an accurate phrasing which confers on the gesture an incredible musical fluidity. It is worth remembering that Italian mime dancers did not follow the rhythm but adjusted their mime actions to the melody, regardless of any possible phrasing. Finally, one should not forget that the nature of the Italian vocabulary was significantly tempered by Ashton's refined taste, by what is generally indicated by non-English people as the restrained and innately elegant manners of the English. There are many examples of how Ashton adopted and reworked old mime gestures. An interesting and controversial one is to be found in his ballet *Ondine*, where 'as he has often done, Ashton devised a characteristic port de bras for Ondine and the other water spirits' (Vaughan, 1977, p. 298). Still, that distinctive gesture – arms stretched upward with the elbows slightly bent, the hands crossed at the wrist, palms and fingertips together – bears an unmistakable similarity to one of the oldest signs of Italian ballet mime, that for 'fish'. Although there is no evidence to prove that Ashton knew that gesture derived from *Commedia dell'Arte*, the similarity between the port de bras – which conveys Ondine's 'watery' nature – and the old conventional sign suggests more than mere coincidence.

The complex range of descriptive and expressive gestures that characterise Ashton's choreography does not derive exclusively from the Italian tradition of the nineteenth century. Russian mime is another informing factor. It is generally accepted that Italian and Russian ballet mime are similar, but such an assumption is erroneous. Although a certain contamination between the two forms can be detected, it should be remembered that Russian ballet mime of the late nineteenth century differed considerably from the Italian vocabulary of gesture. Italian ballet mime was imported to Russia thanks to great Italian ballet stars such as

Virginia Zucchi, whose skills were quickly learnt – or imitated – by their Russian colleagues. Yet the Italian sign language consisted mainly of codified movements which could limit considerably the personal inter-pretation of the performer. This was a problem that was particularly felt by the Russians, who managed to translate that idiom into a more malleable language, more suited to the individual's rendering of a charac-ter. In discussing *La Fille mal gardée*, Tamara Karsavina recalls Mathilde Kschessinska's brilliant mime skills (Guest, 1960, p. 26). Unfortunately there are no sources documenting Kschessinska's bravura. Still, according to some of her private pupils, when she was teaching at the Studio Wacker in Paris, at the end of her classes she used to grant private students a bonus: she taught them some exercises of unusual ports de bras and some mime gestures. Apparently, while demonstrating mime sequences, she often insisted on how the Russians had modified the signs of the Italian vocabulary, making them clearer and somehow more elegant. (Incidentally, a similar claim, although in relation to ballet tech-nique, is found in Legat, 1932, p. 22.) As an example, Kschessinska referred to the conventional gesture for 'marriage', affirming that the Russians – namely herself – had added an extra movement to the origi-nal gesture, that of adjusting the ring with the thumb and the index of the right hand. Now the combination of the two movements, the Italian sign and the Russian addition, can be seen in Lise's mime passage that Ashton received from Karsavina, his 'Goddess of Wisdom' (Guest, 1960, p. 10).

The process of modification of the old Italian canons of mime lan-guage, led by the Russians, reached its peak with Mikhail Fokine, who contributed significantly to the 'modernisation' of the art of ballet, evolving a 'freer, natural style' and requiring that 'the whole body should be expressive' (Beaumont, 1945, p. 87). Mime conventions, therefore, gradually gave way to a range of movements which mirrored and suited the dancer's personal interpretation, often deriving spontaneously from it. An analysis of mime in Ashton's ballets cannot but take into account this other type of Russian mime. Although Fokine did not reject the old mime vocabulary, his language of gesture focused more on suggesting ideas than expressing concepts or telling facts through a codified system of signs. In many of his ballets there is a wide range of movements which, although expressive and indicative of a certain mood or feeling, cannot be related to specific words. Examples can be found in *Le Spectre de la rose* (1911) where both the Young Girl's movement of surprise and

76

the gesture with which the Spirit 'reveals' himself to her do not belong to the Italian vocabulary. It has been suggested that, to a certain extent, Fokine's principles informed the dancing of Anna Pavlova, Ashton's muse. An investigation of the few visual sources on Pavlova demonstrates that the ballerina's language of gesture was an individual concoction of free, expressive movements and conventional, stylised gestures stemming from the ballet tradition. Yet as far as the existing source material is taken into account, Pavlova's dancing did not include the use of codified signs in the Italian style. Probably, Fokine derived some of his ideas on movement from the art of Isadora Duncan. Although the argument is still a controversial one, there is little doubt that, as far as some 'free' expressive gestures are concerned, Ashton too referred more or less directly to Duncan. Still, because of their particular nature, those movements cannot be considered as part of the mime range.

Further developments of Fokine's ideas were brought forth by two other Russian choreographers: Léonide Massine, from whom Ashton learned 'about style and about the beauty of port de bras' (Vaughan, 1977, p. 7) and Bronislava Nijinska, in whose ballets Ashton danced while a member of Ida Rubinstein's company.

A complex, rich and often redundant language of gesture is a distinctive component of Massine's choreography. Still, only a few of these movements derive from the nineteenth-century vocabulary, for the majority consists of gestures created to provide the dancing with some dramatic 'natural' characterisation. In most cases those movements are nothing but a stylised version of common daily actions. Their presence in Massine's choreography reflects the influence on early twentieth-century dance of the dramatic theories expounded by theatre theorists such as Konstantin Stanislavsky and Edward Gordon Craig, who were both against the conventions, particularly the gestural ones, of nineteenth-century drama. Some dance historians have erroneously considered Massine's gesticulation as merely ornamental. On the contrary, it is through that gesticulation that Massine's characters acquire dramatic credibility. The boundary between drama and ballet is therefore crossed, even though this may result in an overpowering use of mime. In both *The Good-Humoured Ladies* (1917) and *Le Astuzie femminili* (1920) (later called *Cimarosiana*), some of the female characters have a recurring outward movement, with arms bent, elbows down, in which the forearms move slightly away from the shoulder and the hands flap downwards, breaking the line at the wrist and ending with the palms up. This movement, which echoes the stylised manners of both the seventeenth and eighteenth centuries, conveys the superficial and whimsical nature of the characters. Interestingly, it occurs in Ashton's *A Month in the Country* (1976), where it becomes Natalia Petrovna's most distinctive and recurring gesture, performed with many variations throughout the ballet. Although both the dynamic of the gesture and its meaning are similar to those in Massine's works, it is the way Ashton uses that gesture that differs from Massine's. In the latter's works, the movement is like a caricature, and appears to be a complement to the dancing to enhance the comic effect. In Ashton's ballet the gesture becomes an integral part of the dancing; as such it can be regarded as the preparation or the continuation of a port de bras even though it retains its narrative identity.

It is difficult to state the extent of Nijinska's influence on Ashton's language of gesture, mainly because of the particular use, or lack of, narrative movements in her ballets. It could be argued that symbolic and allegorical gestures characterise Nijinska's works. Yet the nature of those gestures is never clearly defined, and one might wonder how appropriate it would be to refer to them as Nijinska's 'language of gesture'. This topic remains open to discussion.

This brief analysis of mime in Ashton's ballets would not be complete without mentioning another significant informing factor, namely the choreographer's sense of theatre. To his innate mimetic skills, such as his well-known impersonations, he combined both a great deal of practical experience – having worked in places such as music-halls – and an extensive knowledge of theatre arts. It is not coincidence, therefore, that canonic movements performed by either vaudeville comedians or pantomime actors characterise some passages of Ashton's ballets. The most obvious example is to be found in *Cinderella* (1948): Ashton's characterisation of the Ugly Sister was more in the glorious tradition of English pantomime than in the tradition of the balletic 'travesty' mime roles (Vaughan, 1977, p. 233).

Finally, a technical factor should be considered. Ashton studied and worked mainly with dancers trained according to the teachings imparted by Enrico Cecchetti. His mime vocabulary, therefore, is constantly informed by those principles, particularly in terms of geometry, posture and lines; the smoothness, the roundness and that calibrated elegance of Ashton's narrative and expressive movements derive from the application of Cecchetti's technical and stylistic formulae.

'Ballet mime' is regarded today as a lesser artistic subspecies, if not an obsolete and disturbing accessory to ballet. As far as Ashton's choreography is concerned, however, the importance of his unique and distinctive language of gesture cannot be overlooked, for it constitutes an essential ingredient of what is generally recognised as 'Ashton's style'.

Notes

1. 'Il sogno del coreodramma: Salvatore Viganò, poeto muto', Teatro Romolo Valli, Reggio Emilia, Italy, 1981.

References

Ashton, F. (1951), 'Notes on Choregraphy', in W. Sorell (ed.), *The Dance Has Many Faces*, 2nd edn, 1966, New York, Columbia University Press.

Beaumont, C. (1945), *The Ballet Called Giselle*, London, Beaumont.

Guest, I. (ed.) (1960), *Famous Ballets: La Fille mal gardée*, London, Dancing Times.

Legat, N. (1932), *The Story of the Russian School*, London, British-Continental Press.

Ritorni, C. (1838), *Commentarii della vita e delle opere coreodrammatiche di Salvatore Viganò*, Milano, Guglielmini e Redaelli.

Sorley Walker, K. (1987), *Ninette de Valois: Idealist Without Illusions*, London, Hamilton.

Vaughan, D. (1977), *Frederick Ashton and His Ballets*, London, A & C Black.

Romeo and Juliet

Theatricality and other techniques of expression

Katherine S. Healy

1985 was the year of *Romeo and Juliet* in many companies. The Royal Ballet broadcast Kenneth MacMillan's production with Wayne Eagling and Alessandra Ferri in the title roles. In New York, American Ballet Theatre was also performing MacMillan's, and the Joffrey Ballet had just mounted John Cranko's production. That spring, Frederick Ashton began preparations to revive his production of *Romeo and Juliet* for the summer season of London Festival Ballet (now English National Ballet). The revival of this work, which Ashton had choreographed for the Royal Danish Ballet thirty years earlier, was inspired by the single-minded vision of the artistic director Peter Schaufuss, whose mother, Mona Vangsaae, and father, Frank Schaufuss, were the original Juliet and Mercutio in the Danish production.

From March to July of that year, with intervals to allow for performances and rehearsals of other ballets, Ashton came a few times a week to Festival Ballet House in Kensington to rehearse *Romeo and Juliet*. As the first cast Juliet, I had the privilege of working with Ashton in most of these rehearsals. I was also fortunate to be able to work with Niels Bjørn Larsen of the Royal Danish Ballet as he reconstructed the Copenhagen production from an 8-mm black-and-white film and from his notes. The intensive preparations included two-hour private pas de deux rehearsals with Ashton at least three times a week.

Ashton's production of *Romeo* contrasts strongly with most other productions widely seen in the West in that it focuses more on the emotions of the lovers than on the societal struggle evidenced by the family feud between the Capulets and the Montagues. Therefore, significant time was devoted to the preparation of the two title protagonists, and I had ample opportunity to observe the mounting of the entire production from its inception to its finish.

The element that Ashton stressed the most in the preparation of *Romeo and Juliet* was that of the theatrical. By this I mean the methods and vast knowledge of stagecraft with which he facilitated the presentation and projection of the characters' dramatic, intense emotions on stage. A theatrical effect that was clearly visible to the public was of paramount importance, and took precedence over the complications of steps or technique, unless they facilitated or revealed the desired effect. I intend to discuss his emphasis on the theatrical and how it was employed in this particular production, as well as his specific technical preferences in timing, accentuation and port de bras. I will analyse these categories by focusing primarily on the role of Juliet, drawing upon videotape and journals and notes that I kept at the time, as well as my recollections.

When rehearsals began, several dancers were learning the role of Juliet, including Lucia Truglia, Virginie Alberti and myself. We were supposed to learn the role with Larsen, and then after a few weeks, Ashton would come in and rehearse us himself. In working with Larsen, Kirsten Ralov and Frank Schaufuss (who performed the first cast Lord and Lady Capulet and Escalus respectively), I learned how to project the gestures that tell a story. There is a certain sombre rhythm that infuses their mime, rendering it crystal clear. I learned that if I was asked a question in mime, it should be asked slowly and clearly. Then I should wait a moment before answering – also slowly, clearly, and with generous gestures. Otherwise the dialogue essential to a dramatic production would lapse into obscurity, doing nothing to further the plot.

When I was told, about nine weeks beforehand, that Ashton had chosen me to dance Juliet both in the premiere and in the second performance on 23 and 24 July 1985, I cancelled my original plans to compete in the International Ballet Competition in Moscow that June. Because I should have been competing, I was not scheduled to join London Festival Ballet on their tour to Copenhagen, so it was decided that I would remain in London and work with Ashton privately while they were away.

He cast a very long shadow over many facets of my dancing: my comportment, port de bras, mime, acting and characterisations. I subsequently danced Juliet in John Cranko's production many years later. I have found that often I understand the true dynamics of a role only after I have danced it. I had a professor once who said that one can truly understand a particular culture only if one speaks the language of that culture. It is an apt analogy for a technical analysis of roles. Such analysis is facilitated by speaking the language of a particular production and existing within its context.

Dancing Cranko's Juliet made me realise how much Ashton's production is the story of the lovers, particularly Juliet, as opposed to a sprawling epic of societal clashing. Ashton's Juliet is independent. She is always dancing. She shows a precocious ability to dissemble during the ball when she commands the assembled company to continue with the festivities after Tybalt discovers her alone with Romeo. In Cranko's version, she simply runs to cower with her nurse (who is conspicuously absent in Ashton's ball). In Ashton's Juliet, indecision, despair and her individual initiatives are expressed through dancing almost until the end of the ballet. By contrast, it is illuminating to note that, after Cranko's bedroom pas de deux at the beginning of Act III, Juliet has no more steps to dance. She walks, she runs, and she sits, but, save for two relevés into arabesque, she does not dance. She is a pawn who fulfils her position in the ballet by the fact that she exists as the marriageable daughter of the Capulet family. Compare those relevé arabesques with Ashton's intricately danced mime scene, as she relates her predicament to the Friar. Moreover, Ashton truncates the opening scene of the ballet in which the audience is introduced to the long-running conflict, while Cranko presents a full-blooded crowd scene complete with fruit-throwing and a cast of thousands.

Ashton also adheres to fine literal points drawn from Shakespeare's play. For instance, the clawing movements given to Tybalt at the opening of the ballet are a direct allusion to Mercutio's characterisation of Tybalt in Shakespeare's text as the 'Prince of Cats', the 'ratcatcher' and the 'Good King of Cats'.

Another example is the name of Mercutio's love interest. Ashton discards the character of Rosaline altogether, and along with it the arrival of the guests at the ball in Act I, thereby emphasising the absolute love of Romeo for Juliet. Instead he creates a girlfriend for Mercutio, whose name, Livia, is drawn from the guest list that Romeo happens to read for the Capulet Ball. A third example is the repeated, sweeping gesture that Ashton's lovers make to the sky during the balcony scene pas de deux, a nod to Romeo's invocation of the stars as a simile for Juliet's eyes.

Ashton had two major corrections for me. First, I had to stop 'dropping my wrists'. He meant I should discard the broken wrist flourishes that are a distinguishing characteristic of the Balanchine school, of which I was a product. When I was eight years old in the School of American Ballet, one of my teachers, Elise Reiman, spent an entire lesson teaching twenty little girls how to create the illusion of air manipulating their hands as they executed different port de bras movements. But Ashton was adamantly opposed to any independent movement of the hand from the arm because he said it broke the visual line of the arm for the audience, and the clarity of the position was lost. The wrist correction was the most essential in the tomb scene when Romeo dances with Juliet's dead body. Owing to the exigencies of rigor mortis, it was important that there be no floppiness whatsoever in Juliet's 'movements', particularly in the wrists. Ashton follows Shakespeare's text in the manner of Romeo's and Juliet's suicides (by poison and stabbing, respectively). When Juliet stabs herself, she faces front, thereby placing the phallic symbolism of the method on clear display for the audience. The marriage is finally consummated for all of eternity in the method she uses to unite herself with her dead husband.

While the wrists should always remain unbroken, the fingers were allowed to demonstrate inner turmoil. Ashton stipulated that the fingers of both Romeo and Juliet tremble during their first meeting in the ball. Juliet's fingers were also supposed to tremble during her third act scene with Friar Laurence and in the potion scene – whenever she holds the vial of potion.

The other main correction he emphasised was that my head should not be kept straight all the time: if I put my head up, then I must *really* put it up, and if I turned it to the side, then I should *really* turn it to the side. Otherwise, he explained carefully, the movement would not register visually with the audience. He added head movements during the extended series of Juliet's hops during which Romeo partners her in a manège. He felt that the head movement provided a connection to the spectators as the characters travelled around the back of the stage facing away from the audience, because it allowed brief glimpses of their facial features. In like fashion, he preferred épaulement, the orientation of the body, to be exaggerated so that it would register from afar. This applied throughout the piece, not only for Juliet, but also most notably in the sweeping dances for the guests at the ball, the newly created pas de trois for Romeo, Mercutio and Benvolio in Act II, and in the early morning dance of the mandolin players in Act III. As the players are perched atop the rostrum across the back of the stage that structures the action throughout the ballet, they are farthest away from the audience and therefore the most difficult to see.

The rostrum and the stairs that lead up to it, in fact, serve the distinct purpose of facilitating the display of various tableaux, throwing the various characters into relief as the story progresses. One of the notable relationships that it highlights is Juliet's to Paris. As the rehearsals progressed, I began to wonder if Juliet likes Paris until she meets Romeo. When I asked Ashton, he said yes, and I realised that that was why the role of Paris was not just a cipher, but an actual dancing role. Paris is given the opportunity to see Juliet and Romeo slip away together during the course of the ball. Juliet is still bemused by Paris even after she meets Romeo. In the first cast's version, after she has agreed to marry Paris with that internal yet visible gesture of great personal anguish directed at the Nurse, she watches him walk away, almost as though she regrets the circumstances that will tear them apart. The final punctuation of this relationship is her horrified compassion when she discovers his dead body in the crypt. Ashton wanted a visible shudder to run through her body as she realises that the attractive young man is dead. This relationship emphasises the bond between Romeo and Juliet. Paris is *not* undesirable, and therefore the attachment of the two title protagonists must indeed be a strong one.

Ashton took pains to situate Juliet in the context of the whole production, attending to each detail of the story and adding new texture to the character. He reminded me that in the nursery scene, pre-Romeo, I should be joyful at the news of my planned marriage. Originally, after Romeo kills Tybalt, Larsen had told me to come out, stand to one side on the rostrum and watch the proceedings as Romeo is banished. When Ashton saw this, he said to me, 'You should react,' again following Shakespeare's text. It was a clever idea, inasmuch as the audience can see that Juliet is aware of her predicament. It is the only time that Juliet makes an appearance in any of the market scenes. I pleaded with the Prince of Verona, although he could not 'see' me, I wept, and at Ashton's behest I was taken off the stage at the close of the act in Lady Capulet's arms. I was not sure if I should be doing more or less in this 'lamentation', as I thought of it. Ashton never commented on it. After the premiere, he talked about working with Rudolf Nureyev, because he knew I liked him. He told me how difficult it was to convince Rudolf to do what he wanted.

'You could never keep Rudolf still onstage,' he remembered. 'The Swan Queen would be going through her thing, and there would be Rudolf jumping around on the side, until finally I would say, "For God's sake, stand *still!*" '

I feared he was thinking of my little lamentation. Imagine my relief when, after my third performance, his only correction was that I should stand closer to the centre of the rostrum and make my 'lamentation' bigger!

The rostrum is also part of an overall strategy in the Ashton production to freeze important visual moments. Ashton wanted each position held for as long as possible, almost to allow time for someone to snap a photograph. It reinforces the idea of a tableau, wherein the audience can retain an image of Juliet and Paris together during the ball, or Juliet and Romeo spotlighted during their first meeting in centre stage, or Lady Capulet mourning Juliet's feigned death in Act III.

His coaching incorporated the balletic equivalent of the etiquette and deportment taught to debutantes in finishing school. I was not supposed to look at my mother, Lady Capulet, in the eye whenever I curtsied to her because it was not 'proper'. In other scenes, however, my eyes were supposed to talk. Walking forward with Romeo in the ballroom scene, my eyes were supposed to convey my nervousness by their agitation and uncertainty. Ashton always invoked Margot Fonteyn as the greatest exponent of conveying feeling through the eyes. The movements of the eyes were actually choreographed to the music in the moments before Juliet's potion scene in Act III. This cedes into the bodily swaying that emulates a clock's ticking as Juliet tries to decide if she should drink the potion or not. Swaying of the body in *Romeo* refers to indecision – being pulled in one direction or the other, as in the potion scene, the flight to Friar Laurence and the subsequent scene with Friar Laurence.

Other parts of my body were given similar attention. If my arms had to hang down by my sides, then they had to be held behind my shoulders. If I was walking down the stairs in the ballroom, I had to put one foot directly in front of the other, turn out all the way, straighten the leg, point each foot fully before it touched each stair – all without bouncing or looking down. I was never allowed to stand still on the stage in any other position except for a tendu or else what in the Balanchine school is called B-Plus (where one leg is placed behind the other in a bent tendu).

'You are a ballerina,' he admonished. 'You must *always* stand like one.'

Whenever I kissed Romeo during the balcony scene or the bedroom pas de deux, Ashton would instantly remind me to stand properly. After a while, it became a reflex. For years, I could not stand simply with two feet together onstage in any ballet no matter what I was doing – even when that was specifically required by the choreographer!

Ashton embellished the nursery scene through the use of rapid pointework. The épaulement was exaggerated, and all the quick series of pas de cheval were changed from the éffacé leg to the croisé leg in order to achieve a prettier line. He asked for specific hand movements during the pas de cheval. The pas de cheval motif progresses from Juliet's almost hysterically happy rendition in her nursery to a more dignified manifestation by her attendants at the ball during their dance with Mercutio. It culminates in a final slow, forbidding tempo magnified by the passel of flower girls who arrive in the third act, reflecting and emphasising Juliet's coming of age and her impending collision with reality.

Act III was also revised for Juliet. He significantly expanded the scene in which Juliet decides to seek help from Friar Laurence, making her clearly mime that she has the idea to visit Friar Laurence, and having her sway back and forth in an agony of indecision. Ashton and Alexander Grant coached me precisely for the big 'Ulanova run', their name for Juliet's flight to Friar Laurence. I ran and ran and ran, trying to achieve what they wanted – head, arms, cloak and torso thrown back, feet leading the way in quick powerful steps. Alastair Macaulay wryly commented that 'Ashton had also helped Healy to make certain other effects, such as whipping up a storm of audience applause' with this (1985, p. 37). That was certainly not the goal: it was an expression of despairing flight and determination. There again, an example of a theatrical *effect* upon the audience.

Someone had told Ashton that I used to skate in John Curry's Skating Company, and he was interested in the different positions of skating spins. As I worked with him, I found that, despite his eminence and position, Ashton was very curious and open-minded about other performing arts. I was duly called upon to explain and demonstrate the layback spin – a spin executed in an attitude derrière combined with a deep cambré back. Ashton decided that Romeo should do this just before drinking the poison in the tomb scene. Three more laybacks were inserted for me, always during moments of great despair: once when Juliet runs to the Friar in front of the curtain, and two again during the potion scene, which were more difficult because he wanted them to be very slow and controlled. The laybacks functioned as an off-balance indicator of agitation and disorientation and served to unify the two main characters – both execute this step during stressful moments. For good measure, Ashton created a baroquely ornate manège during Juliet's scene with Friar Laurence that included a relevé arabesque turn in penchée that was also originally derived from the camel spin in figure skating. (Other Juliets later altered this manège because, as I am a left turner, it involved pirouettes to both the right and left, and most ballerinas prefer to turn only to the right.)

Objects acquired personalities, becoming a powerful semiotic method in Ashton's production. The medallion that Romeo presents to Juliet at the end of the bedroom pas de deux becomes the stand-in for Romeo. Romeo's medallion and the vial of sleeping potion wage a silent but highly visible battle for control of Juliet's mind during her solitary anguish in Act III. It is a subtler means to describe this dilemma than say, that used by Rudolf Nureyev in his production, where the ghosts of the characters of Tybalt and Mercutio wrangle over the hypnotised Juliet. Ashton stipulated exactly how I was to open and close the vial, how to throw away the lid so the audience would really see it, how I was to hold the vial generally, how my hand should tremble when I held it and how to drink it, until it took on a life of its own. 'It should be alive,' he would explain to me patiently.

Sometimes he subverted theatrical convention. Flowers evolved into a macabre motif. Ashton inserted a new moment in the wedding scene in Act II. In a re-creation of any standard curtain call, Romeo was to present a bouquet of flowers to Juliet, whereupon she was to pull a single flower out of the bouquet and present it back to him. The metaphor is exquisite. In formal balletic etiquette, such a gesture by the ballerina occurs at the end of the evening when the ballet is finished. Here, however, in the context of Shakespeare's play, Ashton uses this clichéd yet touching exchange to signal the formal close of the comedic portion of the ballet with the traditional dénouement of the wedding, thereby providing the transition to the tragedy that will follow. Romeo clutches the pathetic little flower throughout the next scene until he is confronted with the unpalatable choice between Tybalt's glove challenging him to a duel and the flower symbolising his doomed union with Juliet. This is an earlier example of a struggle between objects that come to represent people. Flowers thereafter appear always in the presence of tragedy; the lilies of the flower girls when they arrive to awaken Juliet on her wedding day and instead find her lifeless body, and Paris's touching bouquet when he comes to the crypt to mourn the premature death of his young bride-to-be.

A prime example of Ashton's theatricality is Juliet's last excruciating crawl towards Romeo after she has stabbed herself at the end of the ballet. Ashton creates one last moment of suspense – the audience is left hoping that she makes it all the way to Romeo's lifeless body for one final embrace. It is a subtle method to arouse sympathy in the public for the characters that has nothing to do with ballet technique or steps. I spent a lot of time crawling on the floor during several rehearsals. Ashton wanted me to crawl using only my arms to propel myself forward towards Romeo. It is exceedingly tempting, if one is obliged to crawl, to do so using every part of the body. I almost blew it the night of the premiere, because after I stabbed myself I fell to the floor too far downstage in the heat of the moment. I had to scramble upstage before I could even think about heading towards Romeo. Four counts of six pass quickly when one is allowed to use only one's arms to get there. I was alarmed by the prospect of the curtain closing before I made it to Romeo's body, but fortunately, I made it just in time!

I feel that these detailed revisions and corrections are significant because Ashton concentrated mainly on coaching the first-night cast. He was concerned about the opening night. 'The critics are preparing to crucify me,' he remarked to me, about a week and a half before the premiere.

Many times he worked with Peter Schaufuss and myself either alone or with Alexander Grant and the choreologist Fiona Grantham present. When the company returned to London from Copenhagen, I showed all of the Juliet revisions to Grantham for the notation record. In addition, Lucia Truglia, the second-cast Juliet, requested that I be called out of my own Swanilda rehearsals twice in order to review the Nursery and Act III revisions with her, despite the fact that Grantham had already taught her the new parts (which the latter had notated when I showed them to her). I was very happy to help out, although there was no question that it was not my responsibility to teach the role to the other Juliets. As it happened, first Matz Skoog, the second-cast Romeo, was sidelined with a minor injury in May and June, then Truglia, and then Skoog again. Hence, they had not rehearsed very much until shortly before the premiere. As I recall it, only one private rehearsal was scheduled for Skoog and Truglia alone with Ashton. Following that one rehearsal, the second cast (and the third cast Juliet, Virginie Alberti, who danced with Schaufuss later in the opening week) ended up being rehearsed by other balletmistresses in the company, mostly without the benefit of Grantham's notation.

Gradually a second, less detailed version began to emerge in which the characterisations were influenced more by Nureyev's previous production for the company than by Ashton's. Judging by muttered remarks that I heard from time to time in various quarters, I think that the disparity was due not only to a shortage of rehearsal time and mixed-up logistics, but also perhaps to misplaced loyalty to the Nureyev production. In any case, many of those differences can be attributed to the variety of individual interpretations. I had understood that one must try to honour the choreographer's wishes, but it is sometimes difficult to draw a clear line where set choreography ends and interpretation begins. All I knew was that many of the details and choreographic elements that Ashton had specifically set on us were not executed by the other casts that season. That this was visibly the case is evident from a review by Alastair Macaulay following that season where he states:

> All of these moments are only clear with the first-cast Katherine Healy. . . At the first two performances she was, however, singularly unspontaneous. But as I went on to watch the other Juliets I realized with dismay how many crucial details had not been passed onto them . . . Several of Juliet's most poignant gestures never passed beyond the first-cast interpreter. (Macaulay, 1985, pp. 36–7)

My perceived lack of spontaneity was due to the fact that Ashton had coached me so much that every moment *was* choreographed. As for 'details not being passed on', each of the other casts had the chance to go to the same rehearsals to which I was called, except for the time during the Copenhagen tour; and it has been my personal experience both in Festival Ballet and in other companies that when one is the second or third cast, one is required to learn the role exactly as the first cast learns it.

I became the sole torch-bearer that season for the original, detailed version when Peter Schaufuss left to fulfil a guest engagement in Japan after the week of the premiere, and Ashton no longer came in for daily rehearsals. As I began to rehearse with a new Romeo, Raymond Smith of Canada, for the subsequent performances in the Royal Festival Hall, I found myself second-guessed by ballet-mistresses who had not been present at the original rehearsals but who had rehearsed the other casts. I was constantly questioned about whether I was *really* sure what I had done in the pas de deux with Schaufuss. After all my rehearsals with Ashton for the premiere – of course I was sure. When I would reply that it was what Ashton wanted, I was usually met with a blank stare and renewed, covertly hostile queries. I was able to stay with Ashton's original version that he had set on me with some difficulty, and it was unfortunate that Raymond Smith sometimes got caught in the subtle rounds of crossfire. I felt an indescribable loyalty to the version I had rehearsed for so long. For one thing, I had worked very hard on it. For another, Ashton had taken a very big chance with me, and I did not want to let him down by abandoning his wishes. He cared about all those details and was meticulous to the last moment: for example, Alexander Grant rushed to my dressing room about an hour before the premiere to say that Ashton had decided that he wanted me to kiss the cross that hangs from Friar Laurence's waist as Juliet exits from her second scene with the Friar. Shortly afterwards, Ashton told me himself, in case Grant had forgotten.

I think it is of interest to consider *Romeo*, partly because it is a lustrous jewel in the Ashton œuvre and partly because it can function as a paradigm for his other works. When I danced Lise in *La Fille mal gardée* several years later I found that several of his precepts were equally applicable to that comic piece, such as the purity of line in the port de bras, the Ashtonian philosophy of holding positions for that extra second in order for them to register with the audience, and the importance of clear mime. *Romeo* also merits consideration because Ashton had the courage to put his work and his reputation on the line at such a late stage in his life. He often humorously referred to the premiere as 'D-Day'.

But even though he was under pressure, he was unfailingly kind and supportive. He told me at dinner after the premiere not to worry about what the critics were going to write. According to him, they had all said to him 'But she's sixteen – she can't act!' He told me that he stuck to his guns because he felt he would be able to *make* me act. Whether or not he succeeded, I think there was a calculated reason that he chose a young ballerina to dance the role. His Juliet, more so than his Romeo, is always actively – through *her* dancing and *her* mime that he expanded in the third act – trying to rebel against and overcome the forces of fate that are stacked against her love for Romeo. After all, she marries Romeo knowing that this is in direct conflict with the plans her parents have for her, whereas Romeo marries her while he is still nominally free of any obstacle except for his family name – he kills Tybalt *after* the wedding, not before.

So many knowledgeable denizens of the ballet world said to me before I danced my first Juliet that, 'You have to be mature before you can understand the role.' I do not agree with that, even now, when I am supposedly mature. A mature heiress of a family such as the Capulets would allow her actions to be governed by a pragmatic *Realpolitik*. Either she would have recognised the futility of the whole exercise and not married Romeo to begin with, or she would have committed bigamy and married Paris in order to keep the peace. But Juliet is an idealist, who believes in an all-encompassing love, and has not yet lost her illusions. She kills herself over what is essentially a brief, five-day love affair. Although such a suicide is certainly possible in an adult, it is much more likely to be committed by an impetuous young adult who has not yet succumbed to cynicism. In that sense, I think Ashton was making a point about the plot. It functions plausibly only as the story of youthful folly and idealism, particularly with regard to the female heroine, who is the focus of the entire last act of his production.

Perhaps now, as an experienced ballerina, I would have made the choice to let all of Sir Frederick's coaching diffuse through my dancing so that I would have been more spontaneous, but I think that by doing exactly what he wanted, I received the finest balletic education possible from a master.

References

Macaulay, A. (1985), 'Ashton Amid the Alien Corn,' *Dance Theatre Journal*, Winter 1985, pp. 34–7.

Following the Fred Step

Adrian Grater

The 'Fred Step' is known to all who have had a close association with Ashton's choreography as it features somewhere in most of his works. From its name, it would be reasonable to assume that it takes a consistent form; but upon closer examination, one finds that it comes in so many guises that it is sometimes difficult to understand how it has come to be recognised as a single entity.

Ashton is said to have adopted it as a 'lucky step' after first seeing it performed by Pavlova in her *Gavotte*. It is defined by David Vaughan as 'posé en arabesque, coupé dessous, small développé à la seconde, pas de bourrée dessous, pas de chat' (1977, p. 9). However, for the purpose of establishing a 'basic version' against which others might be set, I have enlarged upon this slightly to include the changes of level that I believe are inherent at the start, arriving at the eight-count phrase shown in Figure 1. This would match perfectly the music to which Pavlova's *Gavotte* was set (Lincke's *Glow-worm Idyll,* which might be more familiar when set to the lyrics 'glow little glow-worm, glimmer, glimmer'). It is also the form usually taken when performed by Ashton himself, for example as one of the Ugly Sisters in *Cinderella,* as Mrs Tiggy-Winkle in *The Tales of Beatrix Potter,* or, in 1984, when he escorted Fonteyn from the stage at the end of *Salut d'amour,* a moment which must surely be etched in the memory of all who were fortunate enough to have been present.

Limitations of time have prevented me from researching Ashton's earlier works – that is, those for which no movement notation scores exist – so for information on these I rely upon Vaughan. His first reference to the Fred Step is in relation to *Les Masques* (1933), in which he says it is 'disguised by the port de bras, arms interlinked, bent upwards at an angle from the elbows', which was fully demonstrated in Shelley Berg and Jill Beck's conference presentation *Approaches to the Revival of Les*

92

Figure 1. The basic version of the Fred Step.

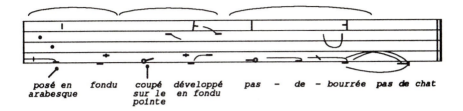

posé en   fondu   coupé   développé   *pas*   -   *de*   - *bourrée*   *pas de chat*
arabesque   sur le   en fondu
                   pointe

Masques (see pp. 38–46). Vaughan also notes its appearance in a 1934 film, *Escape Me Never*, but gives no details (1977, p. 112).

I pick up the story in 1937, when the step appeared in *A Wedding Bouquet*, performed by Ninette de Valois playing the part of Webster, the housemaid (interesting to note here that de Valois herself used a version of it in her ballet *The Rake's Progress*, which she had created two years previously – perhaps the subject for further research?). In *A Wedding Bouquet*, Ashton uses a fairly familiar structure, whereby the step is linked with another short phrase and then the whole is repeated to the other side. Here, the pas de chat is omitted from the 'basic version', but it is enhanced by a pas de bourrée piqué en pointe – a surprising embellishment for a housemaid in her late thirties. Even more surprising for such a character is the fact that one version of the linking step is a series of hopped ronds de jambe en l'air. Never let it be said (as if it ever would) that Ashton was predictable.

In *Cinderella* (1948) Ashton uses the step to wonderful effect as a vehicle for a small *mise-en-scène* in which the Dancing Master is attempting to prepare the Ugly Sisters (Ashton and Robert Helpmann) for the ball, first demonstrating the 'basic version' with absolute precision hand-in-hand with a dreamily delighted Ashton, only to be jealously snatched away by the dominant Helpmann. It is also danced by Cinderella herself, when she performs it in the kitchen to her imaginary Prince (in reality, the broom). As in *Wedding Bouquet,* a phrase is added and it is then repeated, but with a slight timing variation, to the other side. An interesting point here: within the added phrase there is a little hop in which the 'supporting' foot jumps over the raised foot, and which, on paper, bears a striking resemblance to a pas de chat (see simplified recordings, Figure 2). Although the thought never occurred to me when seeing this performed countless times 'live', having seen it in notation I can't help wondering if it may have started life as a pas de chat (which would have fitted perfectly with the Fred Step motif), and evolved during rehearsals – perhaps initially even through a mistake – into this rather unusual form. Sadly, one will never know.

Figure 2. *Cinderella* (1948). Simplified notation of 'hop-over' from Cinderella's Act I solo compared with normal pas de chat.

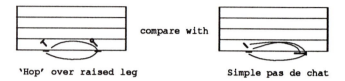

'Hop' over raised leg   Simple pas de chat

We move next to *Daphnis and Chloe* (1951), in which there are a number of quotes, one being a phrase of nine counts near the end which, I believe uniquely, substitutes the finishing pas de chat for two crisp changements. There are also several phrases of seven which are dealt with simply by omitting the last pas de chat, but one of these particularly caught my eye because the 'linking' step unusually *precedes* the Fred Step and, by finishing with the missing pas de chat, gives the Fred Step a sense of completeness – see Figure 3.

Figure 3. *Daphnis and Chloe* (1951), Shepherdesses. The 'linking' step, finishing with a pas de chat, *precedes* the Fred Step from which the pas de chat is omitted in order to fit the musical phrase of 7 counts (performed in a circle).

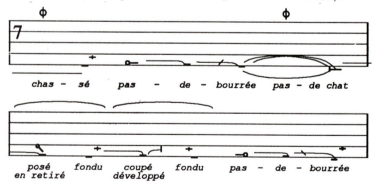

Another point of interest about this extract is that it has a most unusual type of repeat, which starts out to the other side but, by curtailing the chassé to enable an extra step to be inserted, finishes to the same side – compare Figure 4 with the top stave in Figure 3.

Figure 4. The start of the repeat of Figure 3, which, by shortening the chassé and inserting a step on count 4, manages to set out on the other leg but finish on the same leg.

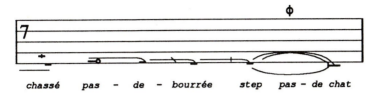

chassé   pas - de - bourrée   step   pas - de chat

Moving briefly out of chronological order, for a purpose that should soon become apparent, I shall jump to the only controversial example I know of, for which the claim by many, including Vaughan, that it is another example of the Fred Step is refuted by others in the profession. The example in question is at the end of the Scherzo in *The Dream* (1964) when it is 'turned to comic effect when done very fast, by the fairy who finds herself alone on the set . . . and does not know which way to turn' (Vaughan, 1977, p. 342).

Figure 5. *The Dream* (1964). Moth at the end of the Scherzo. A pas de chat finishing with the leg out to the side, followed by an incomplete pas de bourrée and a held posé to retiré derrière; coupé to repeat.

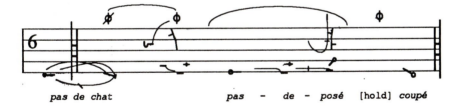

pas de chat   pas - de - posé [hold] coupé

Although it is clear that this includes most components of the Fred Step, I confess to numbering myself amongst the doubters, so I searched for reasons to justify it being identified as such. I may have found the answer in *La Fille mal gardée* (1960), where at the beginning of the Flute Dance one of Lise's friends does an abbreviated Fred Step as she calls the others to join her before they all dance a repeated passage of posé développés *followed* by the phrase illustrated in Figure 6. This phrase not only bears a remarkable similarity to *The Dream* extract, but it is automatically associated with the Fred Step that immediately precedes it.

Figure 6. *La Fille mal gardée* (1960), Flute Dance extract. Compare with *The Dream* extract in Figure 5.

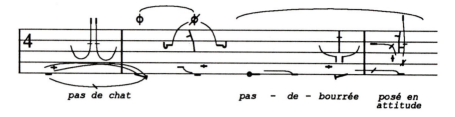

pas de chat   pas - de - bourrée   posé en attitude

Perhaps this association was subconsciously retained when it was seen, four years later, in *The Dream*?

This was not, of course, the only example of Ashton's 'lucky step' in *Fille*, which, perhaps by coincidence, could arguably be considered one of his most successful ballets. It can also be seen in the finale, where the Friends perform the 'basic version' but with the pas de chat being replaced by a preparation for two relevés assemblés which round off the phrase, as well as in a fittingly 'down-to-earth' version for the Act I peasants, performed almost entirely en fondu. The original version of this is illustrated in Figure 7, although it has since become more expansive by taking the first posé to an arabesque with an open arm.

Figure 7. *La Fille mal gardée* (1960). Act I peasants, 6/8 rhythm. Performed mostly on plié and omitting the arabesque and pas de bourrée.

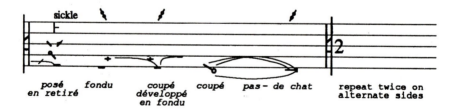

posé   fondu   coupé   coupé   pas - de - chat   repeat twice on
en retiré   développé   alternate sides
               en fondu

Seeing the step performed while holding a sickle provides an immediate link to *Illuminations*, which, although choreographed originally for New York City Ballet in 1950, did not include the Fred Step until it was mounted for the Royal Ballet in 1981. Here it is performed by eight girls as a variety of characters, such as a chimney sweep, postman, baker and so on, each carrying an appropriate prop. As the girls are imitating drunkards there is obviously a good deal of flexibility in interpretation, but its

Figure 8. *Illuminations* (1981). An unusual phrase of seven.

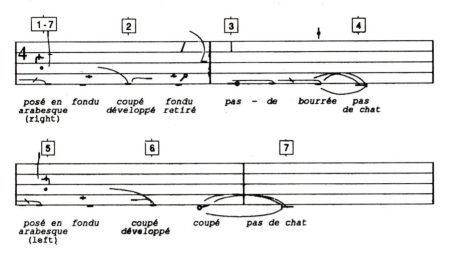

basic analysis is as an unusual phrase of seven, counted at half speed, comprising the full step with an accelerated pas de bourrée, repeated to the other side without the pas de bourrée.

I personally found that the développé fondu on counts '2-and' provided an unexpected challenge, as they reverse the usual pattern of *extending* the working leg with the fondu. In my efforts to try to master the movement rather than just the notation (essential if I was to be able to teach it as part of the workshop which was, after all, the focus of the presentation) I have to confess that, more often than not, 'muscle memory' took over and forced my legs to follow the more familiar path.

In the autumn 1994 edition of *Dance Now*, issued just before this conference, David Vaughan draws attention to the pas de deux from *Die Fledermaus* (1977), pointing out that it includes a version of the Fred Step that finishes with a soutenu rather than the more familiar pas de chat. This occurs twice, and on both occasions it is interestingly phrased as it uses four bars of waltz, with just one count per bar (this includes a finishing port de bras and lowering to dégagé not shown in Figure 9). As a result the 8-count phrase of the adapted Fred Step, instead of being on '1–2–3–4 . . .' or '1–and–2–and . . .', is on an even '1–and–a–2–and–a–3–and . . .' Although performed without emphasis, this results in the rather unusual situation of the lowering to fondu on count 2 effectively being accorded the same status as the posé arabesque and the closing to soutenu that occur respectively on counts 1 and 3.

The soutenu is also featured in one of my favourite examples of the

97

Figure 9. *Die Fledermaus* (1977). Extract from the pas de deux (only the girl's movements are illustrated).

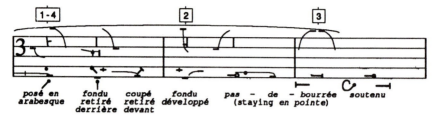

posé en arabesque   fondu retiré derrière   coupé retiré devant   fondu développé   pas - de - bourrée (staying en pointe)   soutenu

Fred Step, when it is performed by the Girl's friends in *Les Deux pigeons* (1961) as they are greeting Lady Bountiful. This is rather too long a passage to include here in notation, but it is where the Friends stand in a semicircle around her as she greets them in turn, discreetly doing the first part of the step (no pas de chat), while the whole sequence is punctuated by occasional soutenus, arms in fifth, by those who have already greeted her or who are waiting to do so. Understated but totally effective – surely a hallmark of much of Ashton's choreography.

There are many other examples of the Fred Step not touched upon here (how could I fail to mention that wonderful exit in *Month in the Country*?), and even those that have been considered have only been looked at fairly superficially through their basic form and structure, while they really beg for a deeper analysis of the way in which Ashton was influenced by the context, the music and the muses. However, I hope that those that are included here have been sufficient to have given a taste of the variety of forms that Ashton gave to this, perhaps the most famous motif in the world of dance.

At the risk of stating the obvious I would like to point out in closing that, just as Pavlova left an indelible mark on Ashton, so Ashton has left an indelible mark on many of today's choreographers. A fitting example of this is David Bintley who paid tribute to the master by quoting him, through variations of the Fred Step, in his 1993 work *Tombeaux*. There are many references in the work, but I concentrated on three in particular, and was fascinated to notice that they were all *turning* steps, a form which, to my knowledge, Ashton himself never used. The first of these is in the male solo at the beginning of the ballet; another is performed initially by 16 dancers who gradually stop until just two are left to perform the final repeat; and the third is during the final pas de deux, which includes a particularly pleasing effect as the dancers appear to use

Figure 10. *Tombeaux* (Bintley, 1993). Male solo at the opening of the ballet, to 9/8 music (counts are added for ease of reference).

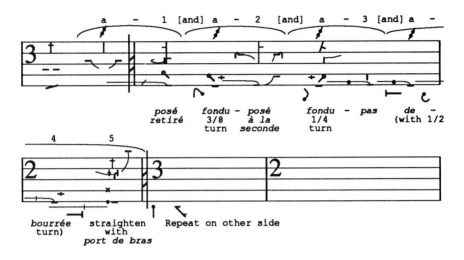

Figure 11. *Tombeaux*. Extract from group section with multiple repeats of 'incomplete' turning Fred Step performed by diminishing number of cast.

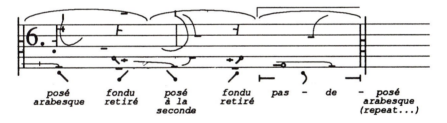

their ports de bras to cause each other to turn. In performance the connection with the Fred Step can be hard to discern, not only because of the turning characteristics but also because of their timing; but in notation form the link is more immediately available, as the basic movement can be looked at in isolation. To those who read Benesh notation to any extent, this should be evident in the following extracts from the solo and group versions.

From Pavlova, to Ashton, to Bintley, this simple sequence of infinite variety . . .

My thanks to Anthony Russell-Roberts, David Bintley and Robert Jude for their help and co-operation in the preparation and publication of this workshop. Also to the many Benesh choreologists whose movement scores were my primary source of reference and without whose skills, care and quiet dedication to the task of recording our dance heritage it would not have been possible.

Figures 1 to 9: Choreography © Ashton (dates as indicated).
Figures 10, 11: Choreography © Bintley 1993.
Benesh Movement Notation © Rudolf Benesh 1955.

References

Vaughan, D. (1977), *Frederick Ashton and His Ballets*, London, A & C Black.
Vaughan, D. (1994), 'Frederick Ashton and His Ballets: a Final Chapter', *Dance Now*, Vol. 3 No. 3, Autumn 1994, pp. 2–13.

Two Letters

Jane Pritchard

Few letters survive from Frederick Ashton to his friend and mentor, Marie Rambert. She did, however, keep material of real importance to herself, and among her collection of papers at the Rambert Dance Company archive are two written at significant times in Ashton's life. Although neither is dated and the envelopes in which they were sent have not survived, the first originates from late August 1928, when Ashton had been in Paris for about a month as a member of Ida Rubinstein's company; the second was written in the summer of 1935, and explains Ashton's decision to become a full member of Ninette de Valois' Vic-Wells Ballet. To place the letters in context it is important to remember the range of Ashton's experience during the first decade of his career in dance – a decade of enormous variety and opportunity, opportunities that Ashton would generally seize, and which provided the base for his subsequent career.

The decade under consideration begins in 1925 when, on 10 April, twenty-year-old Frederick Ashton stepped on stage at the Palace Pier, Brighton, as a member of the Duenna Dancers for a special Good Friday performance; it runs through to the autumn of 1935 when Ashton accepted the 'security' provided by de Valois, becoming chief choreographer and a principal dancer for the Vic-Wells Ballet.

It gave me a regular salary, which I hadn't had before, and I was immensely appreciative of the luxury of using proper dancers at last and having proper facilities. (Dominic & Gilbert, 1971, p. 76)

Even before this decade began, Ashton had seen the dancers whose images infiltrate so many of his works. Anna Pavlova had excited him with her 'extraordinary grace and plasticity' (Dominic & Gilbert, 1971, p. 2) in Lima, Peru, in spring 1917; and later, in London, he would

101

watch her at the Royal Opera House, Covent Garden. In April 1921 Isadora Duncan inspired him with her 'marvellous tragic impact' and wonder-ful run. 'Even when she was galumphing around she was still very impressive' (McDonagh, 1970, p. 18). And he had had the opportunity to see Diaghilev's Ballets Russes on many occasions. Precise choreographic details from the performances he saw found their way into his own later choreography – the *Gavotte Pavlova* enchaînement which became the signature 'Fred Step'[1] and the rose petals streaming from Duncan's hands as she ran downstage[2] are the most obvious examples, but films documenting early ballets, such as *Mars and Venus*[3] clearly show the influence of Massine and Nijinska. Some of the reviews of *A Tragedy of Fashion* suggest it could be regarded as a spoof on Ballets Russes choreography, a perfectly valid interpretation when another item in the Riverside Nights revue was a send-up of Chekhov.[4] In the long run, however, it is the style and movement quality of the great performers he saw, and the choreography in which they danced, that had a lasting impact.

At the outset of his training Ashton took a few Cecchetti-based classes from Léonide Massine before being sent to Marie Rambert for tuition. When Ashton could afford it, he took classes with other teachers, for example with Nicolas Legat, but Rambert welcomed him back even when he could not pay for class. Quickly they became real friends, and she was enormously supportive of his early endeavours. As Ashton acknowledged in one of his last interviews, Rambert was 'an extraordinary cultured woman, well-read and . . . her presence alone was a constant source of stimulation' (Wohlfahrt, 1988, p. 56). Rambert's concern to develop her students' all-round awareness of the arts, so that they acquired a full cultural education, surely influenced Ashton's own self-educative preparation for productions – what he often referred to as his 'homework' – immersing himself in relevant music, literature and visual arts. It is a view expounded in his first article on choreography in the *Dancing Times* in May 1930:

> Anyone contemplating the arrangement of a ballet should first become so well acquainted and imbued with the spirit of whatever period he chooses to portray as to allow the style to flow naturally and unselfconsciously through his work, inspired by the music, and avoiding always exaggeration of style which leads to mannered as opposed to truthful conception. Thus saturated he is free to take inspi-

ration from whatever conflicting sources it may come, and frequently these may be as diverse as the painting of Breughel, or provincial musical comedy. (Ashton, 1930, p. 124)

Although the pictorial and literary base for Ashton's works could be significant – and his earliest choreography included *Capriol Suite* (partly inspired by Arbeau's *Orchésographie*), and *La Péri, Foyer de danse* and *Four Saints in Three Acts* evoking Persian miniatures, sketches of ballet dancers by Degas, and the paintings by artists as varied as Giotto, Goya and El Greco respectively – it is a mistake to overemphasise the importance of narrative and pictorial elements in ballets of great choreographic beauty. Ashton himself claimed:

And consciously, all through my career, I have been working to make ballet independent of literary and pictorial motives . . . . If the ballet is to survive, it must survive through its dancing qualities . . . it is the dance that must be paramount. (Ashton, 1951, p. 33)

This belief in the importance of choreography in its own right was one he shared with Rambert, and through her teaching he acquired a real appreciation of style. They both loved the choreography of Marius Petipa and many of Rambert's classes would end with enchaînements drawn from variations from *The Sleeping Beauty*.

Within the 1925–35 decade Ashton worked on many stages. Among them were the tiniest venues in London, including the Trocadero, where he danced in his own and Buddy Bradley's choreography in late-night cabaret for a year, April 1932–33;[5] the Mercury, where Marie Rambert's Dancers gave three long seasons in 1931, and another in 1934; as well as regular Ballet Club performances on Sunday evenings and Thursday matinees;[6] and the Arts Theatre where he appeared in Lydia Lopokova's 1930 *Masque of Poetry, Music and Dancing*.[7] But he also performed and later choreographed for the largest London venues. These included productions in huge cinemas – the Shepherd's Bush Pavilion and the Regal at Marble Arch – performing divertissements accompanying films; and variety programmes at the London Coliseum and at the Royal Opera House, Covent Garden during the 1928 Italian Opera season. In addition he was seen at major British touring venues with the Nemchinova–Dolin Ballet in the autumn of 1927,[8] as well as the other major European opera houses in Paris, Brussels and Milan during the 1928–29 tour with Ida Rubinstein's company. Ashton's appearance in such a great range of presentations, both artistic and commercial, enabled him to learn his craft very thoroughly.

Ashton had considerable experience as a performer before joining Ida Rubinstein's company. What he gained most from the experience of working with that particular organisation was an apprenticeship as a choreographer. Ashton had begun to choreograph in London by being bullied to arrange works for Rambert, whose own perceptive eye guided his efforts; but in the Parisian studio, with Bronislava Nijinska he could study a master choreographer at work. Nijinska created seven original ballets while Ashton was a member of the company,[9] and regularly taught daily class. As Ashton later said 'her classes were sort of choreographic lessons', and in two interviews he observed:

> The thing that a choreographer needs is an eye. He has to do his training through his eye. . . . Nijinska, in particular, helped me tremendously. I never took my eyes off her when I was with Rubinstein. I used to come and watch all her rehearsals, just to see her work. I used to sit in the corner all day long, just watching her. (Dominic & Gilbert, 1971, p. 31)

> I was totally captivated by her personality, by the way she spoke and tackled problems. To someone like myself, who had meanwhile decided to become a choreographer, she probably transmitted more than to a dancer. (Wohlfahrt, 1988, p. 56)

From the readily accessible information on Ida Rubinstein's company it is difficult to judge its true merits. The most frequently quoted source is Diaghilev's dismissive letters to Serge Lifar, damning every aspect of the productions during the opening season of four performances at the Paris Opéra (Lifar, 1954, pp. 269–73). Diaghilev's opinions were those of a jealous rival whose own company would follow Rubinstein's into the Opéra,[10] and certainly newspaper reviews were more enthusiastic. Nevertheless the company was hindered by Rubinstein's insistence on starring in each ballet. Her determination and stellar personality could not compensate for lack of technique in ballerina roles, however carefully choreographed. Ashton described her as 'absolutely hopeless . . . All the work that we did, building up for her entrances, would always sag right down' when she appeared (McDonagh, 1970, p. 15).

Frederick Ashton in *Les Enchantements de la fée Alcine* by Léonide Massine, with Ida Rubinstein's company.

When Ashton wrote to Rambert, the dancers had been rehearsing with Nijinska for about a month. The letter, eight pages long but all one paragraph, is written in a way that suggests the ink just flowed from Ashton's pen as he tried to convey the excitement of the work. At the top he has added a postscript: 'Please excuse grammatical errors, spelling & punctuation & writing, in fact everything'. The letter is written from

The first page of Ashton's letter to Marie Rambert in 1928. Reproduced by kind permission of the Rambert Archive.

the apartment he had been lent by Lennox Berkeley, 4 rue du Ruisseau, in the eighteenth arrondissement, north of Montmartre. Later he moved to the Hotel St Georges in the centre of Paris.[11] He repeatedly recalled that at this time he lacked money for regular baths (Macaulay, 1984, p. 3),[12] but while with Rubinstein he could certainly afford to buy books (Morris, 1994, p. 131; Nugent, 1994) and sheet music – his

Gymnopédie No. 2 by Erik Satie, acquired in Paris in 1929, survives in the Rambert archive.

The letter reads:

My very dear Mim

I hope you won't consider that you have had to wait a long time for this letter but if so it is only that I might have the more to say to you. Life is very strange here or so it still seems to me & I never realised before how really far Paris is removed from London, as a town it is more beautiful but for everything else give me London, from a work point of view Paris it is undoubtedly better no distractions and no friends, but rather lonely at times & though in my heart of hearts I am not liking life here I feel as though I had known no other, so concentrated is it on one purpose & there seems no other existence outside the "village" life of the Salle Janffroy. The Company is very large & the competition very keen indeed, but I am by no means the worst dancer & I think that though Nijinska has no especial reason for liking me from the point of view of work or life she is not entirely negative to me & that is already something in so big a company. Nijinska is a wonderful woman more wonderful than I had even imagined, her efficiency is overwhelming & her knowledge & vitality something quite super-human & inspiring. She gives a brilliant class, very difficult & never dull & in doing it one realises over & over again that the best system of dance training is obviously Checcetti (I can't spell his name, disgrace!) her arms are I should say entirely based on his & her bar is the same except that she introduces various sorts of developees before the petit battement which one afterwards does in the centre & she very seldom makes us do rond de jambes en l'air. Nearly all her steps in the centre are jumping, she demonstrates the whole time & smokes incessantly her own jump is wonderful & gives one some idea of what Nijinski's jump was like in quality. She is a beautiful dancer & a dancer above all her ugliness. We have two groups for classes & they take place alternate weeks at 9am & 10am after them we rehearse till lunch & back at 3 or 4 till dinner & then back at 9 or 10 till 11.30 or 12pm. Generally one doesn't rehearse more than twice a day sometimes 3 as she takes people in groups till the ballet is finished & then calls full rehearsal. Rubinstein never appears, she has been once to look on only, & has now gone away for a holiday. But I have been going 3 times a day as I have been understudying. She has finished one ballet & as would be my luck it is Russian rather Childrens Tales-Firebird-Noces like people pile themselves on each other but we do real vigorous dancing 6 men. The music is by Rimsky-Korsakoff. The second she has just begun is rather Carnaval like & romantic & is by Shubert-Liszt. I haven't done anything in that yet but understudy in the corner. Massine arrives on the 1st September I hope he will be kind to me.[13] For I am being very diffident & feel really of no count as a dancer as yet and I fully realise what a wonderful experience it is I think better than Diaghileff because of the lessons. I also realise how little strength I have, what a meagre physique I have, I get thinner instead of fatter or more muscular and how hard & long one must work to be anything as a dancer & how the years do tell in it. I also realize how much worse I should be without your excellent teaching & grounding as I see I have more finish than most people & I hope God will give me muscles in time. I am more ambitious than ever and I long & pray that I will succeed, but life is hard and there is so much against me one thinks. I must stop now I am tired, if there is anything you would like to know please ask me as I may have not told you something you would like to know. Well dear Mim, I think of you a lot & I wish you were here many things would amuse you as they do me, and I am constantly more than grateful to you for making it possible for me to enter this Company. My love to you. Fred

It is conspicuous that men writing about Nijinska usually find it necessary to comment on her appearance. George Sari, a colleague of Ashton's in Rubinstein's company, wrote:

Oh! what a genius! Personal beauty does not count with Nijinska – everybody adores her and no one stops to ask, 'Is she beautiful? her eyes? her hair? her lips?' To say she is Nijinska – the artist, the genius, is to have said all! (Sari, 1928, p. 9)

His report confirms many of the details in Ashton's letter and adds:

Rules are rigid but everyone adheres to them and the rehearsals are truly wonderful! All the women of the company rehearse in black tunics with flesh tights and shoes, whilst the men wear black tights and white shirts. (Ibid.)

The works Ashton refers to are *La Princesse cygne* (*The Swan Princess*), inspired by the opera *The Tzar Sultan* in which, according to the programme, Ashton danced as one of eight men (Les Jeunes Gens), along with another British dancer, Rupert Doone, and three young Polish graduates of the Warsaw Opera Ballet who would become notable dancers in the 1930s: Shabelevsky, Jasinsky and Matlinsky. The *Carnaval*-like work was *La Bien aimée* (*The Beloved*), where indeed Ashton appeared as one of the carnival masquers who arrive at the end of the work.[14] In most works for Rubinstein, Ashton appeared in groups of four to nine named dancers, rather than with the anonymous corps de ballet.[15]

While the first letter was written at a time of an exciting private experience Ashton wanted to share with Rambert, the second is an explanation of changing public relationship.

After his season with Ida Rubinstein's company Ashton returned to a variety of jobs in London, including helping Rambert with the foundation of the Ballet Club. His choreographic work became more individual, and, following the creation of *Capriol Suite* and *Pomona*, Ashton was acclaimed by Arnold Haskell as 'the first young choreographist of importance to develop after the close of the Diaghileff era' (1931, p. 448). Although closely associated with Rambert's work Ashton only choreographed five ballets,[16] and a further two divertissement items for the Mercury stage. These were chamber works specifically designed in detail for the tiny space and sophisticated audience. Ashton's work for the Mercury was complemented by ballets choreographed for larger venues. As a freelance choreographer Ashton was kept busy, but he undoubtedly welcomed the opportunity to take up a full-time position within an 'artistic theatre' where it was no longer necessary to compromise, as he felt he had to in the commercial theatre to 'abandon technique and originality in favour of broad general effects' (Ashton, 1933, p. 4).

1935 was a year of realignment in the world of British ballet. The newly-established Markova–Dolin Company,[17] a full-time touring venture presenting eight performances a week, drew on the resources of both the Vic-Wells Ballet and the Ballet Club. It was against this background, and the annual visits of the Ballets Russes companies, the establishment of a new group by Leon Woizikovsky,[18] as well as his decision to accept de Valois' offer of a full-time job, that he wrote to Rambert from Scotland:

Dearest Mim

I have come to the conclusion that civil war has broken out in the world of ballet, & there is nothing more destructive in the world than civil war, much worse than a foreign invasion. In the peace of Argyllshire I see it all like a messiah (not Marguerite but probably like Baron Aloisi[19]) I shall be powerless to avert the inter-consumption of ourselves. Like a future teller I thing [*sic*] that the next twelve months must be for you a period of stocktaking. I dont think that you should beat yourself against the prison bars in fits of bitterness, nor do I think that you should stop your great work of course but I think that you should go slowly in a neutral way & watch the results of the warfare & like America step in at the right moment[20] I would not enter the guerrilla & risk a defeat because Sadlers Wells & Markova have more ammunition with which to fight, & now I see that Leon has also a company & altogether there is too much activity. I would have your season at the Ballet Club. I wonder if you believe that I say this in deep consideration & because I really love you & do not like you to be outside anything I do. You know that I realise that you are the most powerful & constructive influence in my life & I would really never do anything to hurt you that was in my power. But my strength is limited & I am no colossus like Massine I [?] sadly realise & I doubt if my slight form would be able to hold such powerful genius. I know that it hurts you that I go to Sadlers Wells but you also I hope realise that if I do go I must work to the best of my ability. I hope that you are not too upset about Façade but that is not really my doing but Willie [Walton] who wants royalties. For my part it also gives me a good dancing part to hold my own against Bobbie & Harold. But I can write no more now all this seems so petty compared to the great loss of poor Nijinska.* How really terrible. I hope god will grant her great works to distract her poor suffering mind what relief can she possibly have & what comfort can there be for her, she adored her son as you know. La vie La vie.

Do write to me soon.

Always your

Freddie

*Leon [her son] was killed motoring with Nijinska sitting at her side. Singaevsky [her husband] driving & her daughter seriously injured near Paris

Rambert did, indeed, follow Ashton's advice and continue her experimental and chamber presentations. The following January saw the creation of Antony Tudor's *Jardin aux lilas*. *Façade*, originally created for the Camargo Society, which had become a popular work in the Rambert repertory (and indeed remained so until 1968) was the only Ashton work danced by both companies in the 1930s. Music was by William Walton and in the final 'Tango Pasadoble' Ashton had given himself a strong character-role in which to stand up to comparison with the Vic-Wells leading dancers – Robert Helpmann and Harold Turner. The news of Nijinska's tragedy serves as a reminder that Ashton followed Nijinska's life and career with interest, eventually enabling her to mount *Les Biches* and *Les Noces* on the Royal Ballet dancers in the 1960s. Her influence on Ashton can be seen in a number of ways, and during his first season with the Vic-Wells Ballet Ashton re-used the score and narrative of one of the ballets he appeared in with Rubinstein's company – *Le Baiser de la fée* – and choreographed another, *Apparitions*, with thematic similarities to *La Bien aimée*. In these and the other works choreographed in the first seasons at the Vic-Wells he took full advantage of the resources available to him, but his success, and the overall development of his choreographic skill, undoubtedly drew on the experiences of his first decade in dance when Rambert was such a constructive influence in his life.

I would like to thank Anthony Russell-Roberts and the Rambert Dance Company Archive for permission to reproduce the two letters in their entirety.

Notes

1. None of the recent reconstructions of the *Gavotte Pavlova* contain the 'Fred Step enchaînement.
2. Ashton specifically included this in the last section of *Five Brahms Waltzes in the Manner of Isadora Duncan* and adapted the idea in, for example, *Voices of Spring* pas de deux.
3. The films recording early Ballet Club productions made by Pearl and Walter Duff may be viewed at the National Film and Television Archive, London, and at the Dance Collection, New York Public Library for the Performing Arts, Lincoln Center, New York.
4. This sketch 'Love Lies Bleeding or The Puss in Russian Boots' was item 10, following *A Tragedy of Fashion* after an interval in *Riverside Nights*. Chekhov was as topical as Diaghilev's Ballets Russes then performing at His Majesty's Theatre, London. Nigel Playfair, Manager of the Lyric Hammersmith, had

directed one of the first British productions of a Chekhov play, *The Wedding*, at the Grafton Galleries in 1917 (Marie Rambert performed in the same entertainment); had given *The Cherry Orchard* a month's pre-West End run at the Lyric from 25 May 1925; and a Chekhov season had just been presented across the Thames from Hammersmith at Barnes Theatre.

5. Contracts for all but star performers at the Trocadero where performances began at 11.30 p.m. nightly except Sunday ran for a year. 'Magic Nights', in which Ashton featured opened on 4 April 1932 and the following production, 'Revels in Rhythm', on 3 April 1933.

6. Regular Sunday evening, and Thursday matinee performances began at the Ballet Club on Sunday 10 January 1932. The 1934 public (rather than club) season ran 15 May–27 June.

7. For the *Masque of Poetry, Music and Dancing*, which ran for eight performances from Wednesday 10 December to Tuesday 16 December 1930, Ashton choreographed and appeared with Lopokova and Harold Turner in the ballets that closed each half: 'Follow Your Saint: The Passionate Pavan' and 'Dances on a Scotch Theme'.

8. Ashton was with the Nemchinova–Dolin Company performing in variety from 5 September to 24 December 1927. During that period they gave two seasons at the London Coliseum 5 September–8 October, and 28 November–24 December. In the interim they undertook engagements in regional theatres including Bristol Hippodrome (week beginning 17 October); the Palace Theatre, Leicester (14 November) and Manchester Hippodrome (21 November).

9. *Les Noces de Psyché et de l'Amour*, *La Bien aimée* and *Boléro* were performed at the opening programme of the Ida Rubinstein Ballet at the Théâtre Nationale de l'Opéra, Paris, on 22 November 1928. *Le Baiser de la fée* was added at the second on 27 November; and *Nocturne* and *La Princesse cygne* at the third on 29 November. *La Valse* was premiered on tour at the Théâtre de Monte-Carlo on 15 January 1929.

10. For their first, 1928, season at the Opera, the Ida Rubinstein Ballet performed on 22, 27, 29 November and 4 December. Diaghilev's Ballets Russes performed there on 20, 24, 27 December and 3 January 1929.

11. In a letter of 9 October 1928 from Edward Burra to Barbara Ker-Seymer he writes: 'We have done nothing but rush from end to end of the town searching for Fred after penetrating about 40 miles into Old Montmartre (the heart of the apache quarter you know) to the Rue de Ruisseau we were told . . . that he had removed a day or two ago to the Hotel St. George Rue Bonaparte . . .' (Chappell, 1985, p. 46)

12. By contrast with Ashton's repeated comments that dancers in the company were poorly paid, Jasinsky, in an oral interview at the Dance Collection, New York Public Library for the Performing Arts comments on the luxury

of receiving a full year's salary when performing so rarely and a return fare from Poland!

13. Massine created two works for the Ida Rubinstein Ballet. *David* was premiered on 4 December 1928 and *Les Enchantements d'Alcine* received its first performance at the Opéra on 21 May 1929.

14. *Schubert-Liszt* was the working title of this ballet as confirmed on Benois' designs for the ballet. For reproductions of some of these see Barran (1994).

15. Nijinska later paid tribute to Ashton's contribution to the company when she said that 'in character dances he was among the best. He stood out by his exact rendering of style and his flawless accuracy in the details of my choreography. Ashton did not dance solo parts . . . but he knew how to render individual what he did in ensembles . . . He was also very musical' (Dominic & Gilbert, 1971, p. 10).

16. *La Péri* (1931), *The Lady of Shalott* (1931), *Foyer de danse* (1932), *Les Masques* (1933) and *Mephisto Valse* (1934).

17. The Markova-Dolin Ballet (1935–37) was commercially funded by Mrs Henderson and Vivian Van Damm Productions Ltd. Its first performance was at the Theatre Royal, Newcastle upon Tyne, 11 November 1935.

18. The Ballets de Leon Woizikovsky operated in 1935 and 1936, then becoming the nucleus of Colonel de Basil's 'second' Ballets Russes company for touring Australia. They opened a season at the London Coliseum on 10 September 1935.

19. The reference to Marguerite is unclear. Baron Aloisi (1875-1949) was much in the news in 1935 as an Italian advocate of the League of Nations whose mission was destroyed by the rise of Mussolini and the Italian invasion of Abyssinia.

20. A reference to the American intervention in the 1914-18 war.

References

Ashton, F. (1930), 'A Word about Choreography', *Dancing Times*, May 1930.

Ashton F. (1933), 'Ballet and the Choreographer', *Old Vic and Sadler's Wells Magazine*, December 1933.

Ashton, F. (1951), 'Notes on Choreography' in W. Sorell (ed.) *The Dance Has Many Faces*, 3rd edn, 1992, Chicago, A Cappella.

Barran, J. (1994), *An Exhibition of Designs for the Russian Ballet*, London, Barran.

Chappell, W. (ed.) (1985), *"Well derie": The Letters of Edward Burra*, London, Fraser.

Dominic, Z. & Gilbert, J. S. (1971), *Frederick Ashton: A Choreographer and His Ballets*, London, Harrap.

Haskell, A. (1931), 'A Note on the Choreography of Frederick Ashton', *Dancing Times*, January 1931.

Lifar, S. (1954), *A History of Russian Ballet From its Origins to the Present Day*, trans. A. Haskell, London, Hutchinson.

Macaulay, A. (1984), 'Ashton at Eighty', *Dance Theatre Journal*, Autumn 1984.

McDonagh, D. (1970), 'Au Revoir?', *Ballet Review*, Vol. 3, No. 4.

Morris, G. (1994), 'Ashton's London Library', *Dancing Times*, November 1994.

Nugent, A. (1994), 'For Freddy, Yes for Freddy...', *Dance Now*, Vol. 3 No. 3, Autumn 1994, pp. 26-33.

Sari, G. (1928), 'Impressions of Nijinska', *The American Dancer*, December 1928.

Wohlfahrt, H.-T. (1988), 'Der Tänzer muß mit der Technik Gefühle über-tragen', *Ballett-Journal/Das Tanzarchiv*, Vol. 5 No. 1, December 1988. (I am grateful to Claire de Robilant for translating this interview for me.)

Gender, Sexuality, Community

Alastair Macaulay

Frederick Ashton was famous for his good taste, and what I have to say is in bad taste. I think that Ashton felt the whole business of critical analysis was bad form – felt that it violated the mystery. But I am also going in for a much worse kind of bad taste. I want to connect Ashton's private life to his public work. And I am committing a yet worse kind of bad taste, for I did not really know him. Though I presume here to speak of Ashton the private man, I speak from a position of ignorance.

No one will be shocked now to hear that Ashton was homosexual. But it was not mentioned – was not in good taste to mention – in discussions of Ashton's work during his lifetime. Still, the fact is that when we speak of the ballets of George Balanchine or Marius Petipa, we automatically connect their vision of women and womanhood and partnering to the fact that these men were married more than once, and to their heterosexual world view. It is time that we began to ask equivalent questions about Ashton's choreography.

We are at a transitional stage of Ashton studies. His biography is being written right now, by Julie Kavanagh – has been under way for several years – and, when it is published, it will no doubt contain many features that will illuminate his work, and other features that will seem more or less irrelevant to his choreography. I confess that I am both impatient for it and nervous of it. It will be fascinating to see which person or persons Ashton had in mind when he shaped or reshaped the character of Beliaev in *A Month in the Country* from Turgenev's original play; but will that knowledge help to make *A Month in the Country* a larger ballet in our minds? In due course, some people will go to see Ashton's *A Month in the Country* only after they have read the biography, and they will be likely to 'read' Ashton's choreography in terms of cause and effect, as we never did during Ashton's lifetime. Well, that is the nature of history and

115

of biography, and of criticism too. And the good news about Ashton's biography is that it is not one of those quick sensationalist efforts that rush to hit the markets as soon after the subject's death as possible, as has happened to poor Nureyev. It is being seriously and carefully undertaken, with (that key Ashtonian word) love.

I look forward to the Ashton biography because there are many questions about Ashton that his work makes me ask. Here are a few of them:

How come a man who could not read a score made ballets so profoundly musical?

How come a man who never taught a ballet class became one of the major ballet classicists of all time?

How come a man whose own sexual practice was chiefly homosexual made a series of ballets which expressed heterosexual love?

How come sexual love, of any kind, became an important theme to this choreographer at a time when sexuality had received little direct attention on the ballet stage?

How come supported adagio – the form of pas de deux usually employed by ballet classicists (I mean the kind in which man and woman keep at arm's length from each other and he holds her hand to support her while she does supported adagio towards or away from him) – interested Ashton relatively little?

How come this man – Sir Frederick Ashton, Knight of the British Empire, Commander of Honour, Order of Merit, who in the last years of his life stayed at Sandringham each year as a guest of the Queen and Queen Mother, and who actually made a ballet about the Queen as a young princess[1] – made ballets that were far less full of hierarchy than his contemporary George Balanchine, who, by contrast, chose to live in the world's greatest republic?

If the biography can help us to answer these questions, then it will help us understand the fount of the ballets that we already love. I can only tackle a few of them briefly here.

Let me whisk you through a few familiar Ashton stories. He saw Pavlova. 'She injected me with her poison, and there was an end of me. From then on, I wanted to be the greatest dancer in the world, I wanted to be Nijinsky.'[2] Well, he found out that he could not be Nijinsky, and this led to choreography. Many years later, Margot Fonteyn was speaking to him about a choreographer she didn't admire, whom she called 'just a frustrated dancer'. Ashton looked at her and said, 'But we're all frustrated dancers'. Fonteyn added that Ashton 'seemed rather surprised at the idea that anyone who could be a really good dancer would bother to become a choreographer' (Dominic & Gilbert, 1971, p. 4). Choreography for him was, in part, the sublimation of his ambition to be a dancer. But it sublimated other things for him too. He was a great mimic, and a very important part of his work with dancers was his descriptions and imitations of the great ballerinas he had seen. As late as the 1970s, he was rushing around the classroom showing female dancers how to do their roles, and saying 'I should have been a ballerina'.[3] Robert Helpmann once remarked that every ballerina role Ashton ever made could have been made for Pavlova; and that, when he suggested this to Ashton, Ashton said 'Yes, she would have been wonderful. Because I think of her when I'm working all the time' (Dominic & Gilbert, 1971, p. 124). So, yes, he would have liked to be Nijinsky, but we can see that he would have liked to be Pavlova too – and that being Pavlova had a more enduring appeal for him.

Of course, Ashton was not unique in his personal involvement with women's roles. Maria Tallchief, who was Balanchine's third wife, said that she could never dance the Swan Queen as beautifully as her husband (Taper, 1963, p. 23). Other Balanchine ballerinas have said the same; and some of them say the same about Jerome Robbins too. But Balanchine and Robbins did not make female roles for themselves, or spend time imitating female dancers of the past or dressing up as women of the Victorian or Edwardian eras. For a man to have a penetrating understanding of femininity is one thing, for a man to need to keep representing himself in female guise is another. Ashton's performances as the Ugly Sister and Mrs Tiggy-Winkle are famous; as many people know, he was a fine Carabosse; if you have David Vaughan's book on Ashton, you will have looked a hundred times at the photographs of him as Queen Victoria and Queen Alexandra; and some of you may know the photographs of him as an Edwardian dowager in Cecil Beaton's *My Royal Past* (Vaughan, 1977, p. 195 *et seq.*; von Bülop, 1939). Ashton made male roles for himself too – in *Façade*, *Foyer de danse*, *Nocturne*, *Les Sirènes*, *Salut d'amour*, and others – and it would be wrong if we thought of him as some kind of drag artist. Interestingly, like Mark Morris (who has also made female roles for himself), he disliked what he called drag – by which he meant, I think, all the *Priscilla: Queen of the Desert* kind of maquillage and coiffures and glamorous frocks. Nor was he without

117

heterosexual experience. But it is very interesting to watch what the ballets tell us about sexuality.

Love became an important theme in his work during the 1930s. It is possible that his time in America in 1934 made him attend to it more seriously; and it is probable that Margot Fonteyn, who became his new muse at this time, helped him to express many aspects of love. She was the Bride in his 1935 *Baiser de la fée*; she said that it was that ballet that first gave her the delight of dancing an Ashton pas de deux (Fonteyn, 1975, p. 55); and she said also that (with the exception of certain Ashton solos), her greatest pleasure came from dancing in duet (p. 135). And Ashton could see, as the outside world could not, how complex a woman, even in her teens, Fonteyn was.[4] As early as 1936, Ashton began to take delight in showing these opposing facets of her – just compare her roles as the crushed vulnerable innocent in *Nocturne* and the unattainable muse of *Apparitions* (both 1936) – sometimes revealing them to her before she acknowledged their truth in herself. He would do the same for other dancers. Antoinette Sibley has spoken of her delight at how he could reveal her as the wild, impulsive, sensual fairy queen Titania in *The Dream* (1964) and then as the stuttering young English Dorabella, hero-worshipping the older artist Elgar in *Enigma Variations* (1968) (Dromgoole, 1976, p. 30). Of course, he was showing us these truths in ourselves too.

But love is not the same as sex. Perhaps he became more interested in sex during the War. At that time, he first started to think of a ballet about Don Juan, even before he investigated the Richard Strauss score that he eventually used. (It is always revealing when a musical choreographer has been prompted to take up a subject by other than musical causes.) And, in *The Wanderer* (1941), he created a striking duet for a pair of young adult lovers which showed more physical intimacy than many British balletgoers were prepared for at the time (Vaughan, 1977, pp. 192–3). It was, however, in the late 1940s when a particular concern with sexual love entered his work. No doubt there was some reason in his own private life at that time for this; and no doubt he was encouraged by contemporary dance representation of sex in such ballets as Antony Tudor's *Pillar of Fire* and Roland Petit's *Carmen*, both of which were brought to London soon after the War. He developed his new interest in sexual love in four particular ballets. In each of them, he seems to have had something different to say about sex and/or sexual love; in each, he contrasted different kinds of love and desire. *Don Juan* (1948) showed him developing new ways of presenting the female body in a way that caused one reviewer to suggest Ashton had been going too often to Roland Petit's Ballet des Champs-Elysées; and it is noteworthy that the subject of the ballet is the connection between sexual love and death (Fonteyn danced La Morte Amoureuse) (Vaughan, 1977, pp. 227–8).[5]

In *Illuminations* (1950), the hero – the Poet – is caught between the figure of Profane Love, with whom he engages in sexual, Petit-type grapplings (the point of which is surely that they are merely sexual), and that of Sacred Love, a remote figure of strange beauty. He is torn: prose or poetry? flesh or spirit? The dichotomy between the ballet's two extremes is, for the protagonist, tragic: which leads to his death (and then an apotheosis). The Poet here is essentially Rimbaud, whose words are used in the Britten score to which Ashton choreographed; and the divide between flesh and spirit which was so striking a part of Rimbaud's own life, is also generally an expression of the divide between homosexual desire and Christian devotion that has generally obtained in the Western world. Since Rimbaud's own practice was homosexual, the complaint has sometimes been made that a more honest portrayal of the subject would have been to have shown the Poet involved not with a woman but with a man. Ashton's ballet is, however, by no means dishonest. It does bypass literalism, certainly. How could it not? It is clearly a picture of the violently changing landscape of Rimbaud's mind, and it deals in symbols. The figure of Profane Love certainly represents the figure of Rimbaud's famous lover and fellow-poet Verlaine in certain features – just as Verlaine shot Rimbaud, Profane Love shoots the Poet – but, with one foot bare and one on pointe, she represents other elements in Rimbaud's poetry too. And it is Rimbaud's poetry and Britten's superbly imaginative musical setting of it that shape Ashton's ballet most of all. Like Sacred Love, Profane Love is a ballerina conception of 'otherness', conveying meanings that could not be achieved were the role to be danced by a man.

In *Daphnis and Chloe* (1951), the duet for Lykanion and Daphnis contains the most poetically explicit, and explicitly poetic, depiction of sex that I have ever known in dance. You can see the excitement of friction between the bodies, the ecstatic *frissons* of the woman, and, as David Vaughan has written, the moment of orgasm, all expressed in dance terms (1977, p. 249). This pas de deux was, I believe, a breakthrough for Ashton, the open-sesame to several later less explicit, but more sustained, and even more poetic, depictions of sexual love.

119

The fourth of these ballets is *Tiresias* (1951). David Vaughan has spoken of the lost Ashton ballets we will get to see if we get to heaven (see p. 6); but I have to say that I suspect, if we get to heaven with him, that *Tiresias* won't be one of the ballets we get to see there. Nobody seems to have admired it much. Still, what a fascinatingly peculiar subject for a ballet. Tiresias, you may recall, is the aged prophet who, in the course of his life, has been both man and woman, and who is able, from experience, to state which sex derives most pleasure from sex: namely, woman. (In fact, only the female Tiresias was shown experiencing love in the ballet.) Constant Lambert and Ashton specifically planned the role of the female Tiresias, the one who enjoys sex the most, for Margot Fonteyn; and this role was probably the most sexual that Ashton ever made on her (Vaughan, 1977, pp. 252–5, 421–3).

From then on, Ashton made a series of ballets in which he shows the sensuousness of woman's response to man, shows her erogenous zones, joys in her sensuality. In some of these ballets, we hardly think of the love as sexual, but we cannot miss the importance of physical contact. In *La Fille mal gardée* (1960), when Colas is consoling Lise for having surprised her in the middle of her daydream of marriage and children, he places a series of kisses up her arm, and she at once responds in bourrées that tremble with desire.[6] And the sensuousness of female response to man is also evident in such later ballets as *A Month in the Country* (1976) and *Varii Capricci* (1983). The final duet of *The Two Pigeons* (1961) begins with the hero's touch on the woman's underarm or shoulderblade area, and the thrilled, arching response she makes to that. And in the final duet of *The Dream*, Titania alternately melts and radiates in Oberon's arms. In both the *Two Pigeons* and *Dream* duets – which are, I believe, Ashton's two greatest expressions of fulfilled sexual love – the phrasing and structure has the sexual quality of Wagner's erotic music in *Tristan*: of initiative and response, of pressure and relaxation, phrase by phrase, question and answer, building up in a crescendo, reaching a moment of full-out climax – and then the tender dying fall.

I stress the sexual element of Ashton's choreography because it may not seem pronounced to those of us who know our Kenneth MacMillan. But not only are Ashton's pas de deux the more poetic, MacMillan actually refers to them when he is depicting sexual love (the pas de deux of Act I of MacMillan's *Romeo* and *Manon* are full of Ashtonisms). But now compare Ashton's pas de deux to those by those other ballet classicists, Petipa and Balanchine. In the supported adagios choreographed on many occasions by Petipa and Balanchine, man and woman often keep at arm's length from each other. He holds her hand or her waist, and the distance between the two becomes as expressive as the proximity. When physical contact is emphasised, as when he rocks her in his arms from behind in the great adagio of *Swan Lake,* or in the highly erotic duet of *The Prodigal Son,* it makes an unusual effect. It is curious, by contrast, how seldom Ashton's duets make any emphasis on this distance between ballerina and partner. There are a few examples; and it may be biographically relevant that they come from the period 1948–56.[7] In Act III of *Cinderella* (1948), there is a striking passage of supported adagio, when the ballerina takes a grand développé in second, and then turns without his support into arabesque where, taking his hand again, she makes a pronounced penchée. It resembles the second movement of Balanchine's *Symphony in C,* but only briefly. It is only a phrase. The 'Being Beauteous' section of *Illuminations* is more prolonged – is indeed Ashton's ultimate version of the kind of supported adagio that emphasises the distance of the woman from the men who partner her – but it is a one-off, unlike other Ashton choreography (and Balanchine had a hand in its making).[8] There is a very striking instance in the pas de deux for the Queen of the Air in *Homage to the Queen* (1953), as recorded on a 1970 film. And, in the pas de deux of *Birthday Offering* (1956), the ballerina makes some spectacular effects at arm's length from her partner – but, in the context of the whole pas de deux, they seem simply to be brief displays of a ballerina's grandeur amid her generally radiant contentment with her partner.

In other words, a woman's need to be independent of, or remote from, her partner – so striking a feature of Petipa, Ivanov, and Balanchine choreography – was something that almost never interested Ashton. In Ashton's duets, the nearness of the bodies is all-important; we constantly sense two bodies seeking union. Does this – the thrill at a man's touch, the excitement in sensual coupling – reflect aspects of his own sexuality? I believe so. During the last years of his life, I be-came increasingly interested by the peculiar subject matter of *Tiresias,* and a mutual friend asked Ashton about it. Ashton replied, 'Oh yes. I was always the woman, you see'.[9] To the extent that this clinched my theory, this was gratifying. It will be interesting to see what the biography has to tell us about Ashton's masculinity and his femininity. What is more interesting, however, is what the ballets tell us about them. And what is most interesting is what the ballets tell us, not about Ashton, but about ourselves. The more we are in touch with both masculine and feminine sides of ourselves, the more we will delight in his choreography.

Now, ballet is a hierarchical art. It not only places classical dancers in ranks – corps de ballet, coryphées, soloists, ballerinas and so forth – it also distinguishes classical from demi-character and character dancers. Ashton, we can see, enjoyed using all these different ranks and genres – but we can also see that hierarchy matters to him remarkably little. Sure, the ballerina of *Scènes de ballet* is supported by four men in one dance as well by her own partner; but those four also partner the girls in the corps. (Just imagine how *The Sleeping Beauty* would feel if the four princes in the Rose Adagio took time off to partner Aurora's little friends.) In *Cinderella*, there are character, demi-character and classical dancers, corps de ballet and ballerinas and prima ballerina. But at first Cinderella herself is very far from being a prima; and in the main scene where all the ranks are assembled together – the ballroom – her position is extremely ironic. Perhaps his most hierarchical work was *Homage to the Queen*, but it did not survive long. In *Birthday Offering*, he created one of those ballerinas-at-a-gathering ballets, in which, like *Paquita* and *Divertimento No. 15*, each ballerina expresses her identity in a different variation. But, unlike *Paquita* or *Divertimento No. 15*, he does not put them in the context of a corps de ballet. They have their crowns and jewels – chandeliers too – but they are seen in private, without subjects. *The Dream*, of course, has its distinctions – ballerina distinct from corps de ballet, classical versus character – and yet Ashton makes less of these distinctions than several other artists who have set the same story.

Hierarchy matters little to Ashton; community matters much more. In ballet after ballet, from *Capriol Suite* (1930), *Les Rendezvous* (1933), and *Les Patineurs* (1937), through to *Rhapsody* (1980) and *Varii Capricci* (1983) it is clear that the star dancers are members of the same community as those in the corps de ballet. The heroines of *La Fille mal gardée* and *The Two Pigeons* are socially equal to the coryphées. In *Enigma Variations*, the more virtuoso classical roles are no more central than the character or demi-character roles. Most remarkably of all, Ashton's great plotless works, *Symphonic Variations* (1946) and *Monotones* (1965–66), are entirely communities of equals.

This stress on equality and community is easy to love. Please note, however, how unusual it is in classical ballet. And it ties in with Ashton's unusual emphasis on physical love. The classic example here is *La Fille mal gardée*, where the loving couple comes together surrounded, and accepted, by the community at large. But the sense of community is equally important in *Enigma Variations*, though the hero there is involved with three different women and numerous friends: he may not find completely satisfying love for himself – unlike two of his younger friends shown in the ballet – but he finds his peace in being part of a community of friends. I believe that Ashton was expressing, or sublimating, the homosexual's need for private lives and private loves to be accepted by a larger, caring, society.

I seem to have struck a melancholy note. Well, melancholy was an important factor in Ashton's make-up. Fonteyn once said that 'I think Fred's perfect day would always contain a few moments of melancholia and regret because it hadn't been quite perfect' (Dominic & Gilbert, 1971, p. 126). And I believe that, though love and sex always interested him, after 1964 he ceased to see successful love as a cure or resolution or happy ending. Indeed, in several earlier ballets also, he showed successful sexual love as being possible, but not for the particular hero or heroine of the ballet. There are three ballets where this is particularly clear: *The Wanderer*, *Illuminations*, and *Enigma Variations*. In each of these, a subsidiary pair of junior young lovers is shown calmly absorbed in one another, expressing a kind of love that the hero cannot attain. Ashton seems to be echoing here W. H. Auden's point: 'I think that no homosexual, if he is honest, is truly happy in his sex.'

Yet melancholy is only one note in Ashton's perfect day, in Ashton's perfect ballets. I find it interesting that there are very few deaths in his work, and very little transcendence – less than in Balanchine.[10] Ashton is often called a Romantic, and in his emphasis on the importance of love and feeling we can see why. But in another, larger, sense he was not a Romantic at all. A Romantic is one for whom this world is not enough, who strives to find an essence beyond this existence. Ashton's ballets are all about this world. Other choreographers have made ballets that go beneath our skin to our inner selves; Ashton's ballets are about our skin, about our social selves, about the way we relate to each other and to the world about us. This is true, I believe, even of the celestial *Symphonic Variations*, with its Suffolk green, and the lunar *Monotones*, with its 'there you have it' gesture. Harmony is an important word for Ashton's ballets; vitality is more important yet.

At the Ashton gala in 1970, Robert Helpmann, nearing the conclusion of the evening, said 'The man is the work, the work is the man'.[11] Well, whatever its genesis, whatever the mind of its maker, what a wonderful vision it is. Ashton's sense of community was so thorough that it percolates right through to his distribution of dance language. There are innumerable examples; two will have to suffice here.[12] *Romeo and Juliet* (or at least Ashton's 1985 London Festival Ballet version of his 1955 ballet[13]) has four different versions of the famous 'Fred Step': for Juliet and Paris in the ballroom, for the courtiers in the ballroom, for the street-scene crowd while Livia is dancing in the foreground, and for the nurse's page Peter. *The Dream* is full of magic circles traced on, or just above, the floor.[14] Hermia, slowly turned in fondu on pointe by Lysander, traces one such circle with the point of her extended leg; and then Titania, in her pas de deux with Oberon, traces another. And both of these are slow, supported versions of other magic floor-circles we see, such as Titania's ground-skimming double pirouettes in the Lullaby.

Fokine, at the beginning of this century, like Jean-Georges Noverre in the eighteenth century, stated that each kind of character should have a different, and appropriate, kind of dance vocabulary, and Ashton in this respect was generally a Fokinian choreographer. Hermia's way of dancing is nothing like Titania's; little Peter is nothing like Juliet or Paris. But Ashton, in showing how these very different characters can nonetheless unconsciously share a very specific step or phrase, was making a point beyond Fokine's ken. Each of us, prima or corps, character or classical, belongs to the same little world, and can be touched by the same magic.

Parts of this paper are taken from a longer lecture on Ashton given in the Threepenny Review's *1989 lecture series 'The Art of Criticism'. The text of that lecture is due to be published by* The Threepenny Review.

Notes

1. *Nursery Suite* (1986), made for Queen Elizabeth II's sixtieth birthday gala at Covent Garden.
2. Ashton said part or all of this many times. See Vaughan, 1977, p. 4; Dominic & Gilbert, 1971, p. 26; and the 1979 BBC documentary on Ashton.
3. Lesley Collier, interviewed by the Ballet Association in the late 1970s.

4. In her memoirs, Fonteyn describes the paradoxical situation whereby she would kiss Helpmann onstage and believe she was in love, and yet slap on the face the first of her stage-door-johnny admirers who dared to kiss her in a taxi (1975, p.57). What she left unsaid, but which we also know now, is that during these years Fonteyn was secretly involved in a highly sexual affair with Constant Lambert (see Motion, 1986). I believe that all these sides of Fonteyn, paradoxically, were sincere. In the mysteries of her own mind, she was a vulnerable innocent, a happily sexual being, and an inviolable nun at the same time. In due course, she became other women too: an unattainable muse, a man-eater, an emblem of international chic, a frightened virgin who longed for sexual fulfilment but feared she would never find it, and a radiant child of nature. I am imagining this, but I am led to imagine it by the roles she danced, and by the way she danced them. Ashton, of course, knew about her affair with Lambert at the time, as few other people did.

5. The connections between Petit's choreography at this time and Ashton's deserve further research. It is at least possible that the foot-tappings of Fonteyn's dances – tapping a pointe on the floor behind – in *Scènes de ballet* (1948) and *Daphnis and Chloe* (1951) were inspired by those in Petit's ballets (though the device also has simply a look of Fred Astaire to it). And it is important to notice that Fonteyn's work with Petit at this time and her offstage liaison with him had a strong impact on her career: the fans called it 'Margot's awakening'.

6. At this conference, Alexander Grant supported this point, stressing that Ashton wanted Colas to place the kiss into the palm of Lise's hand. ('Ashton knew where the erogenous zone was.')

7. At the time of writing, I had not yet seen the 1962 *Raymonda* pas de deux, due to be restored to Royal Ballet repertory in December 1994; it may contain other examples. Possibly the pas de deux in the 1982 *Pas de légumes* (from the 1979 film *Tales From a Flying Trunk*) danced by the heroine and the Potato Prince, is a late example; but I recall this pas de deux as the one disappointing item of an otherwise delectable ballet.

8. Years later, in the central movement of *Sinfonietta* (1967), Ashton devised another dance with the same basic structure of one woman and four male partners, and the same generally remote quality, but no emphasis is laid on the women's separateness from her male partners, who lifts her so that she seldom, if ever, touches the floor.

9. Source withheld.

10. See, or read about, Balanchine's *Cotillon, Le Baiser de la fée, La Sonnambula, La Valse, Don Quixote, Robert Schumann's Davidsbündlertänze.* Death in Ashton is confined to *Apparitions, Illuminations, Romeo and Juliet.*

11. Helpmann at the 1970 Ashton gala, as preserved on film.

12. Two other examples occur in *Cinderella* and *La Fille mal gardée*. In *Cinderella*, we can see how the season fairies introduce the heroine to steps that she then develops in her own dances, but also how the minor courtiers, mysteriously, are already showing us some of the same steps. (Just look at the various uses in the ballet of the jump with feet tucked up together underneath the dancer's seat. Fairy Spring does it; then all four season fairies together; then the Jester; then the Prince's four friends; and finally Cinderella does it, but in a lift, during the ballroom pas de deux.) I had watched *La Fille mal gardée* more than sixty times until I realised that my favourite step in the ballet occurs in two different contexts: first when Lise is dancing alone with her ribbon in the first scene; then when her girlfriends start the finale for Act II. (The step – tricky to describe – involves a saut de basque which arrives and opens, with a relevé, into a small développé in second, which is followed by a quick raccourci.)

13. It was no secret in 1985 that Ashton added a new pas de trois for Romeo, Mercutio, and Benvolio. But, as Katherine Healy (the first-cast Juliet of that production) has confirmed, Ashton made several further changes and additions.

14. Ashton, I suspect, was thinking of the magic rings left on the ground by toadstools.

References

Dominic, Z., & Gilbert, J. S. (1971), *Frederick Ashton: a Choreographer and His Ballets*, London, Harrap.

Dromgoole, N. (1976), *Sibley and Dowell*, London, Collins.

Fonteyn, M. (1975), *Autobiography*, London, W. H. Allen.

Motion, A. (1986), *The Lamberts*, London, Chatto & Windus.

Taper, B. (1963), *Balanchine*, New York, Harper & Row.

Vaughan, D. (1977), *Frederick Ashton and His Ballets*, London, A & C Black.

von Bülop, (1979), *My Royal Past as Told to Cecil Beaton*, London, Batsford.

Interview with Alexander Grant

Julie Kavanagh

Julie Kavanagh: In 1946 you were a student taking class with the company and very soon found yourself dancing one of the Popular Song boys in *Façade.* Could you tell us how that came about?

Alexander Grant: It all started in New Zealand when I won a Royal Academy of Dancing Scholarship to come to London to continue my training. They put me at the Sadler's Wells School. I arrived on 1 February, after seven weeks at sea in a cargo boat around Cape Horn, which was quite an adventure. There was no school because all the older members of my age had been put into the newly formed company at Sadler's Wells – the old company had been transferred to Covent Garden, and a new company to take its place had been formed at Sadler's Wells Theatre. As there was no school I was asked to do my classes with them and stand at the back during rehearsals, to watch what was going on and learn whatever I could. Then came the marvellous day when Frederick arrived to cast *Façade,* which was to be one of the first ballets to be performed by the newly formed company. I was standing at the barre with a boy called Donald Britton. We were similar in height and physique, and I could see Frederick sitting with Peggy van Praagh, the new director, pointing to us and Peggy van Praagh saying 'No, no, no, he's only a student, he's not in the company, you can't really have him.' But Sir Frederick got his way, and I found myself learning the Popular Song with Donald Britton. So that was my first glimpse of Frederick and his work.

Kavanagh: That is a ballet that you now teach around the world and you coach. Can you talk about the qualities that you try and bring out?

Grant: It was a very special ballet, one of Frederick's earliest works. It was a music-hall kind of thing. During the war in New Zealand I was a member of a concert party, and had done that kind of thing entertaining the troops, so I was quite familiar with what was called music-hall and cabaret. This was just a balletic extension of it. I remember in one of the

127

cabaret items I did in New Zealand – 'By the Sea, By the Beautiful Sea', which I sang, to the horror of everybody – I wore a costume that was practically the same as in *Façade*, so I felt very much at home in it. I believe Ashton actually danced the Tango in those early performances, so I had wonderful tuition from him. It is not generally known what a great performer Ashton was. He wanted to be a great dancer. He wasn't really interested in being a great choreographer, which is what he became. I only managed to see him dance in his later years, but I saw him in many roles: Carabosse, in which he was terrific; Dr Coppelius, in which he was wonderful; Kastchei in *The Firebird*; and an Ugly Sister in *Cinderella*. There were many roles which he performed. I learnt a great deal from him, and worked with him in many ballets that I was lucky enough to be a part of. You asked me how many created works of Ashton ballets had I been associated with. I got out David Vaughan's fantastic chronicle [*Frederick Ashton and His Ballets*, A & C Black, 1977] and was able to count them up: twenty-two. I was rather pleased, as Alicia Markova said that she had created eighteen [see p. 170]. I've also danced in nine other Ashton ballets which I didn't create, so altogether I've danced in thirty-one.

Kavanagh: You were pushed on in *Symphonic Variations*.

Grant: Yes, in the early days when I was a very green, new member of the company. They had been working together during the war as a team and hadn't had too many newcomers – male dancers were very hard to find in those days, particularly during wartime. I went on the very first tour of the touring company for two weeks only, to Exeter and Brighton, dancing in *Façade* and Celia Franca's *Khadra*. Then I was told to have a holiday and join the main company in September. So I'd arrived in February 1946 and joined the company in September. I found to my horror – or fright, really – that Brian Shaw, who had created one of the parts in *Symphonic Variations*, was called into the army and I was suddenly told that I had to do it. I had to learn it in a great hurry. Here I was, completely green, with three of the leading ballerinas: Margot Fonteyn, Pamela May and Moira Shearer. I will always be grateful to Pamela May and Michael Somes, who encouraged me tremendously, and of course Sir Frederick, but Pamela was very patient and tolerant with me. I often remind her of that fact, and I think she remembers it quite well.

Kavanagh: Was that a tremendously challenging role?

Grant: It was. You are on stage when the curtain goes up and you know you can't leave until it's finished. You can't go off and think what's next if you haven't learnt it very well. So you can imagine how frightening it was. You also have to watch your spacing. You have to be in the right spacing because there are very few people on a large stage. It wasn't just a question of learning the steps, you had to know exactly where you were on the stage, and also partner those ballerinas. I mostly partnered Pamela May, and even had to do pirouettes with Moira Shearer – so you can imagine this new young recruit from New Zealand suddenly being thrown on in this wonderful new work. It had been a great success, so it was a ballet that we looked on with great reverence.

Kavanagh: It was extraordinary that he followed that six months later with *Les Sirènes*, which was a resounding flop.

Grant: Yes, my first created Ashton role was in *Les Sirènes*. I played a little boy, with a girl called Pauline Clayden; she held hoops which I jumped through. We also had another part in it. I was an attendant to Sir Frederick, who was King Hihat of Agpar (a kind of Shah of Persia). It was set on the beach at Trouville. Sir Frederick devised a most spectacular entrance for himself: he came down onto the beach from a balloon. But of course he never rehearsed coming down in the balloon, and he had forgotten that to come down in the balloon he had to be up there at the beginning of the ballet, and he didn't come down until half way through it. And he hated heights. So there he was, cowering at the bottom of the basket until his entrance. When he came down he was so frightened that he couldn't remember what came next. I was an attendant behind him with a boy called Kenneth Melville, and here he was saying 'What comes next?' all the time. Everything had gone out of his head. Luckily we were all doing the same step, so I knew what came next for him. So he said, 'No more, I'm not coming down in the balloon any more. I'm going to devise an entrance where you carry me on in a bier' – which we then had to do. But it couldn't be wasted, and Robert Helpmann said, 'This is a wonderful entrance. I will come down in the balloon.' And he did. He was a tenor in the ballet too, actually sang in a tenor voice.

Kavanagh: And then in 1947 Massine came to Covent Garden and had a galvanising influence on the company.

Grant: I was very fortunate that I had been chosen by Massine in a ballet that he was reviving, *Mam'zelle Angot*. The principals were Margot Fonteyn, who was my partner, Moira Shearer and Michael Somes. It is generally known that Ashton's first teacher was Massine. Working with Massine and performing a Massine role – he was always interested in that kind of work; and having made a success of this role brought me to Ashton's notice.

129

Kavanagh: He tended to give you quite a few of those wild jumps which you did in *Mam'zelle Angot*.

Grant: Yes. I think that was why Massine picked me. The one thing I could do in those days was jump. Massine was in Manchester in a musical play called *Bullet in the Ballet*. De Valois heard that it was not a great success and was not being brought to London, so she asked him to come and do some ballets for the company when the show closed. He could only spare a Sunday because he was still in the production in Manchester. We all had an audition class on Sunday afternoon in the rehearsal room at Sadler's Wells. I can remember jumping myself silly – so much so that I was chosen as the Poodle for *La Boutique fantasque*. Then I was lucky enough to get the role of the Barber in *Mam'zelle Angot*.

Kavanagh: How would you say that Ashton's choreography was influenced by Massine?

Grant: Very much. You mentioned *Façade*. I always think that the finale in *Façade* is tremendously Massine-like.

Kavanagh: The hands as well?

Grant: No, the hands are very much Ashton. Ashton was born in South America and had this Latin American/Peruvian background of the tango, for instance. The use of the arms, the Spanish use of the hands, that comes into his work.

Kavanagh: People tend to associate you with gentle creatures like Alain in *La Fille mal gardée*. It is difficult for us to imagine that you had a kind of dangerous quality, on and off stage. You told me that you once ran the bulls at Pamplona, for instance. I was thinking of the Pirate King in *Daphnis and Chloe*. I think you told me that Fonteyn was terrified of you.

Grant: She never complained. She was like a lamb to the slaughter every night. I had to run on with her on one hand. I used to run on with her around the stage, then put her around my neck (I see this movement has now been cut), and swing her around my neck horizontally, and then around my body, and throw her onto the floor and then jump all over her. I was very pleased on one occasion, because after *Daphnis and Chloe* there was a big crowd at the stage door for Fonteyn, as there was every night after the performance; I came out and I heard somebody say, 'That's Alexander Grant, the Pirate Chief'. Then: 'He's so small!' I was terribly pleased, because it meant that I looked enormous on stage.

Kavanagh: You also brought a hint of danger to the Jester in *Cinderella*. Edwin Denby used that wonderful phrase 'the beautiful suspense of an animal pounce' to describe your quality of the Jester.

Grant: Ashton had this wonderful ability to bring special qualities out in people. I think he knew that I was willing to try anything, and he was willing me to try anything. You had this wonderful confidence in him, which he gave you, that you could try anything. He did not like an artist who just came into the room and said, 'Tell me what to do.' He didn't tell you: he gave you an idea and a clue from the movement of what he wanted, and hoped that you would contribute and work on it until he said, 'That's right, that is what I want', or 'That is not what I want.' That's the way he worked. You were never inhibited in his presence – he put you completely at your ease and you were able to attempt anything.

Kavanagh: There were wonderful steps he got you to do that weren't in any classical lexicon.

Grant: Ashton had a phenomenal memory, though he had no memory for recreating his own choreography. If he saw one of his own ballets he would know what was wrong, but he could never put it on, he would never remember every step. But he had a wonderful memory: he had a store of steps and movement that he had seen. He could bring something out of a ballet that he had seen twenty years before and suddenly think: well that would fit.

I would also like at this stage to say something that is not generally known. I was rather disturbed with everyone calling him Fred at this conference. He really disliked Fred. He liked to be called Frederick or Freddie. I never called him Fred and he never called me Alex, always Alexander. I am very surprised that my colleagues, who were very close to him, did not know that. It was not really the 'Fred Step', but 'Freddie's Step'.

Kavanagh: Didn't Sophie Fedorovitch start calling him Fred?

Grant: Maybe. He adored Sophie and maybe even the Dame, and that's where it all came from in the company – but he didn't really like being called Fred.

Kavanagh: His mother used to call him Freddles.

Grant: Twenty years ago I wrote a poem about him:

> *Ever ready Freddie*
> *Always entre nous*
> *In any situation*
> *Knew exactly what to do.*

Kavanagh: Can you tell us about the Jester, an enigmatic figure, part Harlequin and part Buttons. How did this conception come about?

Grant: Always you got the character of what you were supposed to be from Freddie himself, in the movement that he gave you. He was so in tune with the music that after any role that he had created on you, you felt that you couldn't possibly do a different movement to that music. But he wanted you to see what you could bring to a role. The Jester, being not a role really but a character, I decided that he was there to entertain the Prince and be his companion. When the Prince meets Cinderella he would lose a great deal of that companionship, as it would be transferred to Cinderella. Being a Jester, he was never going to have the good fortune to find a Cinderella of his own. I tried to convey that, and was amazed that quite a few people got it.

Kavanagh: That slight sadness, the wistfulness.

Grant: The wistfulness, particularly when he found Cinderella at the ballroom, with the train. I don't know whether you saw the television film that we did in America. We were sent to New York for one week, and filmed a live performance of *Cinderella* at the Brooklyn Studios, the old Chapman Studios. The ballet was cut, including the solos for the Prince and Cinderella, a great deal of the ballroom scene and mime for the Jester. I suppose it had to be condensed for television.

Kavanagh: Was the character you played in *Variations on a Theme of Purcell*, the Master of Ceremonies, rather similar?

Grant: I suppose it was. It was a tremendously enigmatic character. All the dancers were instruments in the orchestra and I was a sort of enigmatic conductor, dressed half black and half white.

Kavanagh: Didn't you have a sort of jazzy, soft-shoe shuffle dance?

Grant: Yes, because I did the drum solo. Ashton had a wonderful variety and versatility of movement.

Kavanagh: What about your atypical roles? You had a sort of Ashtonian love pas de deux in *Madame Chrysanthème.*

Grant: Yes I did. *Madame Chrysanthème* was really *Madam Butterfly.* Pierre Loti had written the book *Madame Chrysanthème*, which was made into the opera *Madam Butterfly* and given a tragic ending. Ashton used the original ending, which was an ironical one. Pierre is an ordinary sailor, not the Captain; when his ship doesn't sail, he comes back and finds her counting out the money she has managed to save from his stay.

Kavanagh: Were you happy with the role?

Grant: Yes, again I was playing a character, a sailor. And always after my seven weeks at sea I thought if I never made it as a dancer I was going to go to sea.

Kavanagh: You danced the Young Man in *The Two Pigeons* didn't you?

Grant: Yes. The role was originally meant for Donald Britton, who was very like myself physically. We were more mature than Christopher Gable. Ashton's original idea was that a mature artist was having a liaison with a young girl and trying to paint her. She was playing up, by being restless, and he got very irritated with her, walked out and found some-one else, then realised that the grass was not greener on the other side, and came back. When Donald Britton injured himself, Christopher Gable was put in and the whole idea changed: it was young love from the start. When it was transferred to Covent Garden and Lynn Seymour came into the main company we did it and took it to New York. Ashton went back to his original idea by giving me the part. However, people had got used to the young romantic thing, and I don't think they took to the version.

Kavanagh: What about roles that you would like to have done?

Grant: I always missed Mercutio. I always feel that if Ashton had chor-eographed *Romeo and Juliet* for the company I might have been lucky enough to get it. I was in Ashton's ballet when I was past my Mercutio stage, as Juliet's father.

I would like to tell you about Ashton's love and success in America. These were the early days at the old Met. Coming out of the stage door you stood on a high step with the public below, so that they could see you. You went down the step and straight across the road to Bill's Bar. One year a number of Frederick's ballets which had not been seen in America before were shown, and each work was more successful than the last. When we went into Bill's Bar members of the public would say, 'Mr Ashton, it was wonderful tonight, can we buy you a drink?' He would say 'Yes'. They would say 'What are you drinking?' and he would say, 'Dry martini'. He took very much to American martinis. Sometimes eight or nine would be lined up on the bar waiting for him. We then went on tour. We used to have our own train, and this was a very long tour to Winnipeg. Frederick was never ill, but on this occasion he was clutching his abdomen and saying that he was in pain. I said, 'Directly we get to Winnipeg you will have to call the doctor to the hotel.' The next day I asked Frederick if he had seen the doctor, and he said, 'Yes, he asked if I had been drinking.' He told the doctor, 'Some people drink when they have been a failure, but I drink when I'm a success.' The doctor diagnosed martini poisoning. True story.

Kavanagh: What was the private Ashton like? Was he a melancholy person?

Grant: Yes. He had long bouts of melancholy. I used to visit him in the country. We had this special thing between friends. He would sit day-dreaming. As many of his dancers will tell you, Ashton used to come into the rehearsal room saying that he dreamt movements. It wasn't, I don't think, that he dreamt them, but he day-dreamed them. He would sit and listen to the music of the ballet that he was doing for hours in a quiet way, and the style that he wanted would come into his mind.

We had a kind of rapport where we did not have to speak, we might spend whole days when we hardly spoke at all. We could communicate without speech. Of course, he was a communicator with body movement. This was the great thing about his work, that he spoke with his body and was able to communicate what he wanted to say in movement in such a way that it even conveyed an emotion. It was this emotional content in his work, and the way that he was able to put it into his artists, that I think was so important.

Kavanagh: I would like you to recap a riveting conversation with Pamela May in which you discussed what was being lost from Ashton's work, the dynamics were going, and details like the chassé.

Grant: One of Ashton's favourite steps in all his ballets was the chassé. In fact he did a whole ballet based on them: *Les Patineurs*. The dancers were supposed to be skating on ice – and the chassé, you know, is a sliding movement on the floor. No longer do people do this chassé. I think it's the Russian influence.

Kavanagh: Richard Glasstone told us that they had stopped teaching them [see p. 202].

Grant: Which is terrible, as he had them in all of his ballets. They are now turned into a posé, without the chassé. Maybe it is to do with the floors – in our day we had wooden floors.

Richard Glasstone: It is nothing to do with the floors.

Grant: I don't know why they have been cut out. When I danced, one of the enchaînements at the end of nearly every class was chassé, coupé, jeté. You chassé along the floor and got down to it and pushed off so that you got up into the air, so you had the contrast of being down and being up. Completely disappeared. Little details like that go. What has also gone, which may also be the Russian influence, is the quick footwork. In de Valois' day the company was famous for quick footwork. De Valois herself was famous for it. Her step when she took class, which everybody hated, was jeté battement forward and back. Ashton sent it up slightly in my role as Alain in *La Fille mal gardée* – Alain tries to do it and can't.

Ashton also incorporated a lot of quick footwork into his ballets, and now they don't really concentrate on that. It is a much slower attack, which is a broader Russian movement. When we first went to America in 1949 one of the things that was remarked on was the wonderful quick footwork of the company. Some of the older ballerinas, like Lesley Collier still have it.

Kavanagh: Can you talk about Alain?

Grant: I never knew when I was going to be in an Ashton ballet, and I think one of the reasons we had such a close friendship was I never asked if I was going to be in his ballets, so he was never embarrassed not to put me in. In those days we were not told the cast before we started rehearsing – sometimes we'd be half way through a ballet and then your name would go up to be in it. I wasn't very keen on *La Fille mal gardée* at first. I'd seen a one-act version by Nijinska, I think, in which Alain ran around trying to catch butterflies with a butterfly net.

People used to say to me what is your favourite role, and my pat answer, in my dancing days, was that it is the next one I'm going to be asked to do, as it will be a new challenge. But looking back, I suppose I have to say my favourite role is Alain, simply because what one was trying to say with one's body and one's actions seemed to be understood by the public. And after all, every artist, if they can convey what they are trying to say to a public, is very grateful. Even now people say that is the role they remember, because that is the role that speaks to them.

Kavanagh: You have said that you have to be very careful not to make Alain maudlin.

Grant: Yes, because you can exaggerate it too much. It should also be danced correctly. Because he's a sort of clumsy thing some performers think it can be danced badly, but it can't. None of Ashton's works should be danced badly: the movements were precisely given in order to convey the character of the artist. They have to be danced correctly and well. Even if it's eccentric character dancing you can't just slop around.

Kavanagh: Did you have a model in mind?

Grant: In a way, yes. Not that Frederick said anything to me. I happened to see Tommy Steele in *She Stoops to Conquer*, and I thought that the role could have a certain charm, because Tommy Steele was very charming. He's not an idiot, he's a child-like creature who has been kept from everything. His father has kept him away from everything, given him everything and looked after him. In the first act he wears a suit which he has grown out of. He's still very child-like, it's too tight for him. In the second act he has a suit which is too large for him – his father has bought him a suit hoping he'll grow into it. He's let down by the fact that his father has promised him something and hasn't been able to deliver the goods. He's not stupid, just child-like through not being out in the world. That's often misunderstood by artists who perform the role.

Kavanagh: Can you tell us about Bottom?

Grant: There again I didn't know that I was going to be in *The Dream* until my name went up as Bottom. I happened to see a postcard of an actor who was playing Bottom at Stratford-on-Avon, and he was already transformed into an ass. He had the ass's head on, and you could see that he wore leggings and had little black hooves and gloves. He looked as though he was standing on pointe. Ashton looked at me and said, 'You can't go on pointe, not with your feet.' I said that if my trousers covered my feet, you wouldn't see that I haven't got a beautiful arch. Nothing was said. I'm called for Bottom's first rehearsal and Ashton asks, 'Where are your pointe shoes?' He choreographed Bottom's little pointe dance in one rehearsal, as though I was on pointe, although I was in character shoes. At every rehearsal he then asked, 'Where are your pointe shoes?' I hadn't been able to find any wide enough, so eventually I squeezed into some shoes, and by the time I had to do my pointework I didn't know I had feet. When we were in America, I did manage to find some wide pointe shoes in Capezio, the line was called 'Pavlova' – which seemed like an omen.

Kavanagh: He put you on pointe again in *Beatrix Potter*.

Grant: Yes, my brother Garry, another boy and I were pigs on pointe. The whole film was choreographed in the studio. He made me his assistant on the film. Ashton also played Mrs Tiggy-Winkle. He hadn't choreographed the finale when we started filming, and was worried that they would say: next day we will film the finale. Ashton always had a horror of being asked to choreograph in a hurry. When he was in revues, including Cochran's, very often you would get a big number and Cochran would say, 'Not good enough', and he would have to re-choreograph it by the next day. So he always had a horror of working in a hurry. Anyway, he was asked, made an enormous fuss, and we learnt the finale in a hanger on the lot one afternoon.

Ann Nugent (critic): Which of the twenty-two roles that were created on you, and the ballets that are no longer performed, do you think would come back to life today if they were recreated?

Grant: That is one of the dilemmas that artistic directors have. I always remember *Dante Sonata*, which was performed barefoot, during the war. It had some wonderful moments in it, but whether it would be considered old-fashioned today is a very difficult question. One of Fonteyn's favourite ballets was *Apparitions*. Once, when she had had diphtheria, it was revived for her come-back. I used to think, with the music, that it was a wonderful ballet. Then when it was revived, when I was with English National Ballet, it didn't work – even with no less a person than Natalia Makarova.

I would like to finish with a story about the music for *Ondine*. Covent Garden moved a baby grand into my house for Hans Werner Henze to use while he composed *Ondine*. Henze used to orchestrate from the piano version. Ashton used to phone every day to enquire whether I had heard a tune. One day Frederick rang and Mrs Griggs, my cleaning lady, answered. In response to Frederick's question whether she'd heard a tune, she answered, 'Yes, he's been playing very pretty music all morning.' That evening Frederick phoned me and said, 'Henze's at last written a tune.' I said, 'I can't believe it, I'll ask him.' I informed Henze that Frederick was happy because he'd written a tune. Henze expressed surprise, and said, 'I didn't feel like composing this morning. I played Mozart all morning.' I believe Henze conducted Mozart at Frederick's memorial service.

The ballerina's solos from Scènes de ballet
Lecture-Demonstration

Antoinette Sibley

Antoinette Sibley briefly outlined *Scènes de ballet*'s creation in 1948 for Margot Fonteyn and Michael Somes. Ashton had heard the music while in his bath, and was very taken with the difficult rhythms. He rang the BBC to enquire what it was – Stravinsky's *Scènes de ballet*. Sibley referred to Ashton's use geometric floor and figure patterns: 'I think he annoyed everyone profusely when he was working on this ballet because he used to bring his volume of Euclid and set out all the theorems for the poor dancers to fathom out, to get all those wonderful shapes. Indeed, you can see this ballet from any angle. It's very rare to be able to view a ballet from the front or the wings or the back, yet *Scènes de ballet* works in any direction. It's perfect: he got his theorems right.'

Sibley regarded *Scènes de ballet* as one of Ashton's greatest works and disclosed that it was one of his own favourites. She pointed out that the work was not always a popular success with audiences, and reflected that this might be because it is so sophisticated and hard to understand. She felt that the ballet was best placed second in a programme, as the music was quite hard and dry for an audience to appreciate at the beginning of a performance. She indicated that the work is precious to the Royal Ballet: 'It's a connoisseur's ballet, it's our ballet, it's Fred's ballet.' It is a short work, only 16–18 minutes, 'but such a lot happens in that time. It's absolutely glorious, it's purely classical ballet, very elegant, very chic, and very much a homage, I think in Sir Fred's mind, to Petipa – in fact, we have a section which we call the Rose Adage section. It's a wonderful vehicle for a classical ballerina because she has the opportunity to perform two completely different solos. The first he would refer to as a diamond – glittering and white and shiny – and the second, a dark pearl – mysterious and oriental. So the fascination for a ballerina, a classical ballerina, is really of the highest ilk, like Balanchine's *Ballet Imperial* and

Petipa's *Sleeping Beauty.*' Sibley indicated that the role was 'always a huge favourite of mine. I absolutely adored doing it. I performed the ballet throughout my career.'

Solo I

After introducing dancer Fiona Chadwick, Sibley went on to describe the ballerina's solo as 'a diamond, sparkling and utterly chic. She has diamonds and pearls on her wrists and collar. She comes flying on with everybody else milling around. Suddenly she just arrives on the scene and she has to make her statement.'

Entering from the wings, upstage right, the ballerina runs in a broad sweep across the back of the stage, curving in to centre stage with a grand jeté élancé en tournant, and single pirouette, crisply stopping in croisé, to the right diagonal front, in a wide fourth position, fondu on the front leg, arms in attitude. Sibley indicated that Ashton would re-mark, 'You come in and you *stop*,' so that 'the very first thing everybody sees is the ballerina – diamond. Then everything that you do is very, very quick and sharp.' The dancer swiftly changes the attitude arm line before executing a single pirouette en dedans to finish in fourth croisé to the left diagonal front. Rapid bourrées en avant are snappily interrupted twice by the motif fourth position, arms demi-seconde with the wrists flexed up. Sibley directed Chadwick to perform as many bourrées forward as she could and then 'stop dead, photograph'. She pointed out that the flexed wrist position was to show the dancer's bracelets.

Sibley indicated that a relevé at the end of a phrase of three jumps on pointe and two relevés passés en arrière should be held, 'like a surprise, as if we're not expecting it'. She advised Chadwick to travel further on three posé turns which precede a bourrée sur place with swirling ports de bras and upper body movement. 'As you can imagine he used to go crazy about the body always having to move, which is very difficult at speed,' Sibley reflected. She indicated that Ashton did not mind about the leg being perfectly turned out for piqué en arrière; it was more important to bend the body over the raised leg.

Sibley encouraged Chadwick to travel with a glissade and grand jeté en tournant, from downstage left, bringing the foot well forward on a chassé to fourth croisé, and to 'stop absolutely dead' before repeating the steps. Ashton's use of phrasing appeared to be behind Sibley's suggestion that Chadwick could anticipate a grand pas de chat style step, allowing more time for a relevé, with low parallel arms and upper body stretching towards the audience. She demonstrated, too, that the 'Fred Step' was a time 'when you can relax more and play a bit, use your hips and shoulders.'

Sibley told us that her favourite was a posé into attitude devant followed by a movement in which she directed Chadwick to 'fall over, then catch up with yourself'. This, another example of Ashton's amplification of the *danse d'école*, resembled a small grand pas de basque en tournant. She directed Chadwick to skim across the stage to downstage right with three posé turns, before repeating the bourrée sur place with ports de bras and upper body movement. This is followed by two posé turns towards upstage right before a fleet run across the back of the stage to end upstage left. Sibley pointed out that at the end of the solo two of the men hold the ballerina's arms and help her jump through the air, to be caught by another two men at downstage right.

The solo is characterised by glitteringly rapid yet precise movements, interspersed and contrasted with moments of serene stillness and occasional fluid ports de bras and upper body movements. It illustrates Ashton's expansive use of the stage space by a single dancer in a short solo.

Solo II

Sibley described the second solo as 'very seductive and sensual, the arms very oriental. It's a black pearl, very mysterious. I used to think that I was in a kasbah with smoke and perfume everywhere, but I don't think that Fred ever told me that. The music oozes. The five men are dancing and the ballerina comes on at the end to start her solo. Spacing is vital because we have four men lined up on stage left, lying down, and the main man even further in, who we have to dance around. She suddenly arrives, looking at the main man who is at her feet.'

The dancer runs from the wings upstage right to stand just right of centre upstage. Her weight is on the right foot, left leg behind, the knee relaxed and the foot à terre; the arms are in attitude. Sinuously swaying the arms and hands above the head, she taps the floor four times with her pointe, performs two jumps on pointe before repeating the toe taps with her other foot. A rond de jambe en l'air style movement is followed by two alternate swishes of her foot, before the rond de jambe en l'air movement is repeated twice. After a chassé passé, relevé passé en arrière and single pirouette she finishes in a deep fourth croisé with a fondu on the front leg. Sibley commented that Ashton used to 'make a big thing of that', as Chadwick performed a brief port de bras in which the downstage hand is lifted close to the chest, under the chin, before extending to fifth, the upper body in a back bend, the head and eye line following the hand.

Sibley directed Chadwick not to make the audience realise that both feet were on the floor in the renversé. She should 'only just get there' through controlling her breathing, and not hold the position before starting four coupé développé style movements. Sibley demonstrated these steps with delicate turns of the head, alluring rolls of the shoulders, twists of the lower arms and wrists and subtle shifts of the hips. She suggested that the three jumps on pointe followed by a balance on one foot, 'are almost *through* the music, and then you catch up with yourself on the balance'. She demonstrated that the balance should include some movement in the hip while the undulating arms provide contrast.

Sibley described a rotation as a 'surprise', and advised Chadwick to place the foot as far behind her as possible after completing a développé to second. This would then enable her to 'turn and stop, absolutely stop – you don't have many opportunities in this solo to stop dead.' Sibley indicated that the sharpness of three brittle posé steps, the free leg diagonally forward and low, should be emphasised by the head and shoulders and flicks of the wrists. As Chadwick rehearsed two renversés, Sibley commented, 'He loves renversés in this solo.'

Sibley said that Ashton used to 'go on and on' about the twisting, curved arm gestures which accompanied a series of steps travelling diagonally backwards from downstage left. 'It's like calling up some spirits, using your arms and wrists.' She indicated that Chadwick should bend the body forward on the small grand pas de basque style movement, providing a contrast with the more upright body position of the grand pas de chat style movement. Sibley explained that one of Ashton's pet theatrical comments related to the use of the head. If a dancer looks down, all the audience sees is the back of the head. 'He wants you to look over and out. He used to say "Pavlova, think Pavlova".' Sibley pointed out that the fouetté relevé en tournant at the end of the phrase should be performed quickly, leaving more time to hold the balance on one leg, the hip provocatively jutting out, as the face peers under an attitude arm line.

Sibley described and demonstrated the simple series of five step-turns across the back of the stage as 'the most wonderful step of all. This is my kasbah, through the smoke and the atmosphere. All he wants is arms . . . with a few of his hip things.' Her arms slinky, she opens them out to shoulder height on each step before drawing them back to her body on the turn. The dancer ends upstage left, performing three jumps on pointe with the swaying arm gesture.

Travelling diagonally to downstage right, the dancer hops, on a flat foot, four times in first arabesque, ending with a petit assemblé. She repeats these steps twice using the second and then first arabesque arm line. A relevé in first arabesque precedes a return to the position in which she started the solo. She taps the floor three times, pirouettes once, to be caught by her partner, and finishes in a crossed fourth position with one arm reaching up and away from her partner.

Sibley explained that both solos were extremely tiring, even though they were short. 'As you can see, he wants so much movement. It is actually more tiring than performing something more upright because you do have to use so much of the body, and travel. He always uses such wonderful patterns as you can see here – diagonals, straight across the stage and circles.'

The choreography in this luscious solo is particularly dense. It is characterised by an elaborate use of sensuous gestures of the head, shoulders, hands and wrists. The solo provides further examples of Ashton's modification of the *danse d'école*. Sibley's coaching, and demonstration of both solos, illustrated how Ashton syncopated or subtly played with the phrasing of steps to create an exhilarating tension between the dance and music.

Discussion

From the audience, David Vaughan mentioned Ashton's comment that *Scènes de ballet* could be seen from any angle. He questioned whether it would be interesting to ask Chadwick to perform the solo with her back to the audience. Sibley indicated that it was the corps de ballet's wonderful shapes taken from the Euclid book, the diagonals, straight lines and semicircles, which could be perceived from anywhere in the theatre; the ballerina's solos were performed to the audience.

Richard Glasstone: You used the demi-seconde line in your demonstration, a line seldom seen in general training now. Do you think that this is because the body is being used, or are you conscious of keeping your arms lower when performing ports de bras? Perhaps it's both.

Sibley: I think it stems from learning the role. Michael Somes, the greatest guardian of all Ashton's works, taught me this role. I never saw Margot [Fonteyn] perform, but I did see Nadia [Nerina] and others. When you learn a role you follow what others have done, and then of course you are pummelled by Fred all the time and prodded. You don't actually think. This solo is so oriental as well.

Glasstone: Your arms were in a lovely diagonal in the first variation as well. When demonstrating you never had your arms up.

Sibley: Thank you. I think he uses the low arm line quite a lot, and in *Daphnis and Chloe.*

Jann Parry (critic): Dancers today are encouraged to get their legs higher, which changes the arabesque line. If you look in programmes or at photographs of Fonteyn in arabesque, the angle is completely different. What do you say when you are coaching dancers: 'Don't do it', or 'All right, do it and we'll accommodate it'? How do you adjust Sir Fred's style?

Sibley: In something like *Symphonic Variations* you really can't lift your legs up because the whole point of the line is set. You couldn't have your leg up by the ear with those wonderful lines, and this ballet is another case in point. I don't think that you'd have much opportunity to get your leg up because the music is so fast.

Chadwick: When we rehearse the partnering we are told to take a 90-degree angle, or only a fraction above.

Sibley: It is very much on the line. When we come to *The Dream* there are certain points where, if you have a very high arabesque, as long as the man can do the same as you, it could be used. But you would have to be the same, so we find that although the arabesques are much higher than we ever did, they have to come down because the men cannot lift their legs as high. It is more important where you are dancing identically, in something like *The Dream*, for the legs to be at the same height, so the women adjust.

Parry: Programme photographs of Fonteyn in *Cinderella* when she leans on the Prince's shoulder show a much lower line than that used today, the line is completely different. [See *Dancing Times*, May 1995, p. 835.]

Alastair Macaulay: It's not just a matter of arabesques, sometimes it's a question of how high a développé à la seconde should go. When Sylvie Guillem first did that, she certainly was doing petits développés higher than I had ever seen from Royal trained dancers.

143

Sibley: Sylvie interprets things her own way. I don't think one is trying to stop this if people think that is progress. It's rather like changing one of the complicated lifts of Kenneth's [MacMillan] – you wouldn't change it just to do something extra and peculiar; this is what is set. There are individual interpretations and Fred always encouraged that, but there are certain things that are really sacrosanct.

Macaulay: With the high secondes that you've been showing in this solo, were they always that high in your experience?

Sibley: Oh yes, that doesn't matter at all. That is one of the occasions that it doesn't matter, because then after that you have to be on the ground. Ashton would be very upset, I would say, if the body was put out or made to go into a different shape by getting the leg up. The rest of the body is set, you can't just do something different with the body to get the leg up.

Chadwick: I would have thought that as long as you didn't break the line of the arm . . .

Glasstone: I agree. The leg could be extended as long as it doesn't cross the path of the arm. If you lift your leg higher you have to lift your arm higher. If you can keep the two in balance then you can take the leg higher. A higher movement of the leg is a different thing from a higher stuck pose of the leg. A moving thing within a musical phrase is acceptable, but just sticking it up there and not worrying where the arm is, that's the danger. It's interesting that you say no one would ever think of changing Sir Fred's or MacMillan's choreography because there are people protecting that. Who's protecting Petipa when we stick the legs up?

Pamela May: There are certain of Ashton's ballets where you couldn't lift the leg because of the line or arm gesture. But he wasn't against high legs. Look at *Monotones*. In certain ballets he did certain things.

Sibley: Not our *Monotones*! As you say, he did use his material. He always brought the best out of anybody that he was creating on. He used all their qualities, whether, as you say, they got their legs up, or whether you were a straight line dancer, he pulled that out of you.

May: It had to keep its quality.

Sibley: The quality is uppermost.

Alexander Grant: It is interesting to note that André Beaurepaire's designs for *Scènes de ballet* were inspired by St Pancras Station. The set was actually a disaster, and Frederick was always taking bits off the stage.

Sibley: I heard that at a dress rehearsal there were stairs going off somewhere and that they were removed in later performances.

144

Angela Kane: So much has been said at this conference about the physical demands of the choreography. In coaching, how much is phrasing emphasised? One of the main differences when you see young dancers, or other companies dancing Ashton's choreography, is how the movements link together.

Sibley: I was so fortunate because I was taught by Michael Somes who is one, probably the most musical person around. He worked with Fred on everything throughout Fred's creative times. When he was around, it was drummed into you: you slept it, ate it, breathed it. Fiona and I only saw each other yesterday to try and think back. Yet even as we are working now, we are remembering nuances that he would like. If you do this slowly you could quicken up there. He loved all that anticipating, then holding, stopping absolutely dead, absolutely still, then moving again. It's one of his wonders, his musicality, it is absolutely vital. The steps aren't done right if they are not done with syncopation, or with musicality, making them breathe.

Kane: How do you integrate this when coaching roles?

Sibley: The first person I really taught this role to was Viviana Durante. She had learnt the steps from a choreologist. I then imparted everything I had ever been taught, prodded and turned. You automatically demonstrate the steps with musicality, and the body and the thoughts that Fred would give you, with what he meant or wanted at a certain time. Certain things he was quite elastic on – not the steps, but on ways of doing something. But other things he was absolutely precise on, and he would go on and on about, like the piqué en arrière from the first solo. Every single rehearsal, whether you did it or not, he would still say, 'Travel, body forward, don't turn out, body forward!' He would go on and on, so you can hear it, it's echoing all the time in your mind when you come to show someone else. As Viviana knew the basic steps, I told her the design and where to travel more. I think I'm right in saying that it's always the travelling and the design that are so important. When he did *The Dream* he always seemed to start off with the design of something: 'I want a step going on a diagonal', or 'I want it going around in a circle.' It makes such a difference, how much you travel something to just get there in time and not make it easy for yourself; that's so important in all his work.

Grant: One of the magical things about Fonteyn was that she thought that she was never going to make it on time, when she was right over one end of the stage – and then she was there on the music for the next thing.

Macaulay: One sees a lot of parallels between these solos and other Ashton solos. I saw a parallel to Chloe's boot solo with the foot tappings.

Sibley: Again the arms are very oriental, aren't they? It was completely to the music, the solo was choreographed to give the impression that you were improvising. Ashton explained that he wanted it to happen very spontaneously as if it were just you and the instrument. It's not all turned out; it's very Greek and relaxed. It's not like you would do in class at all.

Macaulay: One of the steps – which you said was your favourite moment, where the ballerina is in attitude front but leaning way back – isn't that like *Cinderella* in the ballroom? Cinderella performs that in the middle of the ensemble dance, she's in profile to the audience.

Sibley: But it is this falling-off thing that I like [in the small grand pas de basque en tournant style step]. The riskier your performance, the happier Ashton was. He never liked you to be safe. He used to say, 'If you are comfortable, you are wrong.' You used to say, 'It's agony, I can't breathe, this is hurting.' He would say, 'That's it, that's right then.'

Macaulay: That links back to a Margot Fonteyn story: she said that if you leaned as far as he wanted you to, you'd fall over.

Sibley: He pushed you to the limit all the time. You really didn't think there was any way you were going to be able to do it, but you did. He brought things out in you that you never thought you were capable of. That's why he was such a genius. You would do anything to please him. You had no inhibitions, you'd do ridiculous things – when he wanted you to show a fountain or whatever – because you trusted him, you knew that his eye was so perceptive. I think that the love we all felt for him he gave back to us. You would do anything for Fred, and then you were rewarded because he gave you new dimensions.

Pas de deux from The Dream
Lecture-Demonstration

Antoinette Sibley, Anthony Dowell

The lecture-demonstration was in three parts. First, Antoinette Sibley and Anthony Dowell discussed their early experiences of working with Ashton on *The Dream*. They then coached William Trevitt (Royal Ballet) and Susan Lucas (Birmingham Royal Ballet) in Oberon and Titania's pas de deux. The session closed with Sibley and Dowell responding to questions from the audience.

Introduction

Dowell recollected that when Ashton was working on *The Dream* he used to ask a member of staff or a senior dancer to watch newly choreographed scenes and ask if they understood and could follow the action that was being portrayed. Dowell indicated that Ashton was very conscious of telling the story in choreographic terms, in the simplest, most economic way. 'As with *Month*, he was very concerned that what he was creating for us really told the story.'

Dowell recalled being initially perhaps a little blasé about his first major created role, as since joining the Royal Ballet in 1961 his progress had been 'pleasantly fast', and he 'just accepted that there was a new ballet and Ashton was going to give it to me'. Admitting that it was a thrill to have been cast, Dowell nevertheless acknowledged that the honour of creating a role in an Ashton ballet probably meant more, at that time, to Sibley. The appeal of the role of Oberon, for Dowell, lay in the creation of a non-human creature. He indicated that, for young dancers, it is easier to develop and hide behind a character than to perform a solo in a classical ballet where their own personalities are exposed.

Once rehearsals of *The Dream* began, Dowell wondered whether he would be required to dance: although he was the central figure and

147

maintained the narrative flow in some of the mime scenes, 'all I seemed to do in every rehearsal was stand in the middle of the room while people danced around me.' Dowell commented on the challenges that the role offers late in the ballet, and expressed his secret pleasure that young dancers still find the role 'an amazing mountain to climb technically'. He indicated that the role has to be sustained by mime through most of the ballet; then there is 'that manic scherzo', followed by an eight-to-ten-minute pas de deux with Titania, which 'requires tremendous stamina to make it live'. He observed that his facility for moving fast was exploited, particularly in the scherzo choreography, as Ashton 'loved people who could spin and move fast'. Both Sibley and Dowell recalled that Ashton choreographed the pas de deux in two rehearsals.

Sibley recollected that, as their names were paired with Merle Park and Austin Bennett when the ballet was announced, they wrongly assumed that they were the lovers having the arguments. This impression was not dissipated at the first rehearsal, even though Park and Bennett performed the same argument scene. Later rehearsals convinced Sibley that they were Titania and Oberon, although they were never told that they had been cast in these roles. Sibley spoke of her delight at working with Ashton on a leading role, which was briefly followed by disappointment that she was a fairy, not a human character. She explained that she had had the experience of playing a real woman in *La Fête étrange* and a girl in *The Rake's Progress*, and wanted to perform other character roles. As rehearsals for *The Dream* progressed, she realised how wonderful Titania was: 'sensual, proud, capricious, arrogant – any number of adjectives describe her.' ('Hot,' interjected Dowell.) Sibley said that this role became one her favourites – she jokingly said that as Pavlova had died clutching her favourite costume (the Dying Swan), she would have to clutch two costumes: Titania and Manon.

Dowell argued that Titania's character can be ill-conceived by some performers. He indicated that there had been something special about the character when he worked against Sibley and Park: she wasn't just a pretty fairy with emotions – she was crazed. He felt there had to be an underlying sensual quality, which young dancers sometimes found hard to portray.

One of the things which Sibley said helped her characterisation was Dowell's comment on seeing a photograph of her as Titania, with Alexander Grant as Bottom – that she looked like Vivien Leigh.

Coaching

Dowell asked William Trevitt for a stretched, almost vertical arabesque line on Oberon's entrance, before the swift run from upstage left to downstage right, to dismiss Bottom. This position contrasted with the second arabesque à terre, where Dowell wanted Trevitt to 'show his back'.

Sibley indicated that many of the comments that she would make were those that Ashton used repeatedly with her and Dowell. She observed that much of the pas de deux has a 'pulling away and coming together' quality. When Oberon leads Titania from upstage left she should pull away from him, performing 'millions of bourrées, as though shimmering'. As Titania bourrées past Oberon, her body should bend low, following the line of the port de bras while maintaining the pulling away quality. When Oberon releases Titania's hand she must move to upstage right, as if looking for a place to execute the next step.

Sibley explained that the turned, supported arabesque figure caused friction during one rehearsal. Ashton said he'd had a dream in which from arabesque, Sibley turned round on one leg, went down and came up the other way. Sibley and Dowell tried many different ways of doing the step in rehearsal and then said it was impossible. Angry, Ashton left the rehearsal saying, 'That was my dream, I know it can work.' The dancers tried many different ways to achieve his vision, and by the time Ashton returned they had succeeded.

The figure is danced twice before the mood of romantic lyricism appears to be briefly broken by Titania darting to Oberon's left and then right side. On each occasion Dowell indicated that Oberon should catch her hand 'at the last minute'. Sibley suggested that 'It's really as if you are looking – is anybody there? – and then as Oberon leads her to en face centre stage: no, nobody is here, we are all alone. That is when you stop, you know that you are all alone.'

Dowell referred to Oberon's support of Titania's rond de jambe à terre en dedans as representing a compass, and Sibley remarked that although they had created this movement, the other casts found it easier to achieve. Titania repeats the rond de jambe with the left leg finishing again in an arabesque, which Sibley said Ashton wanted moon-shaped. She mentioned that Ashton had used a similar position for Pamela May in *Horoscope* (see p. 185). Sibley demonstrated that the body needed to be forward, with a slightly bent arabesque line and a rounded arm line with the palm of the hand towards the face.

Dowell referred to Oberon's jumping sequence on the diagonal as a 'nightmare'. He suggested that Trevitt 'just step and go for your front foot' when performing Oberon's jump, where the upper body is stretched forward over the legs. Dowell indicated that 'sometimes Fred used to choose a classical step, and then ask you to invert it or turn it another way', and that this step was 'almost the reverse of a temps de poisson.'

Referring to a gargouillade with a forward bend of the upper body as the arms alternately circled forward and down the extended leg, Sibley remarked, 'This really is a horrid step, I don't know why I did it.' She suggested that Lucas think of the shoulder action while performing the step. The hands reach the ankle before 'coming up, holding your leg' on the relevé into arabesque. She referred to the jumps on pointe at the end of the phrase as 'like on a lily pad'.

Discussing Oberon's second solo, Dowell revealed that he couldn't remember what the original step was. He remarked that when he has coached dancers who had been taught from notation, there were some 'very odd versions'. He indicated that although a score was written, Ashton changed the choreography in both *The Dream* and *A Month in the Country*: 'they had a life and nothing was ever frozen, he really wanted to play around.' Dowell continued, 'I was a left-turner, so anyone following me had this awful problem of trying to turn to the left or reversing as much as possible. You can't completely reverse it, but a lot of the Oberons who have followed me have performed the whole scherzo turning to the right. I remember Fred once said to me "Why do you have to turn to the left?" It bothered him at first.' Trevitt performed a tombé coupé sauté en arrière, landing with the free leg en avant, grand jeté en tournant, grand jeté en avant, posé pirouette. When he repeated the step Trevitt finished with a pirouette from a preparation from fourth. Dowell emphasised that the quality should be 'seamless'.

Sibley described the spiralling port de bras from an arabesque line to fourth position, from Titania's second solo, as 'like a gathering-in'. As Titania turned pas de bourrée piqué, Oberon, standing behind her, swept his hand above her head and down her back. Dowell characterised this gesture as 'fairy dust time'. Sibley recalled that Oberon and Titania side by side holding hands was a 'magic moment, because you are so dead at this point', while Dowell declared that 'you cannot see!' Pulling away from, yet supported by Oberon, Titania's petit développé devant crossed the supporting leg before a fouetté into arabesque which Ashton wanted

150

'really fast', to face stage left. After extending into a penchée Titania keeps her body low as she lowers the leg to parallel retiré before being turned, by Oberon, to face centre. Dowell remarked that the retiré was 'rather odd', but it had to be shown. Mirroring Titania, Oberon lifts his upstage leg to parallel retiré before 'like gates' they turn their legs out and extend to penché. Dowell indicated that the arm line should be like a diamond when the dancers were in retiré.

As Titania is pulled backwards by Oberon, the upper body doubled over the legs, Dowell observed that, 'This is another thing that Fred used to do. It's like a surprise. It's rather brutal, for the boy, as you almost have to push her forward and pull her back so that she jack-knifes.' Sibley remarked that there was a discrepancy between Dowell and herself on the direction of Titania's next step, two supported soubresauts to a low retiré. Sibley teaches her girls one way, Dowell teaches the boys another. Dowell interjected that there was only one way for the men to perform it.

The jack-knife shape is repeated as Oberon pulls Titania off balance and then repositions her on balance in an arabesque with an open attitude arm line. Sibley observed that 'so many don't do it quite right': the foot should not move between the on- and off-balance positions. She indicated that the step was 'terribly hard – you feel like a sack of potatoes. You collapse and then hold absolutely straight.'

Instructing Lucas and Trevitt not to attempt the jump from this distance, Sibley revealed that she and Dowell were required to practise Titania's caught jump into Oberon's arms, from centre stage to downstage right, when rehearsed by Ashton.

Although the bourrées in the pas de deux are not supported, Dowell mentioned that Ashton loved supported bourrées and tension lifts that were just off the floor. Both Ashton and MacMillan liked the illusion the lifts made. Sibley remarked that when she danced *A Month in the Country* with Baryshnikov, he physically couldn't do the lifts, as they had not formed part of his training. Dowell confirmed that the lifts were changed for Baryshnikov's performances, in the Vera pas de deux. He acknowledged that the manner in which the danseur 'gripped' his partner was an important factor when lifting, a lesson he learnt from Michael Somes.

Sibley indicated that Oberon should pull Titania across the stage as she performs a series of three arabesques, with port de bras from second to second arabesque. Oberon's port de bras from second to fifth uses Ashton's characteristic bend in the upper body, leaning towards Titania.

As Titania and Oberon return to upstage left where their pas de deux began, Dowell remarked, 'You've got her' – whereas Sibley said, 'She gives in, she starts to give in.' As Trevitt and Lucas began the walks forward and rond de jambe, Dowell indicated that the dancers could cross the dégagé devant 'much more'. Sibley, reinforcing Dowell's comment, demonstrated, and observed that Ashton 'used to go on and on, every time we did it, [the foot] must be crossed, so that we both do that shape [the rond de jambe] together.'

As Titania falls to her knees, her arm around Oberon's neck, Sibley commented that this was the point at which Titania completely gave into Oberon. However, 'You still think "I'll get the boy back".' Dowell revealed that Titania's large, supported open walks 'is where you can drop the whole thing, and it just goes for nothing if this happens.' Dowell demonstrated his point, without a partner, bending almost double as though carrying a heavy weight. He disclosed that to mask the fatigue he 'used to put a wing in with my arm and try to disguise it'.

Dowell also mentioned his use of an arm gesture at the end of the pas de deux when Titania is draped across Oberon's bent knee. As Titania's feet touch the floor he used to raise his arm through second to fifth, bending his upper body towards her. Sibley recalled that at this moment of an 'ecstasy of happiness . . . Fred would shout "I can't see your face".' She advised Lucas 'to make sure, in your happiness, that the audience can see your face.'

Discussion

Anon: The striking image of your demonstration, Antoinette, has been your capacity to project forward. Your face and upper torso are constantly at the front. Did you do that when you danced?

Sibley: I think I did have to project because Fred would comment on the eyes, the head, épaulement and the arms. As I think my arms were probably my best feature, I used them all the time. I relied, and would concentrate on my arms and my back, and then Fred would say, 'I can't see your eyes.' It was always his memories of Pavlova and the way she always used her eyes that he would constantly remind us of.

Anon: You reacted strongly to each other during the demonstration. Is that something that developed during your partnership?

Sibley: I do react to him all the time, in everyday life.

Dowell: I loved the opportunity to build on the role. My early performances of Oberon were markedly different from those of later years.

152

The tragedy for a dancer is that when you are young, you initially want to please with your technical ability; later performances are enhanced by your experiences of life. If you are lucky, the artistic and physical capabilities meet at some point.

Sibley: But from the beginning you always had special qualities.

Dowell: I think everyone starts with something; but it was a sketch compared to what it became.

Sibley: These roles were very lucky for us: this ballet became a signature work which we performed for over twenty years, so we were able to develop them more than others.

Dowell: I think the other advantage we had was our partnership. We benefited in rehearsals, for example, because we knew that we could cope with the physical technicalities.

Sibley: The first time I worked with Anthony was in a rehearsal of MacMillan's *Symphony* [1963]. I was second cast to Lynn [Seymour], rehearsing a section where I should have been supported by two boys. However, I had no boys to work with, so I asked Anthony, who I had only seen in *Napoli*, if he could partner me while I learnt my role. Although I had never danced this section before, I learnt it very naturally with Anthony's support. Unlike other dancers, we have been lucky in that our complementary proportions and musicality have enabled us to ride over some of the frustrations and exhaustion of rehearsals. Thank God, and thank Fred.

Alastair Macaulay: There are two things that strike me as unprecedented in *The Dream*; I wasn't watching in 1964, but I would be interested to know whether they were new to you then. Throughout the ballet Oberon performs penchée arabesque; I don't know of any previous choreography where the man lifts his leg that high. Secondly, do you know of any other choreography where the man and woman work parallel together, in the extraordinary figure where you both do penchée side by side? Other choreographers have since copied it.

Sibley: Anthony did have a lovely penchée arabesque.

Richard Glasstone: So did MacMillan – I remember him performing Moondog in Cranko's *The Lady and the Fool* [1955].

Sibley: I think that Fred used our unusual, mirror-like ability to create the double penchée image. Rudolf [Nureyev] went one step further in *The Nutcracker* when we performed the same steps most of the time, which worked wonderfully.

Dowell: One of the wonderful aspects of working with Ashton was that you always felt that your contribution was important, as he made use of your ideas. He wouldn't necessarily come to a rehearsal with steps, but he might say, 'In this phrase of music, I see a step turning with a jump in the middle.' You'd try something and he'd ask you to reverse it, repeat it or try something else. You kept working together. Once you felt free and relaxed with him you could try anything, even fool around. It was a shock after working with such a great creator to work later with a choreographer who used to teach steps in a rehearsal. My first thoughts were: why has he chosen me? I could be anyone. Later I realised that he had me in mind when he choreographed those steps. I think that is why dear Fred was always so sick with nerves on the first day of rehearsals: he came seeped in the music but with an open mind, a blank page, to let you have an input.

Sibley: You were like clay in his hands. You really did feel that you were contributing. Of course one wasn't, but you felt that you were, because you were making up steps that he would then mould to suit you. You were so involved that it gave you a wonderful feeling.

Anon: Ashton was also very nervous on first nights and revivals.

Sibley: We hadn't really thought much about the importance of *The Dream*'s premiere in New York, as we were performing in every ballet that evening. In the interval we were quite gay, laughing and talking however much the sight of Fred, who was barely able to walk across the stage, depressed us. We thought: does he think we will let him down? We hadn't been worried; it was Fred who could hardly get the cigarette to his mouth.

When Anthony and Fred pulled me back from my retirement, Fred used to visit my dressing room before every performance. He would leave his ash in my ashtray as a good luck symbol, whether I was in the room or not. I would know by this that he had been there, and this gave me confidence and reassurance.

Anon: Did he ever change any steps for different casts, or do you when you rehearse his ballets?

Sibley: Yes, he did, in this ballet. Merle and I had a different step in the diagonal pirouettes in the lullaby solo. I liked to turn en dedans; Merle, who was a great pirouettist, preferred to turn en dehors. Fred liked them both. I always teach my way, but I also show the other version in case it proves more suitable for that artist.

Anon: They are always minor changes?

Sibley: Yes. Fred sometimes considered alternatives if it helped.

Dowell: He had to accept that, unlike me, other Oberons would pirouette to the right, so all the entrances and exits in the scherzo would be different. But these are minor things.

Sibley: Taking over roles can be a problem. When my name went up for Chloe, I went to Fred's house and begged him to remove me from the role, as I felt it was one role you couldn't see anyone performing except Margot Fonteyn. I said, 'There are so many reasons – one being she is so dark, I am so fair – please don't do this to me.' He just looked at me and asked if I'd read the original Longus story of *Daphnis and Chloe*. I hadn't. He advised me to read it and commented that Chloe was fair and very sensual, and he thought I would find my own way of performing her. Which is precisely what I did do.

Jann Parry (critic): Can you imagine *The Dream* being radically redesigned, in the way *Daphnis and Chloe* has? It was wonderful to watch the two of you without the costumes; could you see it being designed more simply?

Dowell: I don't think *Daphnis and Chloe* has been radically redesigned. I couldn't see radical changes being made to *The Dream*, as there are many period images in the ballet that remind one of famous ballet lithographs.

Sibley: We have performed in three different productions.

Dowell: Yes, but so far it has remained in Victorian times, it's never been placed in Elizabethan times or in a wood near Athens. I'm not saying it couldn't . . .

Sibley: The first costumes were so much more beautiful, in my opinion. I begged David Walker to let me go back to my original when I came back to dance it. On occasions, we used to wear our original costumes when we were dancing as guest artists abroad. I loved the original pink colour and the roses.

Beth Genné: You mentioned that Misha [Baryshnikov] found it difficult to perform those low lifts. Are there any other steps and ways of moving that 'foreigners' have found difficult? This could help in the definition of whether there is an Ashton style, or if it is an English one.

Dowell: If we talk to people who haven't been trained here, they mention speed. It wasn't that Misha couldn't eventually have performed those low tension lifts that float just off the floor; it would have taken time. I think that most of the big pas de deux that both Fred and Kenneth [MacMillan] created are incredibly difficult for the man, before a variation.

Sibley: Hopping on pointe is something that Fred used. Practically all of the choreography he created for me included hopping on pointe.

155

Anon: Was *Sylvia* modified for Irek Mukhamedov?

Dowell: A little. One of the differences is that instead of keeping one hand on her leg on the overhead lift, his hand is out at the side.

Sibley: That is the type of lift he is used to; it was unusual for us.

Monica Mason: Perhaps it would be interesting for people to know how difficult Irek found *La Fille mal gardée*. I know Donald MacLeary helped him a great deal.

Dowell: Manon too. I think this refers back to Alastair Macaulay's question on penchée arabesque. Rudolf [Nureyev] choreographed an adagio in *Swan Lake*, then I had adage solos in *A Month in the Country*, *Sleeping Beauty* and *Manon*. Men with other training have found them difficult. Another thing that dancers from another training find hard, especially the men, is stepping onto demi-pointe. They tend to step onto a flat foot and then rise to demi-pointe. Just little differences in training.

Fred loved speed though, and I was quite unusual in that I was fairly tall but I could move fast. He liked that; I think it is one of the reasons for Oberon's scherzo. With increased technical polish, one of the things you have to avoid losing is speed. The finesse of physical movement has developed to the extent that I am horrified at some of the films and videos of my performances, and yet I was considered a technical dancer. I see flaws that I would not like to see in my own dancers.

Sibley: When one explained to Fred that one couldn't move as fast as he wanted or get into so many positions quickly, he would just say, 'Yes, you can. That's really what I want. I want that above all else. I want speed and I need movement.' Then he would explain that Pavlova's performances left an abiding impression of movement. Things like turn-out would not be important, but speed and movement were vital.

Dowell: We would dance *La Valse* in our own way, which was comfortable, and then he'd ask us to move our upper torso more. It always felt like the floor was being moved from under us. You'll notice that dancers with great facility of movement in their limbs maintain a straight trunk, which is actually rather expressionless. And you can see why he wanted the upper body to move, but it does upset the centre of balance. Now that we are the observers we can see why he wanted more movement, as it made the steps look expressive.

David Vaughan: You mentioned your adage solos. If I remember correctly, Robert Helpmann had a solo in *Nocturne* in which he performed very slow jumps across the stage. It seems to me that that was what Ashton was always working towards and perhaps could only fully . . .

Dowell: I am not saying that until I worked with him, he hadn't choreographed male adage solos. I think he choreographed what the music said and what he wanted the story to express using the different qualities of the dancers he worked with.

Glasstone: Watching you this afternoon, I have been struck by the warmth and humanity of the work. I think that was Ashton himself, wasn't it?

Sibley: Love, pure love, always. He gave us so much and we would give back automatically to him. We all did, we all adored him.

Dowell: Rehearsals were an absolute joy. He would put off starting a rehearsal and keep chatting. *A Month in the Country* had a very small cast, and we used to sit around and talk for far too long.

Sibley: He wasn't just a genius with the dance; if you went to him with a problem in life he could always give you advice. He was always so interesting, whether he was talking about books, or music, or the latest thing he had done. It was wonderful to be with him, he was so well informed, you learnt so much from him; maybe that also came out a little in the dancing. It wasn't just dancing for Fred, it was life, love, death, every emotion. In *Enigma Variations*, friendship was the strong emotion.

Vaughan: When you were taking part in a gala in Munich, Sir Fred invited me to watch his rehearsal of this pas de deux with you. When you had finished the dress rehearsal he turned to me and said, 'I wouldn't dream of telling them, but these two, right now, are the most perfect dancers in the world.'

The Solo Seal Variations
Lecture-Demonstration

Pamela May

Pamela May, who had a long association with Ashton, and for whom he created many roles, coached two students from the English National Ballet School in the Solo Seal variations. The Solo Seal is the highest performing award of the Royal Academy of Dancing, the organisation founded in 1920 to raise standards of ballet teaching. The major examinations of the Royal Academy of Dancing were revised in the 1950s, and Pamela May was asked to approach Ashton to choreograph the variations for the final award, the Solo Seal. Despite reservations because he had not choreographed for students before, Ashton agreed to choreograph a demi-caractère and a classical variation. After much discussion with May about the technical standard for the pre-professional examination, Ashton chose the music, from *La Source*. May explained that it was her intention to coach the students, who had previously learnt the variations, bringing out the qualities that Ashton had wanted to see in a young dancer preparing to be a professional.

The demi-caractère variation was danced by Simone Spiteri. May broke it down into clear sections, at the end of each phrase of movement giving the points that Ashton had stressed. After the opening phrase of the variation, May already had much to say on details of style. She commented on the 'play of the hand' and the movements of the wrist, and the need to 'run on in the style' of the dance, this variation requiring sharp, quick runs followed by a steady relevé.

Moving on, May reiterated a theme of this conference: that Ashton loved dancers to 'bend', telling them to 'pick up the roses'. Another theme that recurred in this session was that Ashton liked to surprise the audience with a sharp turn or a change in dynamics.

Further on into the variation, May remarked that a typical feature of Ashton's style was that even when a step was repeated, it was rarely done in exactly the same way. The example she cited here was the change of accent, finishing in attitude sur la pointe on the upbeat first, and then repeating the phrase and finishing in attitude plié on the downbeat.

Correcting a swift change of arms, May commented that Ashton loved the use of the shoulders, and she demonstrated how the shoulders could be used to get the body travelling (in this instance, backwards).

When May had finished coaching the demi-caractère variation, she remarked on how difficult it was, requiring considerable strength, and that it was quite unlike any other Ashton solo.

Erina Takahashi then came in to demonstrate the classical variation. May reiterated the need for the run in to be in keeping with what is to come next, pointing out the difference between the two variations: the demi-caractère, sharp and quick, the classical, smooth and expansive, beginning with a wide run in and a generous port de bras, more calm in mood. May encouraged Takahashi to imagine that she was being pulled forward when stepping into arabesque, so that the feeling was one of continuity. May also commented that the dancer must know 'without looking' where she is going to put her weight when moving into the posé arabesque.

Further on in the variation, May repeated the need to bend more, and pointed out another example of Ashton wishing to surprise the audience, this time with a fouetté emphasising the change from a soft and flowing downwards incline to a sharp change of focus upwards into arabesque sur la pointe.

May interrupted the session briefly to inform the audience that Ashton had chosen Lynn Seymour to choreograph this variation on. The classical variation, in particular, demonstrated the elegance and softness of Seymour's style of dancing. Ashton had left it in May's hands to change anything that was too difficult, and she had simplified a phrase that originally had two glissades and two pas de chat, and was particularly hard. However, she had also suggested to Ashton that ending the variation on one knee was hard for the students, but Ashton had looked at the dancer and at May, and said, 'Good for her!' – so it remained as it was.

Discussion

David Vaughan: Were both solos made for Lynn Seymour?

May: He did work on Lynn for both, but I think when we showed it Pamela Moncur did the demi-caractère and Lynn did the classical.

Vaughan: Do you remember the year it happened?

May: It would have been about 1956.

Monica Mason: The variations are deceptively difficult. Even professional dancers wouldn't find them easy.

The Royal Ballet Ashton Programme
Panel Discussion

Pamela May, Monica Mason, Donald MacLeary,
Philip Gammon. Chair: Anthony Russell-Roberts

The first of the conference panels was held at the Theatre Museum as an introduction to the Ashton programme at the Royal Opera House. The programme consisted of *La Valse, Birthday Offering* pas de deux, *Sylvia* pas de deux, *Symphonic Variations*, and *Daphnis and Chloe.* The panel was introduced by Anthony Russell-Roberts, Ashton's nephew, and administrative director of the Royal Ballet.

Anthony Russell-Roberts: We may consider how these works fit in with Ashton's development as a choreographer, and express an opinion on which were landmark works. It would be interesting to review how the popularity of certain works may have shifted over the years, and how Ashton approached the preparation of his works, both choreographically and musically.

First of all, *Symphonic Variations*, which was premiered on the 24 April 1946, with a cast of Margot Fonteyn, Pamela May, Moira Shearer, Michael Somes, Henry Danton and Brian Shaw. Pamela, you were part of the original cast, perhaps you might describe a little about how *Symphonic Variations* came about.

Pamela May: It really came about because Ashton very much wanted to use that music. We were on tour at the time and he had the records; in fact I think he had two sets. He always carried one of those wind-up gramophones – which shows how long ago it was. We had one in the theatre and another in the digs where we all were living (Ashton and Fonteyn – about six of us altogether). So we had the music of *Symphonic Variations* playing from morning until night. Whenever there was a spare moment – back to the dressing room to play the record! Finally, we started the rehearsals and the music was so familiar, it was a wonderful

161

way to start rehearsing. By that time, Ashton had a pretty good idea of all the movements he wanted for every section.

In the pas de deux for Fonteyn and Somes, the partner lifts the girl, and she does this gentle, very soft lift on pointe. She hardly appears to be lifted, it's as if she is drifting through air. It became almost one of his theme steps. I was so thrilled when I saw it, because the first time Ashton used it was for an enchanting pas de deux for me and Michael Somes as the Lovers in *The Wanderer*, which I loved. I think that was the only particular step that I remember him using for a second time – or maybe even a third time, because I remember he used it in several other ballets.

Anyway, unluckily for Michael, but very luckily for us as a whole, Michael hurt his knee just a few weeks before the opening night of *Symphonic*, so it had to be delayed by about six weeks. During that time Michael could come and watch although he couldn't participate very much, but it meant that Ashton could go on improving things. He was lovely to work for because if you had an idea you could always tell him, 'It would be nice if we could do a lift here instead of a kneel,' and all sorts of little things. We really enjoyed working on it, it was like going through it with a toothcomb until everything was absolutely perfect.

Russell-Roberts: Tell us about how the ballet was received at its first performance, how you felt the public, rather than the critics, responded.

May: I think it was a terrific success, it went very well indeed. At the dress rehearsal we actually had two different endings. There's the part in the middle where we hold hands in a chain and run round the stage (I think we called it 'the interlude'), and the ending of the whole ballet was, in fact, to repeat that chain holding hands, and run off backstage, so the curtain came down on an empty stage. I feel it was probably Sophie Fedorovitch who said to Fred, 'It's wrong. They should finish where they started.' Fred said, 'Try it girls, try it!' So we did, and we went back to our opening positions. 'That's it!' said Fred, and so we had it.

Russell-Roberts: Donald, you've had the task of rehearsing for this revival, and indeed other revivals. Tell us about how dancers today approach masterworks of Ashton, and what it feels like for you, having danced in the piece, to be rehearsing it.

Donald MacLeary: I have to say that I'm always shocked by the lack of stamina they have. It is amazing that when they run it for the first time they can't get through it. I don't think it makes any difference whether you've been trained then or now, it's an absolute killer. When I first danced it, it nearly killed me. I couldn't believe it, it looked so effortless and so beautiful, but I tell you, they're all in pain! Luckily we still have Pamela and Michael, who were originals, and I worked at rehearsals with Fred; there are many people still around who have been associated with the ballet, so we know what we're talking about. Once one instils what Fred wanted, you then have to keep doing it and doing it, so they don't look exhausted and at the end they can stand up and not fall over!

Russell-Roberts: Monica, you are known as a very strong dancer; did you feel the same sense of exhaustion?

Monica Mason: Complete exhaustion! I actually never thought that I would get the chance to be in *Symphonic Variations*. Then Fred decided to have what he called 'the large cast'; my partner was Christine Beckley. I didn't have very long to learn it; then I got one run-through and I was on. I remember being absolutely knocked out by the run-through and thinking, 'How will I feel on stage?' We always say we are 'legless' – well I was, totally legless at the end! I think it must be one of the most challenging ballets in the repertoire today.

Russell-Roberts: It does point out the fact that Fred's choreography is very demanding, it's quite deceptive in its lyrical qualities and is exhausting, in terms of concentration, as well as physically.

Mason: Plus, you have to make it look so effortless and remain very calm and serene.

Russell-Roberts: Perhaps we should dwell a moment on the contribution that Sophie Fedorovitch's brilliant design, so full of clarity, has to the production. Pamela, I've got my own thoughts from Ashton about how the designs developed, but you and I were talking earlier . . .

May: Yes, I remember Sophie Fedorovitch talking to us about the backcloth before we actually saw it. She had seen wonderful lines in a book about electricity, and she thought something terribly simple like that would be right for *Symphonic*.

Russell-Roberts: The idea then developed further because she lived in a cattle bar in Norfolk on the edge of the marsh, and the skyscape overlooking the marsh was absolutely incredible – the horizon and a huge sky. I think the idea of the electricity aligned to this huge skyscape was really the inspiration. The design is still full of modernity today, and it seems extraordinary that it was created back in 1946.

Moving slightly away from *Symphonic Variations* – Philip, one of the hallmarks of Fred's choreography was that he arrived in the studio, quite literally, I think it was his expression, 'drenched in the music'. You might like to tell us what it was like to be part of the creative process?

Philip Gammon: It was always a great honour to work with Sir Fred. I found him such a musical person, not least in the way he did his choreography. He never actually wanted to work out counts as such, as so many choreographers like to do. Kenneth MacMillan, for instance, would always want me to work out the dancers' counts before he even started to create the choreography. Sir Frederick was so immersed in the music that he knew it backwards. His musicality was absolutely wonderful. I want to mention a little anecdote about *A Month in the Country*. He got me to play the last few bars of the *alla polacca* many, many times. In the end I got absolutely bored with it and I flung up my arms. Even though I was way out in the corner, Sir Fred never missed a thing, and he saw what I did. He was stuck for some way of ending this particular section, and seeing me do that inspired him to get the dancers to do exactly the same on stage! My name would go on in posterity, for in the score is written, 'Gammon port de bras'.

Russell-Roberts: It's true, Fred was famous for not missing anything, nobody could ever put anything on him. I remember talking to Norman Morrice, then director of the Royal Ballet, who would go round to Fred's house when he wanted something out of him; Fred would have a habit of knowing in advance exactly what it was Norman wanted to get round to, and he would spend the whole evening deflecting! He really didn't miss anything, and although he was a very modest man, he used to say, 'I can see under water,' and I think that's absolutely true. Interestingly, he was nominated Doctor of Music by quite a few universities. That really is a tribute to his musicality, because he couldn't read a score at all and he couldn't play a piano. Yet he was a true Doctor of Music.

Perhaps we should move on to talk about *Daphnis and Chloe*, which was premiered five years later, in 1951. Fonteyn, Somes, John Field, Violetta Elvin and Alexander Grant were in the cast. Perhaps, first of all, we might talk about the design. Pamela, you probably know something of how Fred came to choose John Craxton as the original designer.

May: Our solo pianist at the time in *Symphonic* was Jean Gilbert, who had been taught by John Craxton's father. I think it was through knowing the father that he was interested to know and use the son, whose work he obviously liked.

MacLeary: He did the designs for the revival of *Apollo*. He'd been chosen because he'd lived in Greece, and was very fond of Greece.

Russell-Roberts: Yes, I think that's the essential point: that Fred really did want it to have a genuinely Greek feeling. Several of you in the audience may be slightly dismayed that the Craxton designs have been jettisoned. The set had become very old and dilapidated, and there was a worry that the pirate scene might now look outdated. We had discussed with Fred the possibility of a redesign for *Daphnis* – he had no idea who might do it, but he was very keen to move on. That's why Anthony Dowell felt justified in looking towards a new design. The designer who we've chosen has tried to have a very Greek feeling to the set. Those of you who read Greek might be able to distinguish the names of Frederick Ashton and various others on the hieroglyphics. The pirate scene has been updated considerably.

Now we ought to ask Alexander Grant in the audience: what do you remember of the creative process?

Alexander Grant: You were saying before about Ashton's choreography being exhausting; that particular ballet is the most exhausting ballet I have ever danced. When I reached a certain age it was actually the only ballet that I asked to be taken out of. I went to Sir Frederick and said, 'I'm not doing justice to this any more, please take me out.' And, very kindly, he did. Also something else about the design: he was not at all happy with the red of my costume. He couldn't find the correct red dye, so he went back to Greece, found the right dye and brought it back!

Russell-Roberts: If we now move on to discuss *Sylvia*. Donald, perhaps you would like to describe the pas de deux. I imagine it is technically very demanding?

MacLeary: Yes, it's a lovely pas de deux because it is technically demanding but at the same time there's a beautiful romantic quality. Some passages are really what I think is the essence of Fred. He had a wonderful romantic feeling for things. He liked pushing you all the time – demand, demand, demand – so it isn't easy. Again, dancers today find it very difficult.

Russell-Roberts: We really can't discuss *Sylvia* without making reference to all the versions there were. It started off as a three-act ballet and Fred was never entirely happy with it. Would any of you like to comment?

Mason: Deanne Bergsma and I were the understudies when Fred made it into the one-act for Nadia Nerina, Svetlana Beriosova and Donald. Fred took all the best bits, all the solos and pas de deux, and crammed it all into one act. It turned out to be completely exhausting, and he wasn't interested that it was so very tiring. Nadia would say to Sir Fred during the *Sylvia* rehearsals, 'Aren't you going to take anything out?' and he would say, 'No, I love this bit!'

Russell-Roberts: I'm sure several of you are wondering why *Sylvia* is not revived. It is a project that may well happen at some time in the future; but, apart from many excellent memories from people, all we have as a faithful record is a video with the dancers looking like little white leaves in a snowstorm. However, it certainly could be possible to reconstruct it, and perhaps one day we might look forward to seeing the whole piece again. There is great virtue in doing historical reconstruction so that you can actually see what it was like, and it is very interesting to see how some pieces have endured. Ashton created over one hundred ballets, and if you look at the pieces that are actually easily revivable there are probably less than twenty. That's a point of great sadness.

On now to 1956, to *Birthday Offering*. It was an important piece because it was created to celebrate the company's twenty-fifth birthday. When I read the names of the seven ballerinas involved you will appreciate it must have been a splendid occasion: Margot Fonteyn, Beryl Grey, Violetta Elvin, Nadia Nerina, Rowena Jackson, Svetlana Beriosova and Elaine Fifield, accompanied by Somes, Grant, Shaw, Philip Chatfield, David Blair, Desmond Doyle and Brian Ashbridge. It was the same year that another very important event occurred for the Royal Ballet.

May: The Sadler's Wells Ballet was given its Royal Charter on 31 October 1956.

Russell-Roberts: These days, perhaps, the acceptance of a Royal Charter might not seem that important, but it set an important seal on the company's stature and reflected the international success of the company.

Being set on seven ballerinas, *Birthday Offering* is a real challenge. Donald, is it fair to say that it was set on the particular strengths of the individual ballerinas?

MacLeary: Oh, absolutely.

Russell-Roberts: What is it like to rehearse it for today's audiences?

MacLeary: You just have to try and remember what Fred used to say; you have an image and a record in your mind. Nobody is ever going to look like Margot Fonteyn because she was unique, but he didn't mind that when he rehearsed other people in that role. He tried to get more out of whatever that person had. He would emphasise it, and that's simply what I tried to do, with the thought of him in my head.

Russell-Roberts: Have you found that there are any roles out of the seven variations that are particularly difficult for today?

MacLeary: Monica could tell you about Nadia's – that was a fiendishly difficult one. None of them was easy because they were all choreographed for that person's special talent. To follow on in anything is always difficult.

Russell-Roberts: The interest, then, was not only that it was a wonderful set of variations, but at that particular time it really did make a statement about the tremendous strength of the company.

Mason: I probably taught all the variations at some time or another in the Royal Ballet School, and I always think it is a particularly fun thing to do: talking about the ballerinas, trying to inject a feeling for the time it was created, and what it was like to have such a splendid roster of ballerinas. Also, it helps the students to understand about the heritage of the Royal Ballet. Those variations are extremely challenging for students, but they learn a great deal about the qualities of Fred's work in that way.

Grant: I can tell you something interesting about *Birthday Offering*. Frederick had just seen Cranko's *Lady and the Fool*, in which Beryl Grey was lifted very many times because she had four different suitors. They lifted her all over the place. Freddie said, 'In the next pas de deux I am going to do there's not going to be a single lift' – and *Birthday Offering* has not a single lift.

Russell-Roberts: Pamela, in 1956 you had just retired from dancing. What did it feel like for you? Did you regret very much that you were not in the opening night?

May: I was in the audience on the opening night and, naturally, at many rehearsals, but oh, how I envied those ballerinas and wished that it had all been a few years earlier!

Russell-Roberts: If we move on now to *La Valse* in 1959. Fred chose André Levasseur to design the scenery and costumes, as he had for *Birthday Offering*. It was the first piece that Anthony Dowell selected when he became director of the Royal Ballet, and it shows quite considerably how the company can be seen to have strengthened, in spite of many injuries at the moment. It's a hugely atmospheric piece, with a marvellous score by Ravel.

Mason: Again, I just want to say of *La Valse*: it's an absolute killer. It's an exhausting ballet for both the corps de ballet and the principals, and again, this must completely disguised. Because it's a relatively short piece, sometimes Fred would say, 'We'll do it all from the beginning once again,' and we would look in complete disbelief. Off we'd go again and we would literally be dropping. In the opening of *La Valse*, when the girls are lifted, the whole point is to lift the girls quickly and to bring them down very slowly. I remember the boys completely loathed this.

MacLeary: I actually did it once for the Queen's Jubilee gala after I had already retired. I was thrilled to be asked to be in the gala, but I didn't know what had hit me when I got to rehearsal.

Grant: I might just shed a little light on what you are saying about Frederick wanting you to do it full out every time: his first teacher was Léonide Massine, and he was exactly the same.

Russell-Roberts: Christopher Carr, our ballet-master who rehearsed the ballet, approached this revival with tremendous trepidation because he felt it was one of the hardest acts that he has had to pull together. He has worked tremendously hard, and having brought it together, the ballet looks terribly easy to do; but, of course, the reverse is the case.

It might be worth spending some moments on general matters. It would be interesting to reflect on what it is that makes an Ashton dancer.

MacLeary: I don't think he had a set pattern. Different people inspired him, his genius was getting things out of different people. I think it's wrong to say 'an Ashton dancer'.

Russell-Roberts: Though it is a phrase that you hear all the time. Sarah Wildor, a soloist with the company, commented in a press interview about the neatness and sharpness of footwork. Is that something that maybe an Ashton dancer particularly has to have?

MacLeary: He would get it out of you whether you had it in the first place or not!

Russell-Roberts: Would you say that it's a characteristic or attribute that he looked for particularly?

MacLeary: He loved Pavlova's feet, he was always talking about Pavlova.

May: He would say, 'Run like Pavlova!' Your feet had to move like Pavlova, bourrées had to be like Pavlova.

Russell-Roberts: Another point we should cover is to what extent Fred's ballets sit comfortably on other companies. Until recently, *Symphonic Variations*, and now *A Month in the Country*, hadn't been done by other companies; but increasingly works are being done around the world. It must be, for the recipient company, the equivalent problem to us, for instance, when importing a Balanchine ballet. If we attempt to stage Balanchine works without a Balanchine *répétiteur*, it seldom works. I feel the same with Ashton works. It will be interesting, as a result of this conference, and as a result of general interest in Ashton's work, over the next few years what pressures there will be for the works to be taken into other companies, and whether works like *A Month in the Country* might not suit certain countries.

Mason: I couldn't have imagined anybody not falling instantly in love with *Symphonic*, but it didn't seem to appeal to the Russians at all.

Russell-Roberts: Philip, is there anything further you would like to mention from a musical point of view?

Gammon: We are in for a treat during tonight's performance, because we have in the pit none other than Bernard Haitink. I played for the piano rehearsals for *Daphnis* and that's a terribly difficult piece to play: you're not only playing so many notes but you're also turning pages rapidly. I was amazed at the rehearsal that Bernard Haitink even offered to turn pages for me. What other conductor would do that?

Russell-Roberts: Talking to Fred about his ballets at the end of his career, he was saying, 'You know, I'm really quite bored by many of them, they're far too long!' But he really is the master of economy. If he could say something in two words that others might say at great length, he wouldn't say it in six sentences. You would have thought that at the end of his career he would have looked back and felt that he had made a great achievement, being one of the very great choreographers of the world. However, I think there was a sense of failure. He said to me once, 'I would very much rather have been the greatest dancer that there had ever been.'

Finally, I will leave you with the thought that Ashton is thought to have created an English style. It's a very difficult concept to grapple with, but I am sure that there will be much deliberation and Fred would probably be amazed at what all the fuss is about.

Maybe a further question that some of you might have is: why is there no Ashton Foundation? As Ashton's nephew, it is a difficult question to answer. I think that, much the same as happened with Balanchine, there will come a time when his friends and collaborators to whom he left the ballets will feel that it is the right moment to club together and to form a foundation. I would leave you with the reassurance that matters are in very good hands. What is interesting is to see how we can dig and excavate, and make live today, ballets that are thought to be long extinct. That is a task that I think should be addressed.

Ashton Dancers Across the Generations
Panel Discussion

Lesley Collier, Beryl Grey, Alicia Markova, Merle Park, David Wall. Chairs: Stephanie Jordan, David Vaughan

Stephanie Jordan: I have asked each of our panel members to start with a short commentary on their memories and impressions of Ashton as a choreographer, as well as the importance of Ashton's influence on them at the start of and throughout their careers. We are also talking about the Ashton style, and how he worked with individual dancers. We start with Dame Alicia, who tells me that there are eighteen roles in all that he created for her, and that it would be impossible for her to choose one, so she is going to give us a medley of several.

Alicia Markova: In 1930, after Diaghilev's death, I was back home in England and received a letter from a young man: Sir Fred. Apparently he had sat up in the 'gods' while I was with the Diaghilev company. The letter explained that he had been invited by Sir Nigel Playfair to stage some dances for the play *Mariage à la mode*, and he wondered if I would dance with him in this new play. I did not have any work, and I thought, 'That could be very interesting. He is young, and seems very interested in everything happening in the ballet world.' So I accepted. This was the first time we met, and we seemed to get along very well. He started to choreograph the dances, and in the pas de deux I met for the first time what was later to become the 'Fred Step' – at the time we both knew it was not Fred's step, it was the step Anna Pavlova danced in her *Gavotte*. He suddenly said to me, 'You know that step that she danced?' and I said 'Yes.' He said, 'Let's do that in the pas de deux.' That was the very first time we had that step – it became the 'Fred Step'. Perhaps that will put on record how that came about.

Mariage à la mode was a big success, and we moved into the Royalty Theatre. Suddenly I was invited by Mim Rambert and Sir Fred to be guest ballerina for the Ballet Club. The first ballet he choreographed for me was *La Péri*, for the opening of the Ballet Club. In all the works from then on, from 1930–34, we were always doing something new.

Between Ballet Club performances, I was dancing with Anton Dolin in music-hall. Fred and I really had the kind of relationship that when I was invited to dance – whether it was in the show *Kissin' Spring*, or music-hall, or the 'pure' ballet – I would ask him to choreograph for me, and when he was asked to stage something he would ask for me. So between all that, there must have been eighteen different works that we worked on together in the four years. Apart from that, I was also doing new works for Dame Ninette and others, but it was with Sir Fred that we just kept going. Later he was invited by Massine to do his first ballet for the Ballets Russes in Monte Carlo 1938–39. He had to go to Paris to stage that. It was called *The Devil's Holiday*, a wonderful work; I was so upset that it was never seen here in England. We did it a lot at the Met and on tour. I remember when Fred arrived in Paris he was terribly nervous. I held his hand through that production because it was the first time he had done a work for an international company. When he came to New York to put on *Les Illuminations* for Balanchine, I held his hand too.

Beryl Grey: Part of my experience is my first memory of Dame Alicia in *Les Rendezvous*, created for her at Sadler's Wells. It epitomises all that one remembers about Dame Alicia, her grace, her lightness, her wit, refinement. That link between dancer and choreographer is, for me, what identifies Sir Fred's works. That was his extraordinary talent: identifying a dancer's particular forte, very often an unseen talent, developing it, pulling out more than the dancer realised was within them. This is both a strength and a weakness of Sir Fred's work, because each role is sculptured around the talents of the chosen artist, and it's so difficult to be number two or three in that role. Many of us have seen first-night performances of Sir Fred's ballets and then many years later we see totally different casts. They do it wonderfully, with interesting interpretations, but it never quite captures that special something that Fred was able to draw from his original choice of artists.

My first encounter with Sir Fred was very brief. I joined Sadler's Wells in July 1941 and he was called up into the RAF the next month. Eighteen months later he was given three months' leave of absence to stage a ballet for Sadler's Wells. During that time I had danced leading roles for Robert Helpmann in *Comus*, *Hamlet* and *The Birds*. It was a great contrast to be suddenly picked by Sir Fred, who I did not know at all, and be chosen for a really nasty role – I was to represent Falsehood in *The*

Quest. Why he chose me, I shall never know. Robert Helpmann was St George, and Fonteyn was Una, who stood for Truth. I had an absolutely marvellous time with Fred, because when you start to work with him, you are influenced by what he is. He had an enormous flexibility of attitude in his creativity which almost defies analysis. He was intensely musical, and we all believed that he would spend two or three months soaking up whatever music he had chosen.

The Quest, however, was not so typical of the way Fred would work. In this instance he had only three months in total, and he had asked William Walton to compose the music specially. And for John Piper – who he had asked to design decor and costumes – it was his very first creation, not only for ballet but for the theatre. Fred had to wait, and each day a new sheet of paper would arrive from William Walton. We were in Coventry, and one or two weeks before the gala opening at the New Theatre in April 1943, the music for the last of the five scenes still had not arrived. He told the company that there was no music for the last scene, but that he knew exactly the number of bars he needed. He requested that from William Walton, and choreographed on that basis. When the music arrived it fitted perfectly. It was quite remarkable. It was the only time I have ever seen Fred work without music.

He had this extraordinary feeling for the right movement to music, and inherent good taste, and he had interminable patience with the bodies of his dancers. Although he seemed to ask the impossible, he passed that patience on, and so one worked and worked until one got what he wanted. He would refer to Pavlova often, and would take off Pavlova's use of hands, her bourrées, her pirouettes and her abandonment. If you look at photographs of Fred you see the neck is right back. This is one of the things he went on about when we were working on *The Quest* – I didn't use my upper back enough, my neck enough, I had to be more abandoned.

Fred had a sensitivity about him. It acted as a magnet in his rehearsals and prevented tension. He was such a gentle, courteous, kind person. It produced a most harmonious relationship in all rehearsals that I've ever attended with Fred. We all adored him, and we gave everything we could.

I find his ballets beautifully characterised. You have the element of romanticism, which perhaps was his forte, but then you get these gorgeous comic characters; he could draw a character so clearly. I have an enormous rapport with his intense musicality, because whenever I hear music, I want to dance.

172

Merle Park: What I remember, especially with the *La Chatte* and the pas de deux from *Die Fledermaus* – *Voices of Spring* – was that Fred cut the music. He said that you must leave your audience wanting more. It's a good lesson for young choreographers to leave your audience wanting more, to cut and cut.

The 'Fred Step' that we have been talking about, I am not exactly sure what it is, does it have a pas de chat? Sometimes it has a soutenu and all sorts of things. I think it must be the lilt, because I think Fred's second name must have been 'bend'. He used to say, 'Bend your body' – sideways or backwards, in any direction. He had a bendy body. I never saw him dance, but I guess coming from a hot country, Peru, he must have had a wonderful body, and he expected everyone else to lilt like that. In *La Chatte*, the last solo he created, the 'Fred Step' turns, and I hadn't done it that way before. The first time I ever came across the 'Fred Step' was in *Daphnis and Chloe* when I first joined the company. When you were in a role for him and he thought, 'What can we do now?', and you said 'The Fred Step?', he would say 'That's right, put it in' – and we would put it in in some way or another.

David Wall: My memories of Fred go back a long way before I met him. He was an enormous influence on me as a young student at White Lodge [the Royal Ballet Lower School]. I think I was thirteen, not really totally focused or directed. I was taken to see a rehearsal of *La Fille mal gardée* and that inspired me: I was focused, and knew exactly what I wanted to be when I graduated – a ballet dancer. After *La Fille mal gardée*, *The Two Pigeons* and *Persephone* inspired me, and I had the pleasure of working with the original casts, which was of great assistance in my later career. The only other time I talked about Fred in public, I got my wrists slapped slightly. We had just created a ballet called *Sinfonietta*, and I was doing an interview with, I think, *Vogue* magazine. We were talking about Sir Frederick and wires got crossed. What came out in print was that I did not think Fred was a choreographer, but a man with a great deal of taste. It wasn't quite right, but I will reiterate that I do think Fred's greatness was his taste. He was brilliant in paring down and bringing purity to the stage. I don't think any ballet has inspired me more than *Symphonic Variations* for the very fact of that purity, the musicality, the blending together of the art forms into one magical ballet.

When I was creating *Sinfonietta* he was little apprehensive. I don't think he was totally at home with the music, by Malcolm Arnold. There was a lot of discord in the music, which I think Fred slightly felt. But it survived: its latest performances were by the Royal Ballet School a couple of years ago. After that I did *Prometheus* for him. I didn't think Fred was at his most creative there. It was the bicentenary of Beethoven, the company was going to Bonn, and I think he had almost been forced into creating this ballet. That was never the way Fred created works – he created from the heart – and consequently I don't think that ballet worked particularly well. There were wonderful moments, several very exciting variations, very witty; but on the whole it wasn't a success.

Then we came to create *The Walk to the Paradise Garden*. Merle and I feel that it was as if we walked into the studio and somehow it happened. There is no memory of why we were doing it, what we were doing it for; it just came from nowhere. We were all on the same wavelength, and it was a most pleasurable, creative period. There was a lot of love in that studio. Fred was loving what he was doing, we were loving working with him.

Park: He talked a lot about Pavlova to me, even my hair-style was Pavlova in that ballet, as well as a lot of the arm movements and use of neck. There was a very clever lift at the end, shaped as a cross. His eye for line was extraordinary. I was upside down with my arms out and my back to the audience. I thought my arms were at my sides making a cross, but Fred said I had to have them much further back. It's a bit like flying a radio-controlled aeroplane: you press the other way if you want it to come towards you. The line of the arms was extraordinary, they were right behind me and I thought I was upside down absolutely straight – but it made a cross in the end.

Wall: I remember Fred trying to start the creative process. With *Amazon Forest*, that I did with Margot [Fonteyn], when we walked into the studio Margot and Fred were very much at ease with each other; I was a little apprehensive. We sat on the floor for about forty-five minutes drinking tea. Fred finally said, 'Should we do something?' Margot said, 'Let's have another cup of tea.' So we did. As soon as he got over the initial hurdle of getting something started, it was a wonderful experience.

Park: After *Paradise Garden*, there was a party in the Crush Bar at the Opera House. Madame Rambert was there and said, 'Fred, darling, it is lovely, but it is too much on the floor.' Those were Fred's floor days!

Talking of music, I see Alexander Grant there. I'm sure he could say a lot about Fred and *Ondine*. Fred had great difficulty with that music, and didn't like it at all.

Alexander Grant: Henze wrote the music in my house, and he was so brilliant that he wrote the orchestration straight down. Fred did not have a piano copy to work with in the studio, so he sent the orchestrations to someone else to make a piano copy – who made it sound like nothing. Eventually, Henze had to have it broadcast by an orchestra in Germany, and Frederick, for the first time, choreographed to tape, which he disliked intensely. It was quite a struggle, because he loved to listen to the music endlessly before going into the studio, and he wasn't able to because of the orchestration.

Lesley Collier: I was delighted when Anthony Dowell said that he was a little bit blasé about being chosen for a role [see p. 147]. When you are young you are so full of self-confidence. Young people are wonderful and don't doubt themselves. I had been a student at White Lodge and had seen *La Fille mal gardée*, *Monotones* and *The Two Pigeons*; most of all I had seen Merle in the Neapolitan Dance in *Swan Lake*. They were all a total inspiration to me, though I had no idea who the choreographer was. It was the visual thing, and the musicality that really spoke to me. When I did *The Two Pigeons* for the school performance, Fred, who was on tour with the company in America, came back early to oversee it. He just walked into the studio, and I did it. I waited for some kind of marvellous comment, because it was a ballet I adored, I fitted into, and I thought I was jolly lovely in it. Fred said, 'You're too stiff, just too stiff.' There is a lovely vision of Lynn Seymour in the solo where she goes up and through the body – well, I didn't do that, and he did not know how to make me do it. I was left knowing I was too stiff, and was thoroughly deflated.

I was finally taken into the company after that performance. The years went by and I was allowed to do the Neapolitan Dance, which was a great shock, because Merle had made it look so easy, and so wonderfully musical. I could hardly hold the tambourine, let alone dance with it above my head. I was beginning to realise that his choreography looked as if it were nothing, but was very difficult to get into the body. And it was difficult to follow someone who had already had it choreographed on them. The Neapolitan was a disaster. It came to the next season and I didn't have a performance. With courage I said, 'I don't seem to have a performance.' It wasn't Fred who spoke to me, but a below-Fred person who said, 'I'm sorry, but Fred thought you were too stiff.' I realised that I had to pull myself together and get to grips with this choreographer, who was then becoming a rather marvellous person in my life.

When I was chosen to do *Rhapsody*, I was in total awe of this person who had become so amazing to me, because in every ballet you realise how his musicality is complete orchestration. Fred is the orchestra choreographer. With *Rhapsody*, we started with my very first entrance in the solo, which is very fast. Fred was nervous, I was nervous, and Philip Gammon was raring to go at the piano. Philip was a marvellous help to Fred: he would really take the music apart for him. I think *Rhapsody* is probably one of the fastest footwork ballets, and Fred was insistent that every note had a step on it – not just a step with the feet, but with a change of arm and change of head. He clearly had decided that I was capable of the fast footwork, but he was determined to make me bend, come what may. It was a joy to work with him. We pulled the music apart and we did steps in different ways.

When it came to the pas de deux with Baryshnikov, it wasn't as harmonious as one might have hoped. Baryshnikov is a musician, and he was very quick to know the music. I am only a musician by ear, I don't play an instrument; I felt undermined by this marvellous Russian who was so quick that he almost dismissed anybody who couldn't keep up. This was a nightmare, because though I feel music very well, I was getting left behind. And Fred was just sitting there, he didn't jump to my defence. I used to give him a lift home afterwards, and I said, 'Fred, I feel terrible.' He said, 'You will work it out, don't worry.' But I felt I was not contributing, that it had all been taken away from me. From the joy of the solo, the pas de deux became a bit of a nightmare. In the end we worked it out and I learned Misha's musicality for it, which sort of went against my own hearing. As there were two ways of hearing the music, it was interesting that Fred, who had a very clear idea of the musicality, allowed us to get on with the musicality of it. Although it was distressing at the beginning, it was kind of him in the end. It is interesting that Anthony Dowell talked about the bourrée lift [see p. 151]. The pas de deux begins with this in *Rhapsody*: the girl is taken across the stage, lifted, and then put down. Baryshnikov had had to have the pas de deux in *A Month in the Country* changed because he couldn't do this lift. When Anthony took Baryshnikov's role in *Rhapsody*, it became a 'Fred' ballet for me, and it was quite wonderful.

David Vaughan: You've all had the experience of having a work created for you by Sir Frederick, and I you've all had the experience of taking over a role created for someone else. Dame Alicia, the Tango in *Façade* was originally done for Lopokova and you took it over . . .

Markova: The whole conception of the Tango today is very different from the beginning. Lopokova had a special quality of humour and innocence. When it was choreographed, she interpreted it as a country bumpkin. Sir Fred was the perfect Dago, Lopokova a debutante who had come up from the country. The costume was ill-fitting. It had everything on it: this little hat with flowers, a piece of maribou round the neck, a pink jacket of the very cheapest material, a knee-length orange tutu, and black tango shoes laced up. On top of that were black lace mittens – it was absolutely disaster! There were kiss-curls painted on the cheeks, and when you came on you behaved as if you were absolutely perfect. The whole thing between Sir Fred and the debutante was almost as if he did not wish to touch her. The debutante is naïve; everything he tries to teach her goes wrong. There were roars of laughter all the way through. Just as she thinks she is getting the rhythm of the walk across in front of him, he tips her over in the air. With the fast lift, where he whirls her round onto the ground and they come face to face, again there were roars of laughter. That was why he asked me if I would give some thought to it after its first production for the Camargo Society, where I had done the Polka – which was another joke on Sir Fred's part. He always had little in-jokes and secrets in a way.

If I can just digress from the Tango to the Polka. The original decor was different because there was, as usual, no money, so everything had to be done very cheaply. The set at the back had the farmhouse door, and I was painted in my polka outfit on that door. Before the Polka, in the milkmaid scene, I had to stand in that door and open the lower part, which would reveal the real part of me on pointe with the skirt, while the upper part was the painted image. During the introduction for the Polka, I had to push the door open and stride out – and I strode out wearing bloomers, not the pretty-pretty costume they wear today. On the opening night there was a gasp in the audience – everybody thought I'd lost my skirt. Fred had wanted to surprise them, so at the dress rehearsal I didn't drop the skirt, but at the performance I danced in the bloomers. The Polka was a comment on the music-hall which Fred and I both had experienced. It was a based on music-hall jokes: the fall-over step and my bloomers and boater hat. All the movements in it featured a tilting of the boater hat. The pas de chat steps in the middle should have little wobbling head movements – today they go with the music, but originally it was syncopated, and had lots of detail in it. When I was dancing for Diaghilev, Sir Fred had seen me do double turns in the air, like the men in Balanchine's *The Nightingale*. At the end of the Polka he put in the double turns. He told me that later he had to change it because the girls couldn't cope with the double turn in the air and he couldn't explain to them those music-hall feelings, which shows how he would adapt material for other artists. After Camargo, when *Façade* came to the Ballet Club, we didn't have Lopokova. That was when Sir Fred asked me to do the Tango. I was uncertain, as I'd never done anything like the Tango and the Tarantella, but I said I was willing, although I didn't think I could ever do it like Lopokova. Fred said, 'Fine, you do it your way.'

There were other experiences too. I never knew what he would throw at me. When he decided to do *High Yellow* with Buddy Bradley, the great black director, I had private lessons with Buddy every day for six weeks. I had to learn to do things like 'snake hips', how to dance like a black girl. I was always interested; I didn't mind what Fred threw at me.

Wall: One of the most difficult roles I had to take over was in *The Dream*, which was given to the touring company of the Royal Ballet. It was choreographed on Anthony Dowell, who is a left turner and has a lot of speed in his work. I managed to convert it to the right, but still could not get as much speed as Anthony. After we'd been doing it for about four months, I said to Fred, 'I really do not think this role suits me.' He said, 'Don't worry about it, just do it your way, I am very happy with the way you are interpreting it.' Fred saw each dancer in a very different way, and did allow changes to occur in the choreography when needed.

Park: I agree. When I did *Rhapsody* I could never run on my pointes like Lesley could; I took great big steps. Fred did not mind, he was very fair about it. In Titania, Antoinette did six little turns, posé. I was better at en dedans and he said that it was fine, that it looks the same as long as the body goes 'bend'!

Collier: I had the same thing in *La Fille mal gardée* with the coda step in the second act. I was able to do a lot of things on pointe, and I managed to do this pas de chat staying on pointe in the pas de bourrée. Until then it had been coming down onto the flat and going up. Fred said, 'I rather like that, I think you could do that very well.' I said, 'Well, it's very difficult.' He said, 'Yes I know, but I think that's a very nice look.' He really didn't mind, and the alternative was to repeat this little running step on pointe, which a lot of dancers do, to echo what happens at the end of the Fanny Elssler pas de deux. He was very flexible about things. He wanted people to love his ballets and feel happy and comfortable in them. You did have to bend, you couldn't say, 'Fred, I can't bend.' But if you had a little trick which made you feel comfortable which gave a nice effect of sharpness or something that he liked, he was more than willing to let you do it.

Grey: I cannot remember him changing anything for me. I don't think I dared ask him, I thought we had to do everything he asked. He used to say, 'Make it comfortable.' He would actually try to persuade your body to find and adjust so that the result was exactly what he felt was right for you. I think he was concerned with the overall vision, with the picture, and I think the little details that have been mentioned didn't worry him.

Collier: It makes it very difficult for the people who are looking after the ballets, because they want to stay true to this. After his death, when they did *Fille*, they went back to the original film with Nadia [Nerina], and there were some lovely things there which had got lost or changed over the years. I think it is important to have them back again, provided he hadn't changed things for the better. You see those dancers and what they could do, and there must be dancers coming up that can and would like to do them; and I'm sure he would love to have it back again.

Grey: Change is inevitable because each temperament and each body is different, each dancer's reaction to music is imperceptibly different. I've seen lots of changes in roles that I did, but it is interesting that people interpret things in different ways.

Collier: When we did *Rhapsody*, Fred said that he'd asked Baryshnikov to 'bring his shopping bag with him', and I wondered what he meant. Fred said, 'All his tricks, I wanted him to do all his tricks.' He wanted to learn from Baryshnikov, he wanted to create something that Baryshnikov could be fantastic in – which is why Anthony Dowell nearly died when he had to take it over. It became a different ballet, and it worked both ways – it gave a wider range to one ballet.

Wall: Fred himself was a very good keeper. On several occasions he rehearsed the company in *Les Sylphides*; that was a wonderful experience.

Collier: That's very true. The *Sylphides* rehearsals were far more nerve-wracking than for his own ballets because he was a bit of a stickler for them. One thing that we might have gathered from this conference is that Fred was really a ballerina at heart and he knew what a ballerina should do. If you could look into him, you could become that ballerina; but you couldn't copy it, you had to digest it and give it out again. Fred was a wonderful coach on *Swan Lake* and the Rose Adagio. He did a spectacular Rose Adagio. He was a fabulous ballerina. Everyone has a guiding soul, I think, and Pavlova was his before and after her death.

Markova: Although he had respect for classical ballet, he was crazy about jazz, which I think is important. He used to save his money and go shopping for records. I remember one 'big' record, Rita Kenner in *Ten Cents a Dance*. Another important influence came from his training, particularly the first influence from Massine. Sir Fred had the good sense to go to Massine for a couple of private lessons before he was passed on to Mim Rambert. Fred's sense of movement grew from that. Massine was strict Cecchetti. Fred carried on with this Italian School influence under Mim Rambert, who was also Cecchetti. When he went to Paris, his next great influence was Madame Nijinska. After the Italian School, he added the Russian School and the new ideas of Nijinska. When I first met him he was obsessed with Nijinska. When he came back to England, he was again influenced by Massine, and so it was back to the Italian School. At the same time, Fred was interested in any kind of dance. We would go and see Indian dancing when we were doing *La Péri*. We went to exhibitions, and I studied the make-up and the movements. We studied a great deal before he started choreographing. Perhaps we had more time in those days; we were always at a museum or a show. And music – this was the most important part. He was always asking me, 'Did you hear that lovely piece of music on the radio last night?' He knew that I had worked with composers like Ravel with Diaghilev, and we had a very happy relationship.

Jordan: Can you comment on your own development within a particular role, or on the changing perceptions of an Ashton role?

Collier: In *Rhapsody*, when Merle did my role, it was the first time I was able to go out front and watch. When you are in a ballet, you can't see where you are in it; that's why I like to be second cast, to see where I fit in. When I saw Merle do it, I was appalled – she didn't even look tired. It's the most killing thing I've ever had to do, and Merle looked as cool as a cucumber. The quality there was every bit 'Fred'; there wasn't an atom that wasn't asked for. She was doing everything I did and yet she looked amazing. With that vision in my mind, I went back to *Rhapsody* and calmed down a bit. I think the tension and excitement from the rehearsal studio never left me – a waste of energy really. Merle economised wonderfully without losing a thing; Ravenna Tucker had the same calm, serene approach. I went back to it with a vision of what I wanted. It still killed me, but I had this idea and it felt different. However special it is to have a role created on you, it is equally important to see other people dance it so that you can see where you fit in the whole plan of the ballet.

Wall: The role that I took on which became part of me was in *The Two Pigeons*. Christopher Gable had created it with Lynn Seymour and they then both transferred to the Royal Ballet, who didn't have the production. I was fortunate enough to perform it at least twice a week on fourteen-week tours, so I got to know the role rather well. I didn't try to be like Christopher. It was a wonderfully complete piece for a young dancer – I think I was seventeen when I did it – it had everything, pyrotechnics, the solo was vigorous and vital. It had a lot of humour – not many dancers get the opportunity to work on how to be a comedian on the stage. The opening scene of *Two Pigeons* taught me a great deal which enhanced performances that were to come. It had the glorious pas de deux at the end of Act II. That pas de deux was so simple, an understatement that was so pure.

I think the mark of a great ballet is the number of casts that succeed in it. Everybody says 'I wish I'd seen the first cast.' The more successful casts there are in a ballet – *La Fille mal gardée*, *Two Pigeons*, *Cinderella*, all Fred's ballets – the more success there is in those pieces. I actually took courage into my hands one evening and asked Fred which was his own favourite of his ballets. I was quite astounded when he told me that it was *Scènes de ballet*, not *Symphonic*. *Two Pigeons* was the role I felt was almost mine.

Park: I don't really have one, except perhaps with *Voices of Spring*, which we did so often over five years, every New Year's Eve. It did change. Each time we did it, it would be faster or whatever; but I can't think of a definite role that I developed.

Jordan: At the beginning of his career, did Fred tend to come with conceptions about what he wanted? The impression is that later he was more immediately involved in getting the dancers to bring ideas to him.

Markova: With the period that I'm discussing (the beginning of his career – he'd only done *A Tragedy of Fashion*), when he arrived the first thing he would say to me was 'Feed me, please!' The first time I thought he meant he was hungry. He said, 'No, feed me with steps.' I would reply, 'Which direction, what sort of thing?' He would say, 'I want something brilliant!' I would show him this and that; he knew that I'd already worked with all the great choreographers. Maybe a few days later he would compose something, and sometimes I would say, 'I don't think we should do that. Massine has already used those steps, I'm sure you can find a twist or use something else.' Then he would come up with these wonderful ideas. For instance, the variation in *Rendezvous* – after the entrance, he said, 'I want double pirouette in attitude, closing in fifth behind and the double pirouette en dehors, and as you come out of it, I want you to swivel round as though you're tipsy.' I said, 'That's rather difficult, the double and the double!' And then it was repeated a second time. Eventually I managed to get the control for the pirouettes and the swing, and into the second time. He would make terrific demands for control, but you had to have complete freedom: you had to try and wed those two things together. It was similar with Fokine when I worked with him: from the waist down you had to have a terribly strong technique; from the waist up it was Duncan. I think it goes back to training. With Diaghilev we had the Cecchetti training, which allowed us to serve any choreographer. At that time we had Fokine, Massine, Nijinska, then Balanchine. We had to come with one body but be able to serve whatever was required. Sir Fred also had had Cecchetti, Nijinska, Massine.

Alastair Macaulay: Merle Park, in the light of what Dame Alicia has been saying about the way he took from non-ballet material, could you talk about the way he used social dance for the *Swan Lake* pas de quatre? At the same time, I would like to ask Lesley Collier, as she has insisted that she could not bend (we all know this is not true – she was a very bendy Alice, and it wasn't just upper body, it also moved from the pelvis), could you talk about *Tweedledum and Tweedledee*?

Park: He based the first girl's solo, which I originally did, on the cha cha cha – that was the dance of that day. We had just been on a big tour of Brazil and Rio, and had done a lot of samba dancing after the performances. Fred was always there, he adored it. Antoinette Sibley did the other girl's solo, which was based on the twist.

Collier: You wanted me to talk about Alice. I had always tried hard to please Fred and I did learn how to use my body. A common problem with dancers is that they are not very strong underneath and a lot of the tension is taken in the top – and I was obviously one of these dancers. I was supposed to be strong, but I had clearly never moved in the right way. I think as I did get stronger underneath I was much freer to move on the top, and I also became quite interested in being daring. We've also heard about how Fred loved people to be daring. If you go to the limits, like on a renversé, which is an upside-down step, you almost come back on yourself – so the more you go, the more you come back on yourself. It all became an interesting science for me physically. Not only was I trying to please Fred, I also found it stimulating to see what the body could do. I still do find that fascinating: even as age creeps on, the body may get even more bendy!

Choreographers and Teachers
Panel Discussion

Julia Farron, Pamela May, Richard Glasstone,
Richard Alston, Ashley Page. Chair: Angela Kane

Angela Kane: What was the first experience the members of the panel had of seeing or doing Ashton work, and what were the elements that touched them?

Julia Farron: The first experience I had was extraordinarily exciting. I was already connected through the school to a scholarship, and went to a performance up in the gallery of Sadler's Wells to see the first night of *Les Patineurs*. That, I think, was my first experience of Ashton and an Ashton ballet. I might possibly have seen *Façade* before, but at fourteen I didn't really know much about choreographers. But *Les Patineurs* had an enormous effect because it was such wonderful dancing, and the cast, including Pamela May here, were all so brilliant. People at the time said this was a new move because he had used much more strength of technique in that ballet than he had perhaps been able to before, because except for the great dancers of Rambert like Alicia [Markova], this was the first time the company had got strong and were able to produce a really technically good ballet with all Fred's style.

The first time I worked with him was *Wedding Bouquet*, which was also thrilling. I was fourteen, with no experience except for working with Dame Ninette on *Prometheus*. The very beginning of that ballet was a group of children playing ball, and Madame came to the rehearsal with it completely counted out: plan, pattern, shape, steps, everything. We learnt it in about half an hour then she said go away and practise, and she got on with the next thing. And, of course, working with Fred was different. You didn't come in and learn a step. I remember he grabbed my hand and he walked around holding my hand. Being as young as I was, I was a bit nervous of this hand-holding, but at the same time he was thinking while he was doing this and I was getting some kind of strength from it

183

too, so that I could start working – as Pépé the dog! I was very small, which is perhaps why I was chosen, and also I could work quickly, which he also liked. One of the great problems was that I was five foot tall, but he wanted me to be smaller and I couldn't. I had to curl up like a dog curls up on the floor, and I couldn't get tight enough. 'You're not small enough, get smaller, get smaller' – that was one of the strongest remembrances of that ballet.

Pamela May: I was asked to dance with Sir Frederick before I had actually worked with him on a ballet. This was again one of Dame Ninette's early ballets, *Douanes*. The part was usually played by Beatrice Appleyard, one of the original members of Dame Ninette's company. I think she was ill, and I was suddenly told that I would have to do this 'flapper' dance in *Douanes*, which was a sort of musical comedy, with hitch kicks and things like that, and wonderful rhythm and hip movements – which of course Ashton was brilliant at, especially in those days when he was still dancing. So I found myself on with Ashton, which was a tremendous thrill.

After that, I think the first ballet I worked on with him was *Baiser de la fée* or *Apparitions*. *Baiser de la fée* I remember very well. One of Margot's [Fonteyn] first parts was the bride, and several of us were her bridesmaids. The work in that was terrific footwork, something that again I don't think Ashton had done very much of, but very quick work, which was very tiring for the bridesmaids but very interesting. The next ballet, very soon afterwards, was *Apparitions* where again I had the excitement of actually dancing with Ashton, because when he arranged the ballroom scene he said to me, 'You've got to have me as your partner because we're short of boys and I'll have to be in it myself.' So I said wonderful, I didn't mind. You should have seen that ballroom scene. Ashton was always saying use your body, and that's what he did in the gallop in *Apparitions*, he whirled me around. Although he was small and light, he was incredibly fast in those days. I had the time of my life. I think we all did, in fact, when *Apparitions* was first done.

After that I think it must have been *Les Patineurs*, where I was one of the two red girls; there were two blue and two red girls. I remember Elizabeth Miller and I, June Brae and Mary Honer all working as soloists in *Les Patineurs*; and what a wonderful ballet that was to work with Ashton on. I did many other ballets at that time. I did *Les Rendezvous*, which was again a beautiful dancing part for the corps de ballet. There were four little girls who did all the quick work, and six couples who did mainly pas de deux. When it was first done, there was Markova and Idzikowsky. After that was *Horoscope*, another wonderful ballet, in which all I had to do was try and make my body into a moon. Every arabesque had to be with a curved leg at the back, and arm fairly high, in line with your head. There was a drop curtain, and when it went up I was at the back, standing there as the moon before the music started for me to bourrée forward. Ashton came round after the first performance and said, 'I don't like the way you stand there at the back on a flat foot, couldn't you be up on pointe?' I said, 'I don't think so, I can't stand there for half a minute on pointe' – there was nothing behind, only a curtain, not even something to lean against. 'What a pity,' he said. He was always wanting these extraordinary things.

Richard Glasstone: As Robert Helpmann said in the film of Ashton's retirement gala, 'the work is the man and the man is the work'. I actually met the work twenty years before I met the man. I was a very young dancer in South Africa, sixteen years old; in our little company we did *Les Rendezvous* and later *Les Patineurs*. I started off in the corps de ballet in the pas de trois in *Les Rendezvous*, which is the hardest thing I think I have ever danced. Looking back now, I had only been dancing for a year when I had to do the pas de six in *Les Rendezvous*, and I think one of the reasons I managed it was because we did the same sort of steps in class as were in the ballet. The class was full of very quick footwork, and I had to get my feet around the class from the very first day. So the ballet didn't seem like a different language: it was a continuation of that sort of footwork and port de bras.

Twenty years later, when I started teaching at the Royal Ballet School – I had never met Ashton; he was just the great choreographer – I did a little ballet to music by Vivaldi called *Primavera* [1970]. Ashton came back stage afterwards and said the nicest thing any one has ever said to me. There I was, a young teacher at the Royal Ballet School doing a little ballet for the kids, and he said, 'I liked that you hear the music the same way I do.' I don't think you could have a greater compliment. I don't think of myself as a choreographer in any sort of original sense, but it was nice to think at least that he thought I heard the music properly.

I didn't really meet him again until 1984. He came to the Royal Ballet School to rehearse *Pas de légumes*, and driving back in the car we got talking about Cecchetti. He said so many nice and interesting things which I didn't know, that I said, 'Won't you put it down on paper?' That is when he wrote me that letter which I referred to [see p. 8].

185

Richard Alston: The first live performance of Ashton's work that I saw was just after I left school. I have long-suffering parents who allowed me to leave school early in order to go to art college (they sent me to an extremely expensive school, so I'm sure they regretted it). The whole family had come up to London. We lived on the edge of Hampstead Heath and I saw in the local paper that the second Royal Ballet company was at the Hippodrome in Golders Green. Since leaving school I'd had this weird, strong desire to go and see loads and loads of ballet performances. So I went every night for a whole week, and at the end of the week, on Friday night, Saturday matinée and Saturday night, they did *La Fille mal gardée.* That was the first ballet of Fred's that I saw. I was completely bowled over on the Friday, and went again on the Saturday matinée. I took my parents on the Saturday evening, took a deep breath and said, 'You know on Monday I'm supposed to be starting at art college? I actually want to be a choreographer.' All hell broke loose. And it was Fred's fault.

Ashley Page: I've been racking my brains trying to think of my first experience of Ashton. I think it must have been the dress rehearsal of *Enigma Variations.* I went to White Lodge [the Royal Ballet Lower School] in 1968, when I was twelve, and I think that was probably the first thing I saw that I consciously knew was Ashton's. We had Joan Lawson teaching both straight dance classes and also history of ballet. She was a great influence on all of us at the time, and she would go on and on about Fred in both the dance classes and history of ballet classes. After seeing *Enigma Variations,* Joan explained it all to us: where it came from, what the music was about. I remember being extraordinarily excited about seeing people like Anthony Dowell, Wayne Sleep and Alexander Grant dashing down the stairs. I think it was probably the first time I had ever seen anything like that; before I had only seen the classics, things on television, and had been in *Nutcracker* just a few months before as a soldier. So this was the first time I had seen a one-act ballet.

There was a day, actually, that Fred came to White Lodge – I think it was his birthday or something like that – and I remember him talking to me at the front door. He was this very calm, cool, benevolent gentleman walking around chatting to everyone like he was the father of this place. There is a very famous photograph of him which I think was taken that day, standing by the big cedar in the grounds.

Glasstone: I want to add one thing which I forgot to say. Within one or two years of my dancing in *Les Rendezvous* as a very young raw student, the Sadler's Wells Theatre Ballet under Peggy van Praagh came on tour into Cape Town. That was very important, because I then actually saw *Les Rendezvous* performed as it should be – having just danced it badly myself – and also saw the Sadler's Wells Theatre Ballet under Peggy van Praagh, who was a great custodian of that sort of style. Older people than myself talk about the Diaghilev Ballet as their touchstone; mine was the Sadler's Wells Theatre Ballet under Peggy van Praagh. I remember the fourteen ballets they performed that season with wonderful dancers, including Kenneth MacMillan, who was a very young dancer at the time. But it was having danced Ashton first and then seeing it properly performed by that wonderful company which was very important to me for understanding the style.

Kane: Are there any particular aspects of Ashton's work which influenced your careers? Julia, I think you wanted to talk about the footwork and the fleetness of the feet in terms of the style influencing the teaching.

Farron: I am not at all sure about this exactly, because I think as dancers, our quick footwork came originally from Dame Ninette, who could never do anything slowly; she always wanted us to do class very, very fast. So I think our quick footwork came from Madame, and Fred was always very anxious to use it, and made the best use of it. In those days, I think, the techniques were nothing like they are today. Today they get better and better and better. I speak for myself, obviously, but what we did have was very fast work and very fast movement, and I think most of those early ballets of hers and of Fred's made good use of that. We didn't, perhaps, have the extensions or the elevations that are needed from dancers today. Fred obviously used quick footwork whenever he wanted, and he was able to use it. The more you see of his ballets, the more you realise that this is a very important part of his choreography.

Kane: And because that is an aspect of his style, does that influence the way you then try to teach and to coach the Ashton style?

Farron: I don't think it influences the way one tries to teach; coach, yes – coaching is a very different matter. Teaching students, you are trying to build and prepare the body, always in the classical form – whether it is Cecchetti inspired or Russian inspired or whatever – you are building bodies to be dancers for choreographers to mess about with; this is what is important. I wouldn't say that I have taught a class thinking, 'This is for Fred's ballets.' But rehearsal, coaching, teaching dances out of his ballets, yes – that is a very different scene.

May: I think the only time we might have given the students something of Ashton's to do was if we chose something for a solo part, or even part of a solo or pas de deux, or prepared them for maybe the annual school matinée. Then we'd say, 'This is an Ashton ballet.' But I agree with Julia: it didn't actually come into the curriculum that this is an 'Ashton day' for teaching his work and his craft. You build up to what Ashton was when you get them into the company.

Alexander Grant: Would they have learnt chassé battements – backwards and forward and back?

Farron: Oh yes, of course, but that's not an Ashton step though, it's de Valois.

May: We had a de Valois syllabus to follow, which had every little step: assemblés, sissonnes, jetés coming forwards and then reversed going back, then coming forwards beaten, then going back beaten. That was the sort of thing we did in the class, which was more or less set down by Dame Ninette – which of course Ashton used very much. When you think back to those ballets, he always had a set of little girls who do quick movements, then there was a set of bigger girls, perhaps with their partners, doing the slower pas de deux adagios and getting their legs up. But in those days he nearly always divided into two groups, two kinds of dancers.

Kane: Richard, when we spoke a few weeks ago you mentioned the lyricism required in Ashton, that the boys had as an additional requirement for a male dancer. Did that influence your work as a teacher?

Glasstone: My own training and teaching have always taken for granted that boys have to be able to move quickly; I don't see why boys have to move slowly all the time. How are you going to do the pas de trois or the pas de six in *Les Rendezvous* unless you can move extremely fast? So I think quick footwork is important for boys too. My training always said that boys had to be able to do lyrical work; it was quite natural to me. I have found over the years that some male teachers take a different attitude, but I can only speak for myself. I think that to equate lyricism with femininity is quite wrong: a man can be just as lyrical as a woman

There is one more thing I would like to say about class. I think, and hope we would all agree – and certainly Ashton himself said – that his work was based on classical ballet. Nijinska said the same about her work. One of the things about classicism is balance. There is balance between the use of arms and legs for instance, there is balance in everything – and there has to be a balance in the shape of the class. And the balance of a classical class has, I think, become distorted and generalised over the

188

years, for whatever reason; there is less time spent on quick footwork in the average classical class. You have to have barre work, a port de bras section, centre practice section, which is a repetition of what you did at the barre; you have to have a lot of adage of different types, small allegro and big allegro, travelling jumps and diagonals and round-the-rooms, jumps that are not beaten and then beaten. All that has to be fitted into an hour or two-hour class. Unless there is that balance within the shape of the class, whatever method you teach, to my mind you are not being true to classical principles. If you do maintain that balance, your dancer is equipped to dance any kind of ballet based on classical technique. And I think that has become distorted. Sometimes it is because a particular choreographer has the monopoly over the repertoire – there are lots of reasons, but I think if you are after classical ballet you have to have classical classes, and that classical classes of whatever method have to encompass all those things within each class every day.

Farron: I think it is perfectly true what Richard was saying that Fred was a classicist. His work was based on classical technique. But what he had was this marvellous way of taking steps and movements, and twisting them, turning them, altering them – face the other way, go at a different speed. But he was basically a classicist, and that is why he was such a wonderful coach to classical dancers: he knew what it was all about and he knew what he was aiming for.

May: The first time I did the *Les Sylphides* pas de deux, Ashton was my partner. Although the influence that Pavlova had on Ashton has been talked about a great deal, what I found in rehearsing this pas de deux was the tremendous influence of Karsavina; throughout the rehearsal and solos he was continually saying how Karsavina had done it. He later worked quite a lot with Karsavina, right up to *La Fille mal gardée*, when she gave him all the mime. As a classical dancer himself, he did that solo beautifully: light, with wonderful movement of shoulders, very lovely soft jumps. When he had given up dancing he often used to come and watch the end of class, feeding his brain with steps, reminding him of steps he could take out of class. He used to like to creep in and sit in the corner. It was wonderful: his brain was always alive.

Glasstone: Just to address your point about style. I think a great danger that you get with teachers – including, I have to confess, a lot of Cecchetti teachers (I'm sorry I'm criticising my own brethren here) – is that they think they have to teach a style. You don't have to teach a style: you have to teach a technique. Style grows out of a technique, and it is the

189

choreographer's job and the coach's job to draw out the style. The ballet teacher's job is to develop musicality and technique, and the two must go together. But to say I am teaching 'the Cecchetti style' in the sense that I am teaching a nineteenth-century thing – that is not your job as a Cecchetti teacher or as a ballet teacher. Your job is to teach the dancer to understand the body, to control the body, to discipline the body so that it can do whatever anyone wants. If someone wants in a ballet to recreate the balletic style of Cecchetti's day, then that is a stylistic thing for them to do. What I find fascinating about teaching Cecchetti is that the people who are interested and really understand it nowadays are contemporary dancers. People often think I'm mad when I say I think Cecchetti and Ashton and Cunningham are one. I think they are. I think it is contemporary dancers nowadays who understand all that off-balance business, which is so much a part of Cecchetti, but which has nothing to do with the Romantic period style.

Kane: Julia said very much the same thing when I was asking her about the way you need to train feet to dance Ashton ballets. She more or less said that you need a well-trained dancer – you don't train the feet in a particular way, you need good feet.

Moving on to the two choreographers, Richard and Ashley. Has Ashton's work influenced you in general terms, or are there particular technical, structural, or musical aspects that you have been informed by and have manipulated in any particular way?

Alston: There are loads of things, but I have singled out three things I want to address briefly; they all connect with what has already been said. You talked a lot about fast footwork. When I think about those kind of steps, particularly in Fred's work, I think more of the 'power' of small steps. *Small* steps: it's not necessarily that they are fast. I feel that techniques are getting stronger and stronger, people can lift their legs higher and higher, choreographers want to wrench dancers into stranger and stranger shapes, the language gets in a way broader and bigger. That's why for me Fred was such an important influence, because there was, until recently, a living artist who used the full range of volumes, if you like. So you could actually say something incredibly personal with a tiny little flick of the ankle. Sometimes small steps could express lightness of heart, something troubling the heart, all sorts of things. I have become increasingly interested in how he used the language to express all these different things.

Also, personally, I find there's a sort of physical empathy – as a dancer who makes dances. I can't explain why, but I really love to use my back and to get the body into soft diagonal positions so it's not all square; and again the choreographer who does that most for me is Fred. I just love to use space, to feel space through the back, so you can actually feel the twist around the spine, which gives a three-dimensional aspect. In Fred's characters this often gives some kind of softness or vulnerability, or it becomes very expressive.

The third thing ties in with teaching. My work as a choreographer has often been with quite strident contemporary music, but my work as a teacher is very much concerned with linking the harmony of movement with melody. The connection between movement and music is immensely important. Fred sometimes chose what might be considered quite light-hearted music, but it gives the most wonderful clarity and framework in which, working every day, you learn to dance. There is *dance* in Fred's ballets. There is not always dance in choreographers' ballets, but he makes people dance.

Fred talked to me a little about Nijinska teaching. One of the things that impressed him most – when he was in Ida Rubinstein's company and Nijinska was his teacher – was that she would come in with a huge wedge of sheet music, dump it on the piano, and say, 'Today Mozart'; and the next day, 'Bach'. She had worked out the class according to one sort of musical style, one sort of feeling in music. She actually wanted the dancers to work with that music specifically; she wanted the feeling that a particular composer gave that day. I remember Fred talking about it at quite some length, and it obviously really impressed him – this in a way very intuitive approach to teaching, but still marvellously connected to music. It was that connection with music that was always, always there in Fred's work.

Page: As a performer, I was lucky enough to be rehearsed by Sir Fred in several different roles. One was the poet in *Illuminations*, which was revived for the Royal Ballet in 1981. I was taught the role by John Taras, who was Balanchine's lieutenant (Fred had made the ballet on New York City Ballet in, I think, 1952). Taras was a pretty hard taskmaster, and he really got me moving in this role. Then Fred came in for the last week or so of rehearsal. That was quite an extraordinary experience: I thought he was going to break me completely. Once we got on stage I had to wear this jacket that I felt very restricted by, and consequently I was getting less fullness of movement than Fred had managed to get out of me in the studio. He made John Taras take me back to the studio that afternoon and put on a very thick motorbike jacket that I had with me at the time. He then made me do an hour or two's work on the role in this leather jacket. He said, 'You've got to dance and come out of that thing.' It was exhausting, having just done a dress rehearsal in the morning, but the next night – the first performance – the difference was just amazing: just the feeling of having worked that hard and having to dance through this and out of this costume. I remember Fred coming back afterwards and saying, 'I don't ever want to see you dance in another way, it has to be that way, you have to tear your guts.' 'Tear your guts' was one of his most favourite expressions.

Kane: And that's what you expect from your dancers now is it?

Page: Oh, it is! In fact, I use similar phrases, without actually realising until I've said it. As a choreographer everything that has been said so far applies. The whole thing about small steps is very interesting. A lot of choreographers these days don't seem to want to use small steps – it's all very big broad movement, which is also interesting. But it was the range of Fred's work: he could, within a phrase, move from very broad expansive movement to something very small, and change speed, thereby deepening the textures of his movement phrases.

Having the good fortune to be rehearsed by Fred and danced in a lot of his ballets, there was the whole thing about not doing enough: it is never enough, you can always do more. That's not to say that you've got to go for the top, of course; but you can always do more than you think, get more out of the smallest movement or phrase. That was always a great influence.

I think we are going to move on to the other question about which particular group of works is a favourite. Certainly my favourite is around 1946–48 – *Scènes de ballet, Cinderella, Symphonic Variations*, particularly Act II of *Cinderella*, which I think offers almost an abstract ballet, certainly once Cinderella has arrived. That whole stylistic phase of his work has been the major influence on me as a choreographer. Talking as a choreographer, I remember things like his fascination with a particular line of arabesque, which was what I call the downward 'V' – most of the time I think Fred hated arabesques which were 'up', he always wanted the absolute pure, straight arabesque with the finger in front of the nose. Quite often in Ashton ballets the legs didn't have to be high, you were required to think of keeping them below hip level, below 90 degrees. Particularly in *Cinderella* and *Scènes de ballet*, the downward 'V' and low arabesque line are favourite things of mine. The difference between *Sym-*

phonic Variations and *Scènes de ballet* is that *Symphonic Variations* is much more lyrical. I suppose in some ways people think of *Scènes de ballet* as being uncharacteristic of Ashton because of its hard edge and geometric shapes, and a lot of people think of it, perhaps because of the Stravinsky score, as being much closer to Balanchine. But there is, for me, a quintessential Ashton flavour in there. I know *Scènes de ballet* much more than *Symphonic Variations* because I have been in it. *Symphonic Variations* I know obviously very well, but only visually. I have actually learnt it, but never performed it. *Symphonic Variations* is always put on a pedestal as the 'great' work I suppose, but that group of three works made very close together has had the biggest influence on me as a choreographer. Plus, I suppose, there is such a strong flavour about it, it was very much a period of work.

There is another question about how the work changes over the years. I suppose Fred developed as the dancers were able to do more, as they became stronger technically. I am not sure whether that was Fred pushing them in the rehearsal studio, or whether it came from the class and just the ever-evolving physicality of dancers being able to do more.

Farron: I don't think it was that way at all, I don't think Fred ever demanded of dancers technically what they couldn't do, he demanded the way they did it. But if they had those technical abilities he would use them.

Page: But with each succeeding generation of dancers I think you can see great jumps in the way he used classical technique. Like when Anthony Dowell came and did *The Dream*. Nobody has ever really done Oberon the way Anthony did. Obviously, in every choreographer's work there are certain aspects of things that were made on a particular dancer, and no one else will ever do it like that – like probably David Blair with *La Fille mal gardée*, and obviously the whole Fonteyn thing.

Farron: I think even right back to *Les Patineurs*, no one had ever done it in the way Harold Turner did.

Glasstone: Why are we always saying that dancers are so much better today? There are many dancers today who couldn't do the Turner variation.

Kane: Ashley, you mentioned *Scènes de ballet* and its Stravinsky music. Given the sort of music that you have worked with, was that an influence – the way the choreography is set on the music?

Page: I suppose unconsciously it must have been, because I've been in *Scènes de ballet* and it's inside me. You could say the way I hear and think of music as a dancer and as a choreographer must have a lot to do with being in the repertory that I've danced in, and also going to see things like *Enigma Variations* dress rehearsals you can see how the music is being used. As Richard Glasstone suggested when he mentioned Fred saying 'you hear the music the same way I do', there are different ways of hearing music, and certainly I can't imagine *Scènes de ballet* being done any other way.

Kane: I was thinking of your *Carmen Arcadiae*, the structural relationship between the dance and the sound.

Page: Yes, absolutely. There is a not entirely unconscious relationship when I sit down and think about using a piece of music, particularly for *Carmen* and *Pursuit* – certainly *Pursuit* was a very conscious homage to *Scènes de ballet*, with the tutus and the geometric shapes and that very terse music; *Scènes de ballet* is pretty terse, although there are some more lyrical moments. Fred got inside that score and revealed it as another subject altogether; choreographers can reveal more about the music by the way they use it.

Kane: Richard, is there a particular group of Ashton's ballets – the plotless works, or the demi-character, or the romantic style works from the 1930s – that you'd like to talk about?

Alston: I keep finding new things every time I go back and see a work of Ashton's, so perhaps at that moment that particular work becomes a favourite. I love all the obvious ones – nothing very subtle I'm afraid – *Les Rendezvous*, *Les Patineurs*, *La Fille mal gardée*, *Symphonic Variations*, *Scènes de ballet*. One ballet that always astonishes me in a particular way is *The Dream*, because I find the economy and the speed of the narrative absolutely breathtaking – what he manages to get into a very, very short version of a very, very long Shakespeare story, which other choreographers have spread out over a whole evening. And the particular sensibility that he got out of the Mendelssohn music, particularly I think when it was first done with the Henry Bardon set and David Walker costumes, it really was about a particular group of characters, and it moved through this whole range of comic characters to the pas de deux, which is just astonishing. The speed of all the fairies suddenly stopping dead in their tracks and making these little romantic print images and so on – there are so many moments. It is certainly one piece that I love to go back to many times.

Kane: Does experience of his working process reveal anything about Ashton and his choreography for you?

Glasstone: I have to take a slightly different angle if I may. First of all, if

I can choose three ballets, I would choose *Les Rendezvous, Symphonic Variations* and *A Month in the Country*. When I watched Dowell and Sibley rehearsing *The Dream* [see pp. 147–57], the thing I felt was Ashton's humanity. I am glad you used the word 'plotless' ballet and not 'abstract', because I don't think there are any abstract Ashton ballets: they are all about human feelings, and that comes across so strongly for me, and I think is characteristic of Ashton. It comes across in quite different ways in those three ballets. *Symphonic Variations*, which seems to be abstract, is actually about human beings; *Les Rendezvous* is very flirtatious; and *A Month in the Country* is very moving. My poor wife was in hospital the day of the dress rehearsal of *A Month in the Country* and I was so moved by the dress rehearsal that I went to the hospital and said, 'You have to let her out for three hours tomorrow because I'm taking her to the ballet.' I took her to the ballet, she watched the performance and then went back into hospital. It was just so incredibly moving. By dancing in *Les Rendezvous* one was moved, and by watching it performed. And *Symphonic Variations*, when it is well danced, I find an emotional experience, not a geometric, plotless experience. Even with *Scènes de ballet* you can get that feeling if it is well danced.

Kane: Pamela, did you observe any changes in the working process, the way he made the ballets? What we have found increasingly during this conference is that he went in with a blank page – was that the case in the very early stages?

May: Well, no I don't think it was, though I don't know about all the ballets. In *The Wanderer*, when we rehearsed the pas de deux with Michael Somes, in 1941–42, the theatres had all closed, the company was disbanded for a short time, and we were all over the country. We were all called back to Dartington Hall, the home of Kurt Jooss, where there was this lovely grass quadrangle, dancers' flats, a dining room and a little theatre. It was a world of its own. We were advised that Ashton wanted to start on one of his new ballets. We were there for about a month, and on Christmas morning there was a knock on my door. It was Fred saying, 'Are you going to church?', and I said I probably was. 'I felt like doing your pas de deux this morning,' he said. So I said I would go to church later – we had our own chapel too. We went up to this rehearsal room, and lying all over the floor were pieces of paper. On them were beautiful drawings, with lovely positions, bodies, heads – some were just heads and arms, some were whole bodies. I said, 'Fred this is beautiful, what is it?' He replied, 'Just a few little positions I thought we might use.' Of course,

Constant [Lambert] was there, and I said, 'Why don't we do one after the other with the music?' He said, 'Yes, that's what I thought.' So, you see, he thought a lot of ideas.

Funnily enough, I never asked him if he had drawn these positions himself, or if he had copied them out of books, until a year before he died. Suddenly, I don't know why, I said, 'You remember those positions that you used in my pas de deux in *The Wanderer*, all beautifully drawn out, were they your own or had you copied them?' He said, 'Hmm, I'm not sure, I often did them myself and I also often copied them out of books.' Even walking along the road in France or Spain or Italy he would just scribble little drawings, so in a funny way he was doing so many preparations. He wasn't like Dame Ninette, who had every bar of music with every position of even your little finger. But obviously in his brain he had all these ideas, it was just forming them musically. The minute he saw you move in a position he would say, 'That's what I want', or 'That's not what I want, your arms are in the wrong sort of position, put them somewhere else.' He would know what he didn't want very quickly. We had a wonderful time; we thought we were practically doing the chor-eography in the end – but we weren't, believe me!

Farron: I think a lot of people who didn't work with Fred as much as perhaps we have, used to say, 'Well, you did all the steps yourself.' But, of course, you don't: you give him a sort of spark and then he takes over. I was thinking of what Pamela said about the drawings. It's not that he hadn't thought about it, because one knows that for months and months he has thought, the music is within him, what it's going to look like, the designs, the costumes – everything is there when he starts work. It took me back to working on *The Wise Virgins*, which we did during the war. Before we started, he brought books for us to look at on the Botticelli paintings that he wanted. With *The Wise Virgins* especially, the very spe-cific positions and groupings that we had to take (there was not a lot of dancing in it) were very clear when he came. But the steps that we did were not there; he didn't walk into the room with them, that's true.

May: It was exactly the same with *Dante Sonata*.

Kane: Was there a big difference in his working process between those one-act ballets of the 1930s and early 1940s and when he started with *Cinderella* and later with *Ondine*, when he moved into the bigger, the longer form?

Farron: I don't know. When you work with someone for so many years, you don't see the difference in the process; but I am sure there must have been development in some way. But the actual process of making a ballet was the most exciting thing one could possibly do. For me, my career was built on doing Fred's ballets, especially creating the new ones, and it didn't matter if you had a soloist role or the leading role or if you were in the corps de ballet (which was a dream, because you went to rehearsal knowing you were going to have fun apart from anything else). The one thing I haven't heard anybody mention is Fred's wit. He was the most witty man, unbelievably witty. It comes out, of course, in his work, and his characterisation and marvellous mechanicals in *The Dream, Cinderella, Wedding Bouquet, La Fille mal gardée* – wonderful wit.

Kane: Could I ask both Julia and Pamela another question: could you comment on your work as teachers setting Ashton choreography extracts on students and then Ashton coming in and coaching?

Farron: I didn't go through that process myself, but I used to teach in the repertory classes – with his permission always. You couldn't just go and teach a Fred ballet or a Fred dance; you had to go to him. I asked him if I could teach the *Façade* Polka in my class. He said, 'Do you remember it?' and I said, 'Well, I did it for a long time, Fred.' He said, 'Oh, all right – don't change it!' – which, of course, I wouldn't have dared to do. When I had the graduate class I occasionally used to teach that fabulous *Les Rendezvous* solo which I love so much – I never did it, but it is a simply wonderful variation, and Pamela did it wonderfully. There is a simple exit step; the first time I ever taught it I was very new to teaching. I showed them what to do. They couldn't get it. I explained that it was alternate arm and leg forward with one shoulder forward and one back, but they still didn't get it. It suddenly hit me, so I said, 'Put your hands behind your backs and do it with your body. Not épaulement, but the torso. You can't dance Fred with a stiff torso. Put your hands behind your back and lead with your shoulders, release the arms and let them be completely relaxed and the shoulders are moved by your own torso.' It's difficult to do or teach that variation, or any other Fred variation, because they all use that same thing: they don't just use épaulement or just bend – they twist!

Kane: Pamela, you've talked about the work that Sir Frederick did on the Solo Seal. Have there been other teaching situations where you've actually set some of his choreography and then he's come in and added additional comments?

May: No. He did teach those two solos from scratch. There was nothing that I could say to him. There was a body and a piece of music, and off he went. I would coach the rehearsals and he would come back the next week, and we would go through the dances and he would correct again, like I had done with those children. [See pp. 158–60.]

Kane: Were there any elements that he emphasised again, apart from the bend and the épaulement, other stylistic aspects that he stressed?

May: He always had something to say. You might think it had been beautifully done, perfectly – but there was always something!

Farron: There are so many small details. For instance he would say, 'Don't show the audience the palms of your hands, that's ugly.' You didn't think about that until you looked in the mirror, and now I'm continually correcting that point – fifth position of the arms with the hands not quite turned inwards. He used to say that certain dancers had 'housemaid's knees' – that they weren't always fully stretched or pulled up.

May: My arabesque foot was always a 'flatiron'! He used to say, 'What's that flatiron doing there?'

Glasstone: I was fascinated by what Julia said, because struggling to teach Cecchetti ports de bras (some of which are very complex) to younger students at White Lodge was very difficult. I eventually cracked it when I said, 'We're going to do port de bras without the arms.' In fact you can do port de bras with your arms behind your back or hanging by your sides, and you then discover what your body is doing and the arms go after that.

The thing I want to say about the early experience I have had: I was involved with the students who were going to dance *Pas de légumes* at White Lodge, and Ashton came down to that rehearsal. He was extremely nice to the kids. He corrected certain things – what Ashton wants to see, always, is every position absolutely clearly, but you never stop moving. I want to read you what he said in a letter after that rehearsal. It was extremely complimentary. (When he says 'you' it was not addressed just to me, but to the whole staff at White Lodge and the people who were putting on *Pas de légumes*.) It reads: 'I thought your boys and girls were delightful in the old veg pas. You do wonderful work on them and they are so youthful and fresh and well-mannered, which is a joy to see these days.' So he obviously thought we didn't do it too badly. But it's not me, it's us at White Lodge who did it.

Kane: Ashley, did Sir Frederick come and coach you before the performance of *The Two Pigeons*?

Page: This was the school matinée, the students' performance in 1975. In January we'd been learning the ballet for a few weeks, just bits of it, and then Fred came in to choose who should do the performance. Always in the school year that's a very nerve-wracking time, as so much importance is placed on the school performance. At the same time, Kenneth [MacMillan] was coming in to choose people for *Danses concertantes*, also on the programme. The next day the case sheet went up, and I was very excited to see that I was doing the gypsy lover. Fred came to rehearse us more meatily – again, it was all about everything having to be bigger, more than you think you can do, and again, as Richard was saying, he was very charming and very nice to us, which gave us confidence. It immediately relaxed us and made us focus on the work, and not on being rehearsed by the great Frederick Ashton.

Kane: How much did you realise at that time – or reflect later on – the links between the Cecchetti training that you'd had through the school?

Page: No. Richard Glasstone hadn't got that quite going at that time.

Glasstone: There's something that I've never talked to Ashley about before. When Ashley was at White Lodge, he was an extremely bubbly, warm boy. At the Upper School, he went through a stage when he became very withdrawn. He wanted to be a pure, classical dancer, like Anthony Dowell, and we got quite worried about him. At one point we thought we were going to have to send him to a shrink! When his name went up to dance in *Pigeons*, we thought: this is not what Ashley is going to want, because he wants to be the pure classical dancer, he wants to do *Symphonic* probably. In fact, dancing that role changed you completely. I don't know if you were aware of that, but it brought you out, back to what you were. You obviously gained confidence, whether it was him or the role or whatever.

Page: Well, I think, both. The fact that I had been chosen and I'd actually got through this thing. The other people down to learn this role for him to choose from were physically much more suited to it, and I actually went to Lynne Wallace, who was directing the school performance, and said, 'I can't do this because there are all these other people that are much more suited than I am.' Coincidentally, later that year I did grow a lot, and I did feel more as though I were right for it. Getting into the studio and having been chosen gave me the initial confidence. Then you could relax and just focus on the work, and get as much out of his personality as you possibly could.

Farron: With *La Fille mal gardée*, not long before I retired from the school (I didn't have anything to do with the teaching of it), there were two girls prepared for Fred to come in and choose. His choice was extraordinary, and it made me realise he had a wonderful eye and knowledge of dancers. He chose the one that nobody expected, but it was such a successful choice: Sandra Madgwick. She was a lovely little girl whom I absolutely adored teaching, but she spent most of her time behind the piano because she couldn't bear to look at herself. She didn't like the look of her feet and she didn't like the look of herself as a dancer; she wouldn't come in front of the mirror, or me. She learnt the role, but she didn't think she was going to get it. She did, and she's had the most enormous success ever since. It was like a little miracle.

Kane: Richard, did you observe Sir Frederick at Rambert when he was setting *Five Brahms Waltzes* on Lucy Burge, and then the Mannequin Dance from *A Tragedy of Fashion* for a gala performance?

Alston: I think the clearest thing to say about the Mannequin Dance was that Fred was petrified. It was very generous and courageous of him to allow something from way, way back to be remembered. Diana Gould (Lady Menuhin) remembered the beginning and the end. Basically, Fred had to fill in the bit in the middle.

Kane: So it wasn't coaching, it was rechoreographing.

Alston: He did – he made it up. It was obviously very influenced by the dance of the girl in blue with the gloves in *Les Biches*. He remembered the images. The fascinating thing about him working with Lucy was his tremendous memory for a dancer. It's often spoken about when talking of Pavlova and so on. The things he said to Lucy about Isadora were crystal clear. He would have seen her when he was a young man in South America – and it wasn't just a picture or a shape, it was a memory of physical things. I think when he first started that dance, when he was making it for Lynn [Seymour], he made just the last section first for a gala, and the image he first remembered was when she came forward from the back with those petals. There was a great deal of detail in how to let these petals go, how to hold them, and how they would come out. It was extraordinary memory for movement, for images and for a dancer's particular style, which I can't help feeling must have dovetailed, if you like, into his sensibility about young dancers. His memory had a tremendous sense of a dancer's particular physicality, be it Fonteyn, Pavlova, Isadora, or a young dancer whom he chose from behind the piano.

Kane: I think we ought to open this dicussion to the floor.

Anon: What was the Mannequin Dance?

Alston: This was the solo which Diana Gould had performed as a separate item, but it was actually a solo from *A Tragedy of Fashion*.

Joan Seaman (Ballet Association): Something that hasn't been touched on at all: Ashton lived through six years of an absolutely horrible war. Did it affect his choreography in any way?

Farron: I don't think so. I think the only thing, perhaps, one could say was that when he had been called up and he was given that three months' leave to come and do *The Quest*: it wasn't one of his most successful ballets, purely because, as Beryl Grey said, the music arrived in dribs and drabs, one page at a time [see p. 172]. Some of the ballets that we did during the war were wonderful ballets. *Dante Sonata* was inspired by Poland. I don't think it had any bad effect; in fact, I think it inspired him.

Seaman: The war affected most people in some way.

Farron: Well, in a funny sort of way it didn't affect the Vic–Wells Ballet, because it thrived and grew and developed at that time, and a lot of that was, of course, what he did for us.

May: It brought in audiences that we had never had before at the New Theatre. We had nine performances a week.

Alastair Macaulay: He made some more serious ballets than he had ever made before, and yet in the middle of the dark time of the war he added to *Façade* the Foxtrot, my favourite dance in the whole of that style. The wit still bubbled up in the middle of all that darkness.

Geraldine Morris: I think the war did affect him quite a lot. Certainly when he choreographed *Symphonic* he talked about the amount of mysticism he'd read during the war which influenced *Symphonic*. And the whole trend from *Dante Sonata* to *The Wanderer* and *The Quest* shows a lot of the neo-Romanticism of the painters of the era; and like the neo-Romantics he wanted an end that responds to the event. His work did change quite a lot, and I think you can see it in the pas de deux from *The Wanderer* and in *Dante Sonata* right through beyond *Symphonic*. It would be true to say that it did affect him.

Farron: I took it that the question meant did it affect him adversely, which of course it didn't.

Julie Kavanagh: We've heard so much about épaulement and fleet footwork and so on – is this technique being taught at the Royal Ballet School? Is Cecchetti taught at all?

Monica Mason: I'm not at the Royal Ballet School, but I am very closely connected with it, and I know that Merle Park's aim is to produce a very rounded classical dancer. The training goes from White Lodge to the Upper School, and although I think a lot of people have talked about the change of syllabus and the change of emphasis on the work, I think that the aims are still to produce a classical dancer at the end of the seven years of training. I do think that an enormous difference comes from the repertoire class. It is extremely important that the person who is teaching repertoire, in this case Julie Lincoln, does an absolutely brilliant job. She worked very closely with Sir Frederick and knows his work very well from being a dancer in his ballets and from when he came along for the final rehearsals before a school performance. She has a wonderful memory. She was party to many little 'Fredisms' and can quote them very easily and freely, and does so when she is rehearsing the children now.

Glasstone: I have heard Julie complain that she would like certain things taught differently, because they would make her work easier. I don't know if that's a controversial thing to say.

Mason: She did complain about the lack of chassé when she came to do *Les Patineurs.* She had to start to teach the chassé, and I think it is important that she also noticed changes in the use of the head. But I have to say that when the students come into the company, Julie has done such a brilliant job that we don't notice the difference.

Anon: There is a name that I have not heard mentioned here, unless I missed it: Constant Lambert. I was thinking about the closeness of the years when Lambert and Sophie Fedorovitch died – were you conscious of any difference in Ashton's approaches after that? He must have felt a terrible sadness over both those deaths.

May: There was tremendous collaboration between the three – not just Ashton and Fedorovitch – from the Ballet Club days through Sadler's Wells and later. Constant and Fred worked tremendously together. They used to discuss what music they would use, how much, what could be cut, and so on. Right from the word go when *Rio Grande* was put on – which was Lambert's music, first done, I think, at the Camargo and later at Sadler's Wells – practically every rehearsal one went to Lambert was there playing for us, though not the whole time because we had an excellent pianist in Hilda Gaunt. Throughout the war we had no orchestra. We had two pianos played by Constant Lambert and Hilda Gaunt, and we did all those ballets. A lot of them sounded wonderful – particularly *Les Sylphides* – on two pianos. In that last year, when Constant got so ill and died, it was obvious that Ashton was very, very sad; he missed him greatly. I can't help but think that today, with younger choreographers coming along, they must miss terribly not having a musical director as dedicated as Constant. I don't think there could be another one.

'Stars' from Cinderella
Workshop

Rosalind Eyre

Rosalind Eyre reconstructed a modified section of the 'Stars' from Act I of *Cinderella,* illustrating the complexity of Ashton's writing for the corps de ballet. She indicated that the work was very fast, like 'shooting stars'. The 'Stars' entrance is rapid. The first eight of the twelve dancers enter alternately from upstage right and left with a quick pas de chat, arm in attitude, before running, opening the outside arm to third, to form two lines of four dancers. The last four dancers enter in pairs to form the last line.

In canon, beginning with the front row, the 'Stars' dance a variation of the first step, a pas de chat followed by a run around a partner, without turning their backs on the audience. The port de bras accompanying this step again uses the attitude arm line. In the final four bars of the phrase all the dancers repeat the movement.

Using an effacé line, towards centre stage, the dancers perform temps levé, coupé, temps levé, pas de chat, relevé fifth, pas de chat in unison. Eyre indicated that in this swift section the emphasis is on 'real waisty movement', which should be 'sharp and fast, not soft and romantic'.

The last modified section of the work taught includes strongly characterised taqueté, as the dancers step forwards and backwards, and stepping in fourth croisé, weave in figures-of-eight across the front of the stage.

Eyre's coaching illustrated how Ashton wove simple steps into highly structured, complex designs, performed very fast, and on occasions syncopated to the music. The use of épaulement, clarity of position and changes of level were emphasised. The workshop provided an illuminating insight into the difficulties of coaching to achieve accuracy, uniformity and style.

Solo from Birthday Offering
Workshop

Monica Mason

Monica Mason explained that Ashton had choreographed *Birthday Offering* to celebrate the twenty-fifth anniversary of the first full evening of ballet performed by the then Vic-Wells Ballet. It was a *pièce d'occasion* created for seven of the company's ballerinas: Margot Fonteyn, Beryl Grey, Violetta Elvin, Nadia Nerina, Rowena Jackson, Svetlana Beriosova and Elaine Fifield, and their partners. Mason remarked that when teaching and performing any of the roles one had to bear in mind the qualities of the dancers who created them.

The solo that Mason taught was performed by Beriosova, a Lithuanian dancer who received some of her training in the West, yet retained elements of Russian training, including an expansive movement quality and an expressive back. It is a slow variation which contains particular elements of Ashton's style. The solo does not mean anything in a literal sense, yet it does have a specific kinetic quality. The costume worn by Beriosova was bell-shaped; the arm lines should echo this shape.

The solo begins in the left diagonal back corner, and contrasts the languorous qualities of deep ronds de jambe using a 'long lean twist in the body' with sharp retiré relevé. The rond de jambe 'should describe a very large circle'. Mason emphasised that everything in the solo was governed by direction, and when performing the rond de jambe the dancer should watch her foot. The body should be curved forward on the retiré, giving a 'feeling of the knee being under the chin'.

Mason explained that Ashton adored renversés, and used them in many of his ballets. She suggested that the dancers think of flamenco when performing renversé, and leave the face towards the audience. Performing the step in this manner means that the audience never loses sight of the dancer's face. Mason directed the dancers' attention to the music which would allow them to emphasise and contrast the slow renversé with the following quick piqué steps.

Mason indicated that Ashton wanted the dancer gradually to fold the upper body forward when performing seven piqués en arrière, until the dancer's face could no longer be seen. The solo ends with two sissonnes over, sissonne en avant, a run forward towards the audience, and a pas de chat gathering 'all the flowers thrown to you and then letting them drop through the hands' as the arms are raised to an open fifth.

Throughout the solo Mason contrasted the ability to flow the arm gestures with the intricate and faster moving feet. She reminded the dancers that in classical ballet the spectators watch the upper body; they will not watch a dancer's feet unless or until the dancer leads their gaze to the feet by her focus.

Excerpts from Enigma Variations

Lecture-Demonstration

Peter Wright

As a finale to the Ashton conference, Peter Wright and dancers from the Birmingham Royal Ballet presented excerpts from *Enigma Variations*, which had recently been revived for the company by Michael Somes.

Peter Wright: I can't claim to be a great expert on the choreography of *Enigma Variations*. It was choreographed by Frederick Ashton for the Royal Ballet at a time when I wasn't around, but from the first performance I saw I have always loved it; I think it is one of his greatest works. I like to think of it as a ballet about friendship, but about family too – a 'family' of friends. In practically every classical ballet you have the idea of 'friends'. Swanhilda has her friends, Giselle has her friends, Juliet has friends – the Prince always manages to have a friend somewhere! But they are incidental, and there are hardly any ballets that go into the depth and feeling of true friendship, and I think this ballet really does. It also goes into a lot of other deep and significant emotions between artists and companions to artists. It also has so many opportunities for characterisation – which I tend to find is on the wane at the moment, though I'm sure it will come up again – which calls for artistry and interpretative qualities that are, for me, so important to classical ballet. Technique isn't everything. Someone said (I think it was Pavlova) that technique is only a means to a beginning: it should never be regarded as an end in itself. I think this ballet demonstrates wonderfully that whole focus of what classical ballet really is about and the opportunities it gives the artists.

Enigma Variations has a subtitle taken from Elgar's subtitle for the music: 'My Friends Pictured Within.' The introduction to the programme reads:

Some time before the action of the ballet takes place, Elgar had sent the score of the *Enigma Variations* to the famous conductor Richter in the hope of interesting him in the work. The characters – intimates and friends of the composer – dance their individual variations, at the end of which a telegram arrives from Richter, addressed to their mutual friend Jaeger, agreeing to conduct the first performance.

This is, of course, what Elgar had been longing for, but would never allow himself to believe was going to happen.

It was the success of the *Enigma Variations* which was to bring international fame to Elgar and immortality to the friends pictured within. The action of the ballet takes place in Worcestershire in 1898.

Our approach to this lecture-demonstration is based on how we at the Birmingham Royal Ballet have brought the ballet to life. I like to think of this, of course, as a tribute to dear Sir Fred and this great masterpiece, but I also regard it as a tribute to Michael Somes and what he has done in keeping Fred's ballets alive. We were incredibly lucky because not only was Michael supervising everything, but also we had magnificent help from Anthony Dowell, Antoinette Sibley, Monica Mason and Deanne Bergsma. That was invaluable – sometimes confusing, but invaluable! Sadly, Derek Rencher, who has danced the role of Elgar in every performance, was going to help with this production but was taken ill.

In the case of a ballet like this, the question of casting is all important. When we decided to do it and Tony Dyson, who owns the ballet, had agreed and I'd had discussions with Michael, I did my casting as I thought would be right. I did it very quickly, as it all seemed pretty obvious to me. After that I discussed it with a lot of people, including Michael, but we didn't always agree. However, we agreed on most things. You have to be careful with a ballet like this that you don't just cast it according to the artists who did it originally rather than the characters they are playing. This ballet had the most wonderful original cast, including Svetlana Beriosova, Antoinette Sibley, Anthony Dowell, Wayne Sleep, Derek Rencher, Alexander Grant, Georgina Parkinson, Deanne Bergsma – but you still have to remember the characters they are portraying. This can be very difficult, because the ideal person may not have the technique to dance it, and vice versa. In the end, my very quick-thinking shortlist turned out to be the one that we did. We have got a second cast and some others that are studying it. However, we all did agree on the first cast. It's not always like that with casting, especially a famous ballet with famous interpreters.

Excerpt 1

The two key figures of *Enigma Variations* are Elgar and his wife Alice, Lady Elgar – danced here by Desmond Kelly and Sherilyn Kennedy. The duet establishes the extraordinary and wonderful relationship between the husband and the wife, the artist and the companion. It establishes at once so much about the characters and the relationships in the whole ballet. It didn't happen overnight, it is the result of many rehearsals, and it was often difficult to get things just right – especially with Michael Somes!

Excerpt 2

Jessica Clarke and Duncan de Gruchy dance the two characters in this duet: Isabel Fitton, who was always described as young and romantic, and Richard Arnold, the son of Matthew Arnold, a fairly studious scholar, quite serious but obviously very much in love. This again is not an easy duet to realise, especially today. Fred's idea was about love shining through the restraints of the period. Today we tend to go for it, and relationships develop very fast. In those days they didn't do that: they were very careful about how they behaved. That is far harder choreographically than doing everything full out – you often have to unlearn before you relearn. These ballets grow from performance to performance – you learn and discover by performing. You can go a certain length in rehearsal, but it is not until you get on stage with the audience that you really understand, get your timing right. There are a lot of interesting things in this duet: Ashton's use of music, phrasing, playing with the music sometimes.

Excerpt 3

This is a complete contrast: the Troyte variation, danced by Kevin O'Hare. Kevin had to build up his stamina for this solo: it's a killer, it's non-stop at the same level. Troyte was a very close friend to Elgar, outspoken and brusque. The boisterous mood is mere banter. I know people like this sometimes: they come and they talk and talk and they go on and on and get very excited. And when they've gone, you wonder: what was all that about? I think Troyte must have been a bit like that.

Excerpt 4

Now another contrast: Alain Dubreuil as Jaeger, with Desmond and Sherilyn as Elgar and his wife, in the Nimrod variation. One of the most moving parts of the ballet, this is very much about the relationship between Elgar, his great and dear friend Jaeger, and Elgar's wife too. It expresses this quite superbly, with absolute economy of movement and steps – Ashton brought it right down to the minimum. Its very under-statement makes it even more telling and moving. I'm sure everyone always reads different things into different ballets; I find it very moving that Elgar's wife understood so well that there are areas between artists and their friends that one can't intrude on. For instance, this particular variation illustrates when, on a summer evening, Elgar and Jaeger would discuss Beethoven and other music, and also their professional world. Although all three were very close, they were not necessarily close on everything. One of the great qualities of Elgar's wife was that she was always there and understood that he also had his own world – the world of the artist who is not lonely, but alone, and has to follow his or her own way always. Even after seeing the ballet many times, I still find it very moving.

Excerpt 5

We are going on now to the Dorabella solo created by Antoinette Sibley, danced here by Sandra Madgwick. This solo demands a great deal of body movement. One of the things about watching Sir Fred take rehears-als was the way he was forever prodding people: 'Use your back dear, bend, go, more!' He never wanted people to be rigid. There is a miscon-ceived idea about classical ballet being as though dancers have corsets on – this is certainly not true of Ashton.

There have been many interpreters of this role, and it is can be quite hard for artists sometimes when they have got different versions coming from all sides. Fred was wonderful, because he was quite flexible in a way. He wanted the steps and the timing accurately done, but he always wanted his artists to look right, so he would sometimes give way a bit, saying, 'No, you look better doing it that way.' Even with notation and word of mouth you still get conflicting opinions about how it was originally done and how it may have slightly changed.

The solo is absolutely fiendish in terms of stamina, accuracy of timing, musicality, everything. Originally Sir Fred wanted Dorabella to feature in the next number, which was the one about George Robertson Sinclair, or rather his bulldog – the scene with the dog barking at the children, originally created by Wayne Sleep. Poor Antoinette, after that variation she couldn't move, and so Fred had to give in and Dorabella – understandably! – does not feature in the next section.

Excerpt 6

We now come back to Elgar and Lady Elgar, the final duet, which in this demonstration we will run going straight into the Lady Mary variation, the real 'Enigma' variation. I've put them together because in the original – which we checked in the films made by Edmee Wood when it was first done – Lady Elgar exits at the same time that Lady Mary, the 'Enigma', enters. Lady Mary was a very enigmatic person that Elgar saw on a sea voyage; whether she was a real person or a vision in his head, we don't know. Over the years the choreography changed somehow, and Lady Elgar and Lady Mary didn't meet. Michael Somes thinks it's right that they should meet; other people think they shouldn't, and we don't really know what Fred wanted. Now that we've been performing it a bit, we've evolved our own slight compromise: you're never quite sure whether they meet, look at, or see each other. These are the kind of things that happen when you revive a ballet, even when it's been constantly in the repertory, as this ballet has been, over many years.

The first part is very deep and moving, because Elgar's wife is trying to help him with his feelings of insecurity. He doesn't know how to finish *Enigma Variations*. The ending was always a problem. There are, in fact, two endings – a long one and a short one. In the end, Elgar opted for the long one, but Fred chose the short one, which worked better theatrically. Fred had difficulty, too, getting the finale right. Everything else went through very quickly, but when it came to the finale, it took much longer. In this duet, Lady Elgar tries as hard as she can to help and support Elgar. It's as though she says, 'Go on, believe in yourself, think positive, get on with it.' You can only go a certain way with that and you can't push it. You can only help as much as you can and then let the artist get on – as in the Nimrod variation, where Elgar is worried, and Jaeger says, 'It will be all right, believe it,' but Elgar is still concerned and worried, and then he has to fight the battle on his own. This occurs again in this very beautiful pas de deux at the end, which is followed by the Lady Mary variation, danced here by Cathy Batcheller. Cathy came to us from the Stuttgart Ballet, where she was a principal dancer. She had no Ashton background at all, never worked in an Ashton ballet. Deanne Bergsma and Michael Somes helped her, and Monica Mason too – who I think was the second person ever to dance the role of Lady Elgar – and with that sort of support behind her, she took to it at once.

Discussion

Peter Wright: Desmond Kelly was very close to the production right from the start – he's my assistant director – and worked very closely with Michael Somes. I'd like him to talk not only about the rehearsals, but also about the role of Elgar.

Desmond Kelly: When Peter first broached it to me that we might do the ballet, I thought that we didn't have the people in the company to do the characters. I could still remember the original production from when I was with the Royal Ballet, and memories of the artists in it were vivid in my mind. When we sat down and began talk about it, I realised, as Peter said, that we shouldn't look for people who were like the original dancers, but should find people who were like the characters in the ballet. But we still had to have something of what had been before, so we had to balance it out. It was like a blessed project from the beginning, the casting went well. Before Michael Somes came, we were taught the ballet from the Benesh notation and the Edmee Wood film. We scheduled an hour and a half for the pas de deux, one hour for Troyte – it went very quickly. Then Michael came and put the finishing touches to it. He was very meticulous. For example, there are three walks forward for Elgar, and as soon as the music began and I started to take the first step, Michael yelled 'Stop!' It took hours to get this simple walk just right. Then it came to the same walk at the beginning of the pas de deux. This time Michael suggested that we had to make it different, and we had to try various head positions – it all took a very long time. In the end I thought that Derek Rencher had been so good in the role that I wasn't going to be able to do it. I watched the film and then I thought, 'I can't be like Derek – I'm just going to have to be myself.' Then things started to happen. Peter gave me a wonderful picture of Elgar, and I thought that

211

with a bit of imagination I might be able to look a bit like him. So I parted my hair on the wrong side for me, which was Elgar's side, rather high, and patted it down. I added a moustache, and from then on it was wonderful for me.

Wright: No role comes easily. You have to unlearn before you learn: one comes in with preconceived ideas. We made a point of letting all the artists have a video so that they could study it. Sometimes this is good, sometimes not so good. Some people are very good imitators and will copy too much, some not enough. You never quite get it right, although in this case it worked, generally, very well.

Sherilyn Kennedy: I found Michael a little intimidating. I'd watched the video lots of times, and his biggest criticism was that I was too facial for the style and the era it was set in. Every time I would do something he would shout, 'Stop, too much face – more natural, less is best!' Then Monica Mason came along, and that was wonderful, because I was a little too balletic still, instead of just being a natural human being. Monica was wonderful with me, and with the second cast (Samira Saidi), in helping us be natural.

Wright: A lot of it was trial and error, because certain things that Svetlana had done you ended up doing the way she did, but in the meantime you tried a lot of things that Michael suggested, with more arms or less arms.

Kennedy: He kept saying that I wasn't moving enough in the beginning steps. I'd move a lot, and he didn't like that, and he would suggest more hips. In the end we got it back to subtle movement, but we tried lots of things. Every dancer is different, and what looks best on one doesn't necessarily suit another.

Wright: Duncan and Jessica – I was talking about the pas de deux earlier on and the difficulties of capturing the period, the restraint. Did you find that a problem, having to tone it down and understate?

Jessica Clarke: I think Michael wanted more of it to come from within – he kept driving us to do this.

Duncan de Gruchy: One thing comes to mind at the beginning in relation to the sense of frustration about not being able to express things full out. Jessica goes away from me, so my natural instinct is to stop her quite forcibly, and Michael didn't want that – he wanted it done quite subtly. But I couldn't find a way of doing that – I found it one of the hardest things. I still don't know if I've got it right. It's just one example of something that you want to do naturally, but you can't.

212

Wright: I think there is also a sense in the pas de deux that comes out choreographically – you are always looking around to see if you're being watched. You look from side to side sometimes before looking at each other. That illustrates a lot. I like Ashton's musicality – his phrasing. There is a particular step which created, I think, certain problems. The way Fred finished it made it a very difficult step to do; and you can't do it terribly fast, so there had to be a certain compromise with the music. It's meant to illustrate laughter, but it ended up being a very light and difficult step with the music taken slower.

Kevin O'Hare: I don't know if I'm so keen on this idea of the casting being done from the original characters: I saw a picture of Troyte and he was a bit of an ugly chap – I'd rather it was based on Anthony Dowell! Anthony came in at the very beginning before we had learnt it, so he was able to show us exactly what each step was. We'd had half an hour with the notator beforehand, who taught us the steps, but Anthony showed us that it wasn't all so upright. He explained that the very first steps shouldn't be done with the body upright: you should let the upper body fall back on itself and then get it round onto the other side. There was the other problem that Anthony is a left-turner and I'm not, but we decided to keep it on the left side because if we made too many changes it would alter the shape of the solo.

When Michael came he had no sympathy at all, because he had never done it, and he made me do it about three times in a row. We decided that the best way to get the stamina was that I should have five minutes every day, and do it two or three times without a break. So after class, while everybody else was having a coffee break, I would have my five minutes. We started quite slowly. We decided that it was going to be about 80 beats on the metronome. We started at about 70, and worked our way up. By the time we got to the stage call I was going faster than the orchestra. They gradually got faster and faster, which was good, as Anthony thought it was easier to do faster. It's very different from most male solos: usually you do one step and walk to the side and then you do another step, but with this one you just keep going.

Wright: With most classical solos you can do the last diagonal the way you turn best, because you can run to either corner. But with a solo like this one, which is choreographed a special way, you can't suddenly change one particular bit and turn to the right.

I don't know if any of you have got anything to say about Nimrod – it's so self-explanatory.

Kelly: The programme says that it is based on moments in an evening spent discussing Beethoven with Jaeger. I think it's much deeper than that. It seems to relate more to the ending of the *Enigma Variations,* when Jaeger persuaded Elgar to change the ending and put in the extra music. He didn't want to, but he did it, and then he knew it was right. There was a lovely letter that he wrote saying, 'My dear friend, you were right, it is much better.' All that comes into it.

Wright: I'd like to invite Leslie Edwards from the audience to join us in the discussion. Leslie came up to Birmingham when we put on *Enigma,* and danced Jaeger, the role he created. Fred had very cleverly interwoven the character right through the ballet. This character was a very good amateur cellist, and in the final duet he sits at the side of the stage and plays the cello. Leslie didn't, of course, really play the cello, but he looked very convincing. He was also with us throughout the production, and I know that he has some comments, particularly about the finale. We have already discussed how Fred had certain difficulties with this, as had Elgar himself.

Leslie Edwards: All geniuses have trouble with finales, and we did have slight trouble with this one. I must call upon Alexander Grant to help me out here.

Alexander Grant: Fred was always bothered by finales. With *Beatrix Potter* he'd choreographed the whole thing except the finale, and all through the filming he was very worried about it. He had to do the finale in one afternoon. Finales were obviously a special thing with Frederick.

Edwards: I always enjoyed all the cameo roles I did with Fred, especially *Enigma* because the whole cast was so wonderful. When I was up in Birmingham I had the marvellous experience of going with Michael Somes to see the birthplace of Sir Edward Elgar, so when I opened in Birmingham, I thought, 'Good gracious, I'm appearing at his "local"!' I thought that maybe he had visited that theatre to see Sir Henry Irving or Dan Leno in pantomime. When I saw the little house where he was born, I felt a human warmth, and I realised why we are so moved by the music and the ballet. I do think it's important to understand what the work you are interpreting is about, and every one of these items throughout *Enigma* gives you a sense of pausing for thought.

Grant: I don't know how widely it is known that many years ago Frederick's most unfavourite composer was Elgar. When he said he was going to do *Enigma Variations,* I said, 'But that's your most unfavourite composer!' Frederick always had his pulse on the moment, and said, 'The time is right now, and I'm going to do it.' He had a wonderful memory, and he recalled that, many years before, Julia Trevelyan Oman had sent him a script and designs for costumes for *Enigma Variations*, and he suddenly remembered them when he thought the time was right.

Wright: Sandra, I know you wanted to talk about some difficulties you had with Dorabella, especially that there were several people rehearsing you in the role.

Sandra Madgwick: I was taught Dorabella by our notator Denis Bonner, and was really having trouble picking up the steps because the combinations were quite difficult. Antoinette was coming in, and I was worried because I didn't feel I really knew it. When she arrived, she didn't care that I didn't have all the combinations in my head yet; she was more interested in getting the characterisation across. She explained that Dorabella was full of life, and had this great fun relationship with Elgar, and I really began to feel that everything was happening. Then Michael Somes came and started to put all the actions in and made it even more of a conversation – at one moment I was darting this way, and then it was very soft. The jumps had to be very hard and down, and then up and bright. He worked me very hard in it, and showed me how the body had to bend and how the back had to be very expressive. I wanted to get all these qualities together – everybody's contributions. Then another ballerina came in who had also done the role and showed me what she had done. I started to get confused with all the different versions and felt as though I was being torn between how I felt it, how Antoinette had set it, and how everybody else conceived it. Eventually Michael Somes understood and told everybody to be quiet and let me do it the way I felt it, and to enjoy it.

Wright: Michael was very understanding, because he realised the quandary that you were in. On the other hand, it can be an advantage to have advice from people who have danced a role. Fred did change things for a particular reason, often to help an artist look right in a role. What is good for one artist, though, may not work for another – each artist has to find the right way. There was a particular step where nobody was sure which way the arm should be used; it drove us all mad. There was a quite a subtle difference, but it was important.

Madgwick: Antoinette was very definite that the chassé went down onto the front leg while the arm went sweeping up. Then it was remembered that because I was travelling so much forward, I ran out of space and I was coming too close to Elgar too soon. Then it was decided that the step would have to travel more to the side, and the arm was changed to a much faster movement, with the body inclining backwards. I began to get confused, so I ended up with a compromise – using an expressive upwards arm gesture but keeping the legs going sideways. That felt right for me.

Wright: The nice thing about the step is that as you go down the arm gestures strongly upwards – it makes the step more interesting; and then there's the speed of it too.

Grant: And there's the chassé again, the forgotten chassé! [See p. 134.]

Wright: Alain, is there anything you'd like to say about the Nimrod?

Alain Dubreuil: I think Desmond has said it all. It's about friendship. I felt it quite easy to do with Desmond. We've known each other for something like thirty years, so we have a great deal of rapport. We felt very comfortable doing that kind of work together – perhaps it is because we are friends or that we've had a lot of experience, rather than being new dancers, when just to walk on stage can be quite difficult. The music is also very beautiful and emotionally charged.

Wright: I felt very much that you established a sort of professional understanding between the two of you. Your professional lives have been very close, and I think the understanding of your art comes over.

Cathy, you are a newcomer into this world, having been a principal with the Stuttgart Ballet, although you slotted in wonderfully.

Cathy Batcheller: I had learnt the steps from the choreologist and I had an idea of what the Lady Mary role was supposed to be about, but I was interpreting certain things from the way I saw the movement, trying to find a meaning. Then Deanne Bergsma came in and talked about the role. The way she moved and spoke showed very clearly how I could change the interpretation. In the first entrance, there's a feeling of the bow of a ship cutting through the water, and the movement of the waves of the ocean. I started to feel comfortable.

Wright: Deanne had a lovely way of describing things.

Batcheller: Her manner was calm and tranquil. She was very helpful with the timing of certain actions – in connection with Elgar and the enigmatic qualities. When Michael came, we did the finale. That was my first experience of working with him and I was very nervous: I knew he was going to be very exacting. I understood what he was trying to get out of us at rehearsal, although it was a different way of working, like being thrown into cold water. He wanted to get the most out of us all. When we worked on the solo, he felt that I understood the role from deep down and then it was just a pleasure, I felt I had the freedom from him to dance it.

Anon: What one reads about Lady Mary suggests she's supposed to be a dream, a fantasy. However, you were saying earlier that there was some dispute over whether Lady Elgar sees her, and yet in the finale this fantasy appears and dances with all the other characters.

Wright: That's the 'enigma'. You mustn't take the ballet too literally. There are excerpts representing different people. It's not as though they've all met on that particular day, as in the finale. I don't think there is an actual photograph – this is purely in Fred's imagination – of everyone together. It was a way of bringing the characters together, a sort of poetic licence. I feel as though Lady Mary is unreal – in Elgar's imagination – whereas Lady Elgar is very real. It is all about 'ideas', and one must be careful about being too specifically literal.

David Vaughan: Fred said the finale was partly for symmetry.

Wright: Yes. Somehow in a ballet of this nature, when you have a series of variations, it seems right for symmetry that you do reintroduce everyone at the end.

Anon: But she does go off the stage before everyone else.

Wright: She's not in the photograph, so she doesn't appear in 'the picture'.

John Percival: We had the comment that Sir Frederick had a problem making these finales. Surely the photograph is a metaphor for the whole ballet: it is 'my friends pictured' – so he has a picture taken – with, of course, one of the characters not in the picture because she's left the stage.

Anon: Speaking for the future of all of Sir Fred's ballets that we've heard about during this conference, I'd like to say that it is difficult learning from a choreologist, where you just learn the steps. You then learn the role and the meaning of the ballet from the various people who have come in to teach it. What do you feel is going to happen when the people who are so close to Sir Fred, who worked with him, aren't there to come and teach? What is going to happen to this legacy in the future?

Wright: We can only do our best. We went to endless pains with *Enigma Variations*, as we try to do with all choreographers' work. Notation is absolutely essential when teaching a ballet in the early stages, because it is so accurate. But you must bring in someone who really knows it well to polish it up. I think the ideal way is to have the expert

217

there who knows and understands it at the same time as the steps are being taught – someone like Michael Somes. You can't create miracles; you can't suddenly produce another Ashton who will understand the former Ashton. You have to rely on who is around at the moment who can understand the work. We have a wealth of Ashton works, and I will always endeavour to make sure that everything is accurately recorded on video and notation and that we will have the right people present. There isn't anything more that one can do. One can have the example, as with the video, although one artist copying step by step, finger by finger, head by head, doesn't help that artist much. It can become a stereotype, it doesn't always 'live' – and that was one of the things that Ashton wanted, he wanted his choreography to live through the artist who was performing it.

Things won't always be the same. For instance, we revived Massine's *Le Tricorne* in the same programme as *Enigma Variations*, and unfortunately, Lorca, Massine's son, was unable to be with us until the last six days. We spent a long time unravelling different versions, and then finally when Lorca came along he had his own particular ideas. There was great confusion, and we ended up not having nearly enough time to bring the ballet to life.

These days the size of companies and the size of the activities and productions – whether it be the Royal Opera, the Royal Ballet, the Birmingham Royal Ballet – puts pressure on everything. There is so little time; although everything has grown, union rulings have meant that the amount of time that artists can work has been reduced. Everything is much larger and more expensive. We are luckier in Birmingham because we are much more our own masters. From my own experiences of working with the Royal Ballet at Covent Garden, I am aware of the pressures there, and the timescale of everything is a nightmare. Fred used to say, 'Please don't think that I want to see my ballets put on a lot – I don't. I would like to see them done occasionally, but done exquisitely.' I agree with that. The first part is not such a problem, but to have the right amount of time to get things really well done and to pay the necessary attention to detail certainly is. But we've got to get it right. We've got a great and wonderful heritage, and I feel optimistic because I think we are aware of the problems. The situation at Covent Garden is very different now from the way it was twenty years ago, and although some things are better, others are worse. I think we got our act together pretty well with our production of *Enigma Variations* in Birmingham – through the help of all our contributors – all aspects of it, design and everything. And I think, as Michael said, Fred would have been really pleased.

Monica Mason: I just wanted to mention that Robert Jude [Royal Ballet video archive] came across the film of Fred's retirement gala at the back of a cupboard in a box, and it was only saved a few weeks before it would have completely crumbled away. Robert made a recording of it, which has been shown at this conference.

I think that something that we've always wanted to do, and have begun to do now, is to develop the archive in an effort to try to record our ballets as accurately and as efficiently as possible. It is perhaps not widely known that to achieve some of these recordings we had negotiations going on with the Musicians' Union for over six years in order to get permission to record more rehearsals. So it's not that we don't try. Also, Robert and David Drew have been making private recordings of people; I know Leslie Edwards has contributed already by trying to get people to talk on camera about their lives, their careers and some of their roles, which I think will help younger dancers enormously.

Wright: I also wish that there was more real understanding of notation, and that dancers and choreographers were able to use notation as a musician is expected to use music notation. Notation is often acquired second-hand – learning from a notator who may not necessarily be the best demonstrator of the steps they are reading from the score. If you can understand notation, you can analyse movement and study it for yourself. You can also refer to the old scores – we've got nearly every ballet notated [see Appendix I]. This is not only important for a dancer, it is also very important for teachers who, I think, should use it much more.

Richard Glasstone: I agree with you about notation, and I think it has to go hand in hand with the human being. One of the most wonderful things in this conference has been the demonstrations we've just seen, because they were so detailed and so lovingly done. I'm sure it's those people in the future, as répétiteurs and teachers, who will hand it on.

Appendix I

Scores of Ashton Ballets in Benesh Movement Notation

Apparitions
Birthday Offering
Capriol Suite
Cinderella
The Creatures of Prometheus
Dante Sonata
Daphnis and Chloe
Death in Venice (danced scenes)
The Dream
Enigma Variations
Façade
La Fille mal gardée
Die Fledermaus (Act II, danced scenes)
Illuminations
Jazz Calendar
Monotones I & II
A Month in the Country
Ondine
Pas de légumes
Les Patineurs

Raymonda: Scène d'amour
Les Rendezvous
Rhapsody
Romeo and Juliet
Le Rossignol
Scènes de ballet
Sinfonietta
The Sleeping Beauty (additional choreography)
Swan Lake
Sylvia (one-act version)
Symphonic Variations
Tales of Beatrix Potter
Thaïs Pas de deux
The Two Pigeons
La Valse
Valses nobles et sentimentales
Varii Capricci
The Walk to the Paradise Garden
A Wedding Bouquet

Information provided by the Benesh Institute, the international centre for Benesh Movement Notation. The Institute provides dance companies and choreographers with an efficient and accurate system of notation for the professional recording and revival of dance repertoire, and houses over 400 scores in its library of choreographic scores and related material. There is a special agreement for the educational use of scores, and permission may be granted to use specified scores for study purposes. Currently there are some 250 scores available; this number will increase considerably in the near future. For further information, contact: The Benesh Institute, 12 Lisson Grove, London NW1 6TS.

Appendix II
Notes on Contributors

Richard Alston was one of the first full-time students at the London Contemporary Dance School in 1967. In 1972 he founded Strider, the first independent dance company to emerge from LCDS. In 1977, after two years study with Merce Cunningham, Alston began choreographing for London Contemporary Dance Theatre, Ballet Rambert, Second Stride and his own group Richard Alston and Dancers. From 1986–94 he was artistic director of Rambert Dance Company. In 1994 he became artistic director of the Contemporary Dance Trust and of the Richard Alston Dance Company.

Jill Beck is chair of the dance division at Southern Methodist University, Dallas, Texas. She is an international authority on dance notation and the restaging of dance repertory. She is editor-in-chief of *Traditional Arts in Performance*. She has been a master teacher for the American Dance Festival, served as chair of the theatre and dance department of the City College of New York, and was on the dance and graduate music faculties of the Juillard School.

Shelley Berg is an associate professor in the dance division at Southern Methodist University in Dallas, Texas. She studied at the Royal Ballet School and danced with the Slovene National Ballet and Les Grand Ballets Canadiens. She is author of *Le Sacre du printemps: Seven Productions from Nijinsky to Graham*. She is a consultant to the dance panel of the National Endowment for the Arts, and on the board of the Society for Dance History Scholars.

Lesley Collier studied at the Royal Academy of Dancing and the Royal Ballet School, joining the Royal Ballet in 1965, becoming a principal in 1972. Her first role as a soloist was Lise in Frederick Ashton's *La Fille mal gardée*. Many choreographers have created ballets for her; for many her most dazzling role has been with Baryshnikov in Ashton's *Rhapsody* in 1980. She was recipient of the Dancer of the Year (*Dance and Dancers*) in 1986 and the Evening Standard Award in 1987. She is now a CBE.

Anthony Dowell began training at the Royal Ballet School in 1955, joining the Covent Garden Opera Ballet in 1960 and the Royal Ballet in 1961, where he became a principal in 1966. In 1964 he was chosen by Ashton to dance Oberon in *The Dream* with Antoinette Sibley as Titania, a pairing that initiated one of the world's great dance partnerships. He created a number of roles in Ashton's ballets. From 1977–80 he was principal guest artist with American Ballet Theatre. He returned to the Royal Ballet in 1981 to lead the company's fiftieth anniversary celebrations. In 1984 he became assistant to Norman Morrice, director of the Royal Ballet, becoming associate director in 1985, and succeeding Morrice as director in 1986. He became a CBE in 1973.

Leslie Edwards trained with Marie Rambert and danced with Ballet Rambert and the Vic-Wells Ballet. His talent as a mime first attracted attention in Ashton's *The Quest*. He has created roles for MacMillan, Cranko and Andrée Howard, among others. In 1958 he began teaching at the Royal Ballet School. In 1967 he founded the Royal Ballet Choreographic Group. From 1970–90 he was ballet-master to the Royal Opera. He received the Royal Academy of Dancing Queen Elizabeth II Coronation Award (1984), and the Lorenzo il Magnifico Prize for dance (1991). He was made an OBE in 1975.

Rosalind Eyre trained at the Royal Ballet School and joined the Royal Ballet in 1960. She was made a principal in 1985 and now performs a wide variety of roles. In 1986 she became the Royal Ballet's ballet-mistress, having been assistant ballet-mistress since 1972.

Julia Farron was the first scholarship pupil at Ninette de Valois' school after its establishment at Sadler's Wells Theatre in 1931. In 1936, aged fourteen, she became the youngest member of the Vic-Wells Ballet, having already made her professional debut in pantomime, aged twelve. At fifteen she appeared in her first created role, Pépé the dog in Ashton's *A Wedding Bouquet*. In 1964 she became a teacher at the Royal Ballet School. She became assistant director of the Royal Academy of Dancing in 1982, becoming director in 1983, until her retirement in 1989. In 1994 she was awarded the Royal Academy of Dancing Queen Elizabeth II Coronation Award.

Philip Gammon studied with Harold Craxton at the Royal Academy of Music, where he won the MacFarren Gold Medal, and with Yvonne Loriod in Germany. Since joining the Royal Ballet his many solo piano performances have included *Elite Syncopations*, *A Month in the Country*, and *Winter Dreams*. He played at the memorial services for Frederick Ashton, Margot Fonteyn, and Kenneth MacMillan.

Beth Genné PhD teaches dance history and art history at the University of Michigan, Ann Arbor. Her research on Ashton and Fedorovitch began when she was J. Paul Getty Postdoctoral Fellow in London in 1988. She has published in the *Dancing Times*, *Art Journal*, *Dance Research Journal*, *Dance Chronicle* and *Psychoanalytic Perspectives on Art*. Her book, on Ninette de Valois' early years and her ballet *Le Bar aux Folies-Bergères*, is to be published in the *Studies in Dance History* series. Recently, she curated an exhibition of photographs of Nijinsky at the University of Michigan Museum of Art.

Richard Glasstone graduated from the University of Cape Town Ballet School.

223

He has worked as a dancer, choreographer, and teacher in South Africa, England, Holland, Belgium, Switzerland, and the USA, as well as directing the Turkish State Ballet companies in Ankara and Istanbul. He was for many years senior teacher for boys and head of choreographic studies at the Royal Ballet School. He was the founder director of the Cecchetti Centre, a founder member of the Society for Dance Research, and is a senior examiner for the Cecchetti Society. He is the author of three books and numerous articles on dance.

Alexander Grant was born in Wellington, New Zealand. He won a Royal Academy of Dancing scholarship to Sadler's Wells Ballet School, joining Sadler's Wells Ballet in 1946, becoming a soloist in 1949, and soon after, a principal. From 1971–75, while still performing with the Royal Ballet, he was director of the company's small touring group Ballet For All. In his thirty-year career with the Royal Ballet, he became its greatest demi-caractère dancer. From 1976–83 he was director of the National Ballet of Canada. From 1985–1991 he was a principal dancer with London Festival Ballet (now English National Ballet). He was made a CBE in 1965.

Adrian Grater joined the Royal Ballet Touring Company in 1958, was promoted to soloist in 1964, and joined the Covent Garden company in 1970. In 1976 he became ballet-master for Ballet International, and was director of Ballet For All (1978–79). After training in Benesh Movement Notation he became assistant director of the Benesh Institute (1981), then technical director (1991).

Andrée Grau studied dance in her native Switzerland and in London, where she also studied Benesh Movement Notation. She obtained her MA in social anthropology in 1979, and her PhD in 1983. She is currently a senior research fellow at Roehampton Institute. She teaches anthropology of dance at London Contemporary Dance School, and cultural/social anthropology at Richmond College, the American International University in London. Her publications have appeared in many professional journals.

Beryl Grey began ballet at the age of four, and at ten was given a scholarship to the Vic-Wells Ballet School, joining Sadler's Wells Ballet within four years. She danced Odette in *Swan Lake* Act II at fourteen, and Odette/Odile in the full-length ballet on her fifteenth birthday, a record unequalled to this day. In 1957 she made ballet history, dancing Odette/Odile with the Bolshoi Ballet in Moscow, and Giselle with the Kirov Ballet in Leningrad. She made history again in 1964, travelling to China to dance with the Shanghai Ballet and the Peking Ballets. She continued to dance as a guest ballerina with companies throughout the world until the mid-1960s. In 1966 she became director general of the Arts Educational School, and governor of London Festival Ballet, where she was later artistic director (1968–79). She is the author of two books, *Red Curtain Up* and *Through the Bamboo Curtain*, compiler/editor of *My Favourite Ballet Stories*, and the subject of several biographies. As well as numerous

224

honorary doctorates, Beryl Grey was awarded the CBE in 1973 and created a Dame of the same order in 1988.

Katherine Siöbhän Healy trained at the School of American Ballet. In 1982 she was awarded the silver medal at the International Ballet Competition in Jackson, Mississippi, and won the gold medal at the International Ballet Competition in Varna, Bulgaria in 1983. In 1984, aged fifteen, she joined London Festival Ballet as a principal dancer, and in 1985 was chosen by Ashton as the first-cast Juliet for the revival of *Romeo and Juliet*. She subsequently danced with Les Ballets de Monte Carlo and the Vienna State Opera Ballet, where she is currently engaged. In 1990 she graduated magna cum laude from Princeton University with a BA in art history, and was awarded the senior thesis prize for her work entitled 'Edgar Degas and the Aesthetic of the Ballet Master'. She has contributed articles to *Dance Now*.

Stephanie Jordan trained in both dance and music. She has taught both practical and theoretical aspects of dance in Europe and North America. Her books include *Striding Out: Aspects of Contemporary and New Dance in Britain* and *Parallel Lines: Media Representation of Dance* (co-edited with Dave Allen). Her doctoral dissertation was on the work of Doris Humphrey. She has contributed many scholarly articles and conference papers on dance, and is an established dance critic. She is currently Professor of Dance Studies at Roehampton Institute, where she leads the postgraduate and research programme. She is currently writing a book on music and dance.

Julie Kavanagh is writing the authorised biography of Frederick Ashton. She trained at the Royal Ballet School, where she twice won the annual choreographic competition judged by Ashton, and continued her studies at the University of Cape Town, where she performed with the CAPAB Ballet. She graduated with a first class in English from Oxford University, and has worked on *Vogue*, *Harpers & Queen*, and *Vanity Fair*. She was dance critic of the *Spectator* for six years and has written for *The Times Literary Supplement*, *The Times*, *Dancing Times*, *American Scholar*, *Vanity Fair*, *The Observer*, and *The Independent on Sunday*. She is currently London editor of the *New Yorker*.

Alastair Macaulay is chief drama critic for *The Financial Times*, for which he also reviews dance and music. He has contributed extensive dance criticism to the *Dancing Times* and other publications, and is author of *Some Views and Reviews of Ashton's Choreography*. Since 1980 he has lectured in dance history and other subjects at various colleges, and has been chief examiner in Western dance history to the Imperial Society of Teachers of Dancing. In 1983 he was the founding editor of *Dance Theatre Journal*, and in 1988 became guest dance critic to the *New Yorker*. He has lectured on dance in the USA, Canada, and Italy. He returned to the *New Yorker* as guest dance critic in 1992.

Donald MacLeary joined the Royal Ballet School aged thirteen, with no prior

225

ballet training; three years later he joined the Sadler's Wells Theatre Ballet, becoming a soloist in 1954 and transferring to the Covent Garden company as a principal in 1959, where he was renowned as a *danseur noble* and an exemplary partner. From 1975–79 he was ballet-master, after which he returned to dancing as a guest artist with Scottish Ballet and other companies. He returned to the Royal Ballet as répétiteur in 1981, and was appointed répétiteur to the principal artists in 1985.

Alicia Markova joined Diaghilev's Ballets Russes in 1924, aged fourteen. She returned to London in 1929, and danced with the Camargo Society, Rambert's Ballet Club and later the Vic-Wells Ballet. She created roles in many ballets, including Ashton's *La Péri* and *Les Rendezvous*. In 1935 she created, with Anton Dolin, the Markova-Dolin Company. In the late 1930s she joined the Ballets Russes de Monte Carlo. In 1949, Markova and Dolin again assembled a company, which was to become London Festival Ballet. Since her retirement in 1962 she has continued to teach. In 1973 she became a governor of the Royal Ballet School and the president of English National Ballet in 1986. She is the recipient of many awards, including CBE (1958), the Royal Academy of Dancing Queen Elizabeth II Coronation Award (1963), Dame of the British Empire in (1963), Honorary Doctorate in Music from Leicester University (1966).

Monica Mason came to England from South Africa at the age of fourteen, joining the Royal Ballet two years later in 1958, the youngest member of the company. After a brief period in the corps she was chosen by Kenneth MacMillan to create the role of the Chosen Maiden in *The Rite of Spring*. In 1963 she was appointed soloist, and became a principal in 1968. In 1980 she was appointed répétiteur to MacMillan, in 1984 principal répétiteur to the Royal Ballet, and in 1988 assistant to the director. She became assistant director of the Royal Ballet in 1991.

Pamela May joined the Sadler's Wells Ballet School at the age of fifteen and graduated into the company, which she left temporarily between 1941 and 1943. Ashton created many roles for her. She was a teacher at the Royal Ballet School from 1954, and is currently a governor of the Royal Ballet companies and of the Royal Ballet School. She is Vice-President and Fellow of the Royal Academy of Dancing. She is a recipient of the Royal Academy of Dancing Queen Elizabeth II Coronation Award.

Geraldine Morris trained in Dublin and at the Royal Ballet School. She joined the Royal Ballet in 1964 and remained until 1971. After a BA (Open University, she completed an MA in Dance Studies (Surrey University). She is currently writing an education pack on Ashton's work for the National Resource Centre for Dance, and is working for a PhD on Ashton's syntax and vocabulary at Roehampton Institute. She teaches dance studies at the Royal Ballet School.

James Neufeld teaches English Literature at Trent University in Peterborough,

Canada, where he is also Vice-President of University Services. He has written on dance for the *Journal of Canadian Studies* and *Dance in Canada*, and is a contributor to the *International Dictionary of Ballet*. He is currently at work on a book-length history of the National Ballet of Canada. He has published articles on Restoration drama, and on Canadian poetry and fiction.

Ashley Page trained at the Royal Ballet School, graduating in 1975. After a year with Ballet For All, he joined the Royal Ballet in 1976, becoming a principal in 1984. He has performed many Ashton roles. He began to choreograph in the Royal Ballet Choreographic group in 1981, was the recipient of the first Frederick Ashton Choreographic Award in 1982, and was invited to produce his first work at the Royal Opera House in 1984. He has created works for, among others, Rambert Dance Company, Dance Umbrella Festival, Dance on Four, Dutch National Ballet, Istanbul State Ballet, as well as the Royal Ballet. In 1990 he was awarded the first Frederick Ashton Memorial Commission from Rambert Dance Company.

Merle Park came to England from her native Rhodesia in 1951 to study at Elmhurst. She joined Sadler's Wells Ballet in 1954, was made a soloist in 1958, and a principal in 1959. She interpreted Ashton's musicality well, most notably in the central role in *Symphonic Variations* and Ashton created several roles for her. She became a CBE in 1974 and a Dame of the same order in 1986.

John Percival has followed dance keenly since his schooldays, and began writing about it professionally while at Oxford. He was a dance critic of *The Times* since 1965, and he edited the magazine *Dance and Dancers*. He has written eight books. He believes he has seen more performances by more companies in more places than any other critic today.

Giannandrea Poesio trained as a dancer and an actor. After a brief performing career, he graduated in 1986 from the University of Florence with a thesis on Diaghilev in Italy. A dance and ballet critic since 1981, he has contributed to Italian publications such as *La Republica*, *La Nazione*, and *La Danza*. He is currently London editor for the Italian *Danza & Danza* and *Chorégraphie*. In 1993 he completed his PhD in dance history at the University of Surrey. Since 1990 he has been a regular contributor to the *Dancing Times,* and teacher of dance history at English National Ballet School. Since 1994 he has been lecturer and research fellow at Roehampton Institute. He has also lectured for the University of Florence, the Royal Ballet School teacher training course, and the National Academy of Dance in Rome.

Jane Pritchard is archivist of English National Ballet and Rambert Dance Company. In 1987 she helped prepare the Les Ballets 1933 exhibition, seen in Brighton, Saratoga, and the Lincoln Centre Library for the Performing Arts; she also wrote the company's history for the catalogue. Her publications have appeared in several journals, including *Dance Chronicle* and *Dance Research*.

Antoinette Sibley went to the Royal Ballet School in 1949, graduating into the Royal Ballet in 1956. In 1959 she was promoted to soloist, and a few months later achieved outstanding success when she took over the role of Odette/Odile in *Swan Lake* at short notice. She became a principal the following year and quickly became one of the leading dancers of her generation. She created many roles in Ashton ballets. Her partnership with Anthony Dowell, which began with *The Dream* (1964), developed into one of the world's outstanding ballet partnerships. In 1979 she retired officially from ballet, but in 1980 returned to create Ashton's *Soupirs* with Anthony Dowell for a gala, and continued dancing most of her ballerina roles until 1988. She is president of the Royal Academy of Dancing, and a guest coach with the Royal Ballet. She was created a CBE in 1973.

David Vaughan was born in London and educated at Oxford University. He studied ballet with Marie Rambert and Audrey de Vos. In 1950 he continued his studies at the School of American Ballet, later studying with Antony Tudor, Richard Thomas, and Merce Cunningham. He has worked as a dancer, actor, singer, and choreographer, on film and television, in ballet and modern dance companies, and in cabaret. He is associate editor of *Ballet Review* and the *Encyclopaedia of Dance and Ballet*. He is the author of *Frederick Ashton and His Ballets* and the forthcoming *Merce Cunningham: 50 Years*, for which he received a Guggenheim Fellowship; and he has contributed to *Dancers on a Plane: Cage, Cunningham, Johns* and to Ornella Volta's *Satie et la danse*. He has been associated with Merce Cunningham Dance Company since 1959, as archivist since 1976. He has taught dance history and criticism at New York University, the State University of New York/College at Purchase, the Laban Centre for Movement and Dance, the University of Chicago Dance History Seminar, and the American Dance Festival Critics' Conference. In 1986 he was Regents' Lecturer at the University of California.

David Wall joined the Royal Ballet School at the age of ten and the Royal Ballet Touring Company eight years later, dancing Siegfried in *Swan Lake* and Colas in *La Fille mal gardée* while still in the corps de ballet. At twenty he was appointed principal, the youngest in the history of the company. In 1970 he joined the Royal Ballet at Covent Garden and created many roles. Guest engagements have included appearances in South America, Italy, Australia and Japan. In 1978 he won the Evening Standard Ballet Award for the most 'outstanding achievement in dance in 1977'. He was associate director of the Royal Academy of Dancing from 1984–87, and director from 1987–90. He is a CBE.

Peter Wright made his professional debut with Ballet Jooss, and during the 1950s worked with several dance companies, including Sadler's Wells Theatre Ballet, for which he created his first ballet, *A Blue Rose* (1957). In 1959 he was appointed ballet-master to Sadler's Wells Opera and teacher at the Royal Ballet

School. In 1961 he went to Stuttgart as teacher and ballet-master to the company being formed by John Cranko, where he choreographed several ballets. During the 1960s he was a successful producer of television ballets, and choreographed various West End musicals and revues. In 1969 he returned to the Royal Ballet as associate to the director, later becoming assistant director, then associate director. In 1977 he became director of Sadler's Wells Royal Ballet (now the Birmingham Royal Ballet). He received the Evening Standard Award for Ballet in 1981, and was made a CBE in 1986. In 1990 he was made Special Professor of Performance Studies by the University of Birmingham; he was also awarded an Honorary Doctorate of Music from London University, and was presented with the Elizabeth II Coronation Award from the Royal Academy of Dancing. In 1993 he was awarded a knighthood, and also became president of the Benesh Institute.